D1450637

Excellence in Education

Excellence in Education
Perspectives on Policy and Practice

edited by
Philip G. Altbach
Gail P. Kelly
Lois Weis

Prometheus Books
Buffalo, New York

Published 1985 by Prometheus Books
700 East Amherst Street, Buffalo, New York 14215

Library of Congress Card Number: 85-61565
ISBN 0-87975-296-3 (Cloth)
ISBN 0-87975-301-3 (Paper)

Printed in the United States of America

Frontiers in Education
Series Editor: Philip G. Altbach

Other titles in the series:

Higher Education in American Society
edited by Philip G. Altbach and Robert O. Berdahl

The American University
edited by Jan H. Blits

Contents

116121

7

Introduction

Philip G. Altbach, Gail P. Kelly, and Lois Weis[1]

Between 1983 and 1985 well over a dozen reports were issued on the state of the nation's schools, from the primary grades through higher education. While the reports differ in many ways, all are critical of current educational practices. All recommend a series of changes in curricular content, testing and standards, methods of teacher training, teacher rewards, and locus of control over schools. Since *A Nation at Risk* was issued in 1983, school reform has been at the top of the nation's agenda. Many states have made extensive changes in requirements for graduation and those for teacher certification.

This book focuses on the current reform movement in education. We seek to understand the excellence reports: their analysis of the state of the nation's schools, prescription for reform, and the implications of their recommendations for reforms instituted in response to the struggles of the 1960s. We also seek to understand the implication of the recommendations for current educational practice and to assess the limitations of proposed reforms in light of that practice. We focus on the ideological underpinnings of the reports and what the reports mean for school practice and the shape of American society.

This volume is divided into five parts. In Part One we focus on what the reports actually say; in Part Two we inquire into the social, political, and economic context of the reports. What are they a response to, and whose interests are they likely to serve? What is the relationship between economic structures and proposed reforms? In Part Three we ask how the reform movement of the 1980s might affect the educational policies instituted in the 1960s and 1970s. How, specifically, do the recommendations made by the national commissions affect the push toward equality that characterized earlier reform efforts? What might current reforms mean for women, minorities, and the handicapped? The fourth part of this book looks at the implications of the proposed reforms for educational practice. To what extent will the reforms affect curriculum, teacher preparation and practice, and student outcomes? Are reforms likely to penetrate student and/or teacher cultures? If they do affect such cultures, will the results be as intended? Can they be expected to herald in an era of excellence? In the concluding section, Gail Kelly and Maxine Seller consider the historical implications of past reform movements, using New York State as an example.

We begin this book with an overview of what Philip Altbach calls the "Great Education Crisis." In this essay Altbach places the reform commissions of the 1980s in the context of past reforms like the National Defense Education Act of the 1950s and school integration of the 1960s and 1970s. As he points out, the current reports reflect this country's continuing and generally unsuccessful attempts to use schools to solve a range of social, economic, and political problems. Given that schools did not create such problems, Altbach argues, they can hardly be expected to solve them on their own.

The essays in this volume demonstrate that there is only limited consensus among the many reports on school reforms that have appeared in 1983 and 1984, beyond agreement that our schools need improvement. The three chapters in Part One of this book discuss the reports: they ask what the reports say, how they analyze current practice, and what kinds of reforms they advocate. Gail Kelly's essay underscores the differences among the many reports. She points out that there is no consistent analysis of the schools, and agendas for reform often conflict. Her essay concludes that the reports serve to open a debate about the proper role of government, business, and parents in the reform of schools.

While Kelly's essay underscores the differences among the various reports, Ernest Boyer and Paul Peterson focus on other issues, such as similarities among the reports. Here Boyer argues that many of the reports seek to improve the working conditions of teachers and at the same time strive to reward outstanding teachers. He suggests that we must directly confront the conditions that drive good teachers from the classroom. Boyer also argues that many of the reports share certain basic assumptions about education, for example, that the educational system can encourage equality and excellence simultaneously.

Peterson argues that the reports do not address difficult issues related to education, and that they say little that is not already known by educators, teachers, and parents. He attributes this to the commission process itself rather than the individuals who comprise the commissions. The process demands representation from diverse sectors of society. This, coupled with a lack of real power to implement changes, Peterson argues, means that commissions are not equipped for serious policy analysis, and that the process is largely symbolic.

While the essays in Part One add to our understanding of the excellence reports and raise basic questions about them, the essays in Part Two focus on their political, social, and economic contexts. Joel Spring's chapter underscores the fact that the reports were generated by the conservative Reagan administration. There are, nevertheless, real differences among the reports in terms of their analysis and recommendations. He suggests that this is due to the political origin of the reports. Through a close study of the reports, Spring argues that the political base of each report has shaped reactions to the economy, thereby influencing proposals for educational change. Michael Apple's chapter focuses directly on the linkages between the economy and proposed reforms. He argues that proposed reforms cannot address perceived problems in the economy since these problems are largely unrelated to schooling. The reports tend to assume that America will regain its competitive edge if only we can produce appropriately skilled and trained labor. Apple suggests that this explanation is far too simplistic.

Sheila Slaughter's essay focuses on higher education and argues that the reports are not necessarily in agreement on the way that higher education does or should relate to business. She distinguishes between "liberal" and "technical" reports and suggests that the former will ultimately lose because they do not seriously consider issues of production.

The essays in Part Two situate the reports in their wider social, political, and economic context, while those in Part Three place the reports more narrowly into the context of school reform efforts in the United States since 1960.

Richard Hunter's contribution discusses how the Richmond Public Schools have reformed over the past decades. Hunter argues that the national commissions do not reflect any new thrust in education; rather, they reinforce what some urban districts have attempted all along. Hunter's views are not shared by Carl Grant, Christine Sleeter, or Rosemarie Rosen in their essays. Grant and Sleeter, in particular, argue that the reforms posed by the various commissions on excellence will undermine the very real progress made in the education of women, minorities, and the handicapped. Their careful analysis of the language of the reports suggests little concern for these groups in the drive toward excellence.

While Part Three reflects on the reforms in relation to those of the 1960s and 1970s, the essays in Part Four ask whether and how the reforms posited by the various commissions on excellence will affect educational practice. The essays here are less than optimistic that desired changes in teacher behavior and student outcomes can be brought about. Dennis Carlson, in his analysis of the meaning of the reports for curriculum, argues that the reports will not produce excellence. Rather, he suggests that the model of the curriculum emphasized in the reports, that of a technology for producing predetermined institutional outputs defined as test scores, skills, and so forth, will contribute to a "dumbing down" of the curriculum in that discrete facts and recall will be emphasized, driving out the development of more complex forms of literacy and critical thinking. He also suggests that the model used will contribute to the "de-skilling" of teachers.

Linda McNeil elaborates this theme by arguing that the effect of regulating teacher behavior along the lines suggested in the reports will be to de-skill teachers.

This de-skilling will promote mediocrity rather than excellence. Through two case studies McNeil demonstrates that increased control over teachers leads skilled instructors to water down content, restrict or eliminate student reading and discussion, and to call for less student writing. Unless reforms emphasize teacher autonomy rather than control, McNeil argues, instructional quality will be lowered.

Albert Shanker, president of the American Federation of Teachers, questions whether the current proposals to recruit and retain good teachers in the profession will be effective unless issues relating to teacher work—discipline, class size, professional autonomy, and nonteaching tasks such as hall patrol—are addressed directly. While he views some facets of the reports critically, he also stresses their positive aspects.

Lois Weis, in her analysis of student culture included in Part Four, is similarly skeptical of the reforms recommended by the commissions on excellence. She argues that the reforms neglect the issue of student culture, and, while they strive to improve student outcomes, they will be unsuccessful because they do not truly address why certain categories of students fail.

While many of the chapters in Part Four take a dim view of whether changes in practices suggested by the commissions on excellence will improve student outcomes, not all the essays included here are as pessimistic. Hugh Petrie's contribution argues that teacher practices can be improved if schools of education are reformed. He believes that this is possible and that, in the future, the professional training of teachers will be able to affect changes in classroom practice. This volume's concluding essay by Gail Kelly and Maxine Seller is, like Petrie's, less pessimistic about the current reforms. Through an analysis of the history of school reform in New York State, Kelly and Seller argue that it is possible to change educational practices if reforms are specific and fully funded and clear-cut executive leadership for enacting reforms exists. They maintain that the extent to which the reform movement of the 1980s shares these characteristics will have much to do with whether the reforms have their intended results.

The essays in this volume, as we have pointed out, raise a series of issues about the commissions on excellence in education of 1983 and 1984. Generally, the essays take a critical view, but they are diverse and seek to present a broad spectrum of thought about the context of current reform efforts and the implications of specific recommendations for educational practice and outcomes. Our intent is not only to spark debate about the reports; we also hope that these essays will serve to direct thought about ways in which American schools can be excellent without sacrificing hard-won opportunities for women, minorities, and the handicapped, and for educational equity generally.

NOTE

1. We would like to acknowledge the assistance of Jennifer Newton, who copyedited some of the manuscripts for this book.

The Great Education "Crisis"

Philip G. Altbach

Suddenly, education has become a national concern. Reports, commentary, television specials, and much recrimination have flooded the literature and the airwaves in the past two years. Why has education suddenly taken center stage and what are the implications of the current debates for American education? What is the meaning, and the impact, of the many reports on education that have appeared in the last year?

This chapter provides a broad overview of the factors that have led to the current "great debate." For it is only by understanding the context of contemporary education that one can make sense of the myriad proposals for reform and change. Further, since solutions are necessarily related to past practice and to the societal context of American education, understanding the historical, social, and political factors relating to American education will permit a more realistic appraisal of the crisis and the possibilities for solutions.

Americans are great believers in quick solutions to complex problems. And since everyone has been to school, everyone is an "expert" on education. These two factors have contributed to the recent emergence of education in the headlines. While massive public and media attention contributes to placing any issue, from "crime in the streets" to educational reform, at the top of the national agenda and affects the chances for implementation of changes in national and state policies, it is often the case, as Ernest Boyer has stated, that public concern is a "mile wide and an inch deep." Thus, media attention and the American desire for speedy solutions often mean that "answers" are provided that are neither thoughtful nor practical. It also means that sometimes large amounts of money are spent on solutions that do not necessarily solve the problem.

The current concern with excellence in education is a classic case of how Americans perceive problems and develop solutions. This essay focuses attention on aspects of the current education debate. One must understand not only the specific educational issues involved, but also the relevant background factors. Today's crisis is the direct result of yesterday's policies and of long-standing American confusion concerning the role of the schools in society.

13

The schools have been expected not only to teach children and provide the basic skills needed by a complex technological society but also to solve the dilemma of racial discrimination, to provide opportunities for women and minorities, to socialize generations of immigrants and to bend to changing social policies, such as church-state relations and "sex education." It is significant, for example, that America's struggle for racial equality gained impetus from the 1954 school segregation case, and education has been deeply involved with issues of racial justice ever since. It has proved easier to desegregate the schools than to change housing patterns or redistribute income. The educational system was able to cope with these new demands, but not without considerable trauma and change. At precisely the same time as added social functions were placed on the educational agenda, funding was being cut in many areas. Programs for the handicapped, for gifted children, innovative "magnet" schools, and other educational improvement efforts that were launched with much hope and fanfare in the 1960s and 1970s suffered financial cuts.

EDUCATION AND SOCIETY: FOLLOW THE LEADER

In the United States, the schools have relatively little autonomy in terms of basic policy and the direction of education. Educational institutions generally follow the dictates of society in terms of policy, curriculum, standards, and orientations. when society's goals change, the schools must also change. The current "crisis" reflects the fact that social goals have shifted from a stress on equity and the solution of societal problems through education, which characterized the 1960s, to a focus on academic and technological achievement that will enable the nation to compete in an increasingly difficult world market. Educational institutions change slowly, and the schools are now "out of sync" with broader social policy. The current reform proposals, and the general stress on "excellence in education," are intended to quickly move the educational system toward these new societal goals. Unlike earlier shifts, such as the 1950s' move toward a more science-based curriculum after Sputnik, today's reforms are not being allocated massive funding to help the system cope with the changes.

It is worthwhile considering how the process of change occurs in the United States. The very complex process reflects the many competing constituencies and interests relating to education and to America's decentralized educational structure. In France, it is only necessary to convince the prime minister and the minister of education that a change is needed, and it will become policy; only a major national outcry can reverse the direction. In the United States, with its checks and balances, its constitutional arrangements concerning education, and its wide variety of educational interest groups ranging from teachers' unions to taxpayers' associations, educational policy changes must travel a lengthy and complex path to implementation. Indeed, it is a tribute to the strength of the "excellence idea" that the concept has moved so far so fast.

History shows us that the schools have been a part of virtually every social change in recent American history. Social policy and educational policy are intertwined. During the 1930s, stimulated by the depression and social crisis of the period, educators debated William H. Kilpatrick's famous question, "Dare the Schools Change the Social Order?" Progressive educators involved themselves in the social movements of the day. The schools later adjusted to the population explosion of the 1950s and expansion was the order of the day. Later, when the Soviet Union launched Sputnik, the schools were called on to help prepare the basis for American technological growth. Only a few years later, in the 1960s, social protest and a new recognition that the schools should participate in the solution to the problems of racism, poverty, and other issues led to a burgeoning of school-related social programs. Again, educators responded by adding new functions and made the necessary adjustments. Most recently, the enrollment declines and fiscal problems of the 1970s forced futher adjustment—mainly, scaling back the innovative programs so eagerly established just a few years earlier. Now, American education is beginning to cope with a new "crisis"—the excellence debates of the 1980s.[1]

Thus, the crisis in education is caused directly by social policy and by public opinion. Educational policy makers follow; they seldom lead. We must understand this basic fact if we are to move toward reform and improvement in education.

Americans are notably ahistorical. We forget that we placed a great deal of stress on educational excellence after Sputnik in the 1950s, and spent large amounts of money on improving science education, reforming the preparation of teachers, building schools, supporting libraries, and the like. These efforts achieved a good deal of success. Test scores improved. More students took science courses. American technology could look to well-trained scientists and engineers.

American education also underwent one of its greatest periods of expansion during the 1950s and 1960s. The schools had to accommodate the postwar "baby boom" generation. Millions were spent on new buildings and expanded programs. The teaching profession expanded as well. There was such a tremendous need for teachers that teacher training requirements were temporarily weakened in order to recruit more teachers quickly. Today, demographic realities have changed. The baby boomers have moved through the educational system and are now just about out of the universities. There are fewer school-age children and the projections, at least for the medium term, are for even smaller age cohorts. We are living with the results of the expansion of a quarter century ago—there is an age bulge in the teaching profession that results, at present, in too few teachers retiring. It will mean massive retirements in the coming decades and another inevitable shortage of teachers. There is a surplus of school buildings while the patterns of enrollment have changed significantly. Changing curricular patterns mean that there are too many social studies and English teachers and too few science instructors. Little "new blood" in the teaching profession has meant fewer new ideas and, perhaps, less energy. In short, the educational system is living with the results of the expansion, and then the downturn, in enrollments of the past few decades. Adjustments have been necessary, and they have added to the problems that the system now experiences.

In the 1960s, orientations and values changed. The stress was on solving social problems that were recognized as a result of protest movements. Governmental leaders and the public began to worry about social equality, racial justice, and whether young people could adjust psychologically and socially to a difficult social situation. In addition to this volatile mixture, the war in Vietnam stimulated further protest that affected students, particularly those in colleges and, to some extent, those in high schools as well.

The schools again were asked to help solve these social problems. Massive changes occurred, stimulated from the outside and implemented by educators in response to external demands. The curriculum was altered to allow more individual choice. Requirements were reduced. Discipline was relaxed. Stress on foreign languages, science, and mathematics was replaced by courses on social problems. To an extent, the schools turned away from traditional educational issues and became institutions to ensure adjustment to massive social change.

Alienation among young people caused by the Vietnam war, racial tensions, and the social changes of the period had an impact on the schools and colleges. Student activism took place in some high schools as well as in institutions of higher education. Students demanded more control over their education, and demoralized teachers, administrators, and policy makers gave in to many demands. As if these changes were not enough, the schools were thrust directly into the major social movement of the period, the civil rights struggle. Attention turned to desegregating the education system—court decisions shaped educational policy and tensions rose in many cities. Inner-city schools were confronted with problems of student discipline, and the use of drugs became a matter of concern for schools. While urban schools were most troubled, the suburbs were not spared. In the end, the schools dealt with this multiplicity of challenges, but frequently at the cost of weakening the traditional curriculum.

The schools could not do everything; it was not surprising that Scholastic Achievement Test (SAT) scores continued a modest decline, that the traditional curriculum was diluted, and that fewer students chose to take foreign languages and mathematics. In general, educational standards were perceived to have suffered. Part of the problem was that politicians turned to the schools for solutions to difficult social problem, and educators, happy with increased funding, were willing to attempt everything. In those heady days of social reform, it was assumed that using the schools for social change would not conflict with providing high educational standards. The public looked to the schools as a solution to all of the nation's problems. It paid relatively little attention to what was happening to the curriculum, to the education of teachers, and to the expensive buildings, libraries, and facilities that had been so lavishly provided a few years earlier.

The 1970s were not a happy time for public education in the United States, and it is in this context that the National Commission's recommendations were developed. It is hardly surprising that the tone of the report is highly critical of the educational system. It is important to understand that the recent criticisms of the schools come from a particularly difficult historical and sociological context. Rapid change, conflicting demands, fiscal problems, and a teaching profession and administrative cadre that have seen little movement in a decade provide a combination of circumstances that does not lead to an improvement in the educational quality of innovation in educational practice. Just the opposite is the case. The reports point to many of the problems of the educational systems—problems created by previous policies.

As the 1970s came to a close, it was clear that the schools had not solved America's social problems. In retrospect, they could not have been expected to do so. They did as well as most other social institutions—the church and local government are two examples—but problems of social equality and racial harmony proved difficult to solve.

The schools were hit by multiple problems at the same time. Society turned against the schools. Education had previously been seen as a panacea for social ills; now the schools were abandoned as a means of social change. Public opinion polls indicated that popular esteem for education in general and the public schools in particular had declined. Educators could not respond to the criticisms that were raised. Many educators had been reluctantly drawn into the social programs of the 1960s and did little to defend them. Educators did not take this opportunity to rethink educational priorities—only later were they forced to do so by the reports of external agencies such as the National Commission on Excellence in Education.[2] In addition, demographic factors meant that the number of school-age children declined and this led to enrollment drops; in some areas these declines were of dramatic proportions. Schools with enrollment-driven budgets faced further strains on their already threatened school funding. As a final element of this fiscal disaster, schools needed to take on ever-increasing social and educational responsibilities, many of which proved to be quite expensive. For example, "mainstreaming" handicapped students by integrating them into classrooms with other students, while a noble goal, required considerable educational adjustment and additional expense. New facilities were needed and teachers had to receive additional training. Yet, the schools were simply ordered to follow this national priority without regard for its fiscal or academic implications.

In many cases, regulations from the federal and state levels were imposed on school systems without their being given sufficient funding or even the necessary adjustment time. Quotas for minority groups, bilingual education, and other innovations were imposed on school systems that were already feeling fiscal cutbacks. The schools were simply unable to respond to all of the burdens placed on them. For urban districts, particularly, the pressures of ensuring racial integration, conforming to new state and federal mandates, and dealing with a changing and, in many cases, declining enrollment base were overwhelming. It should have come as no surprise that achievement scores and other measures of educational quality declined. The enshrined philosophy of social adjustment and participation in the 1960s was changing to more concern for discipline and with the "three Rs." Again, the schools were slow to adjust—by the mid-1970s, they were fiscally strapped and demoralized. Combined with these challenges, the Reagan administration slashed funding for education by about 25 percent. These cuts were particularly difficult, since many programs mandated by the federal government had to be maintained regardless of federal funding.

"Unnecessary" school buildings were closed without regard to neighborhood consequences. Enhanced sports programs, better guidance counseling, and many other "frills" that had been so carefully added earlier were cut back or eliminated. Little was added to replace such budget-driven cuts.

WHO IS BEHIND THE REPORTS?

Despite the fact that the problems of the schools are well known, the current debate did not emerge from grass-roots concern. Rather, it can be argued that most of the reports and investigations that have led to the current debate are the result of a coordinated effort by America's educational and corporate elite.

Most of the reports are the product of expensive research efforts; most were developed by committees of "experts" and policy makers concerned with education. The list of individuals involved with the debates reads like a "Who's Who" of the power elite of not only the education establishment but also the world of corporations and commerce.

The commissions and committees that were set up by the foundations and government agencies to look at American education included a combination of university-based administrators and professors, corporate officials, politicians concerned with education, and a scattering of teachers and others. Research data from social scientists was used by the commissions, but it is clear that there was more concern with public policy and with underlying assumptions about the role of the schools in contemporary American society than with reflecting the trends in the studies.

The conservative orientation of those involved with the excellence debate is clear. The most influential of the reports came from the National Commission on Excellence in Education that was appointed by President Reagan's secretary of eduation. Business interests were very important in several of the other reports. Several of the major private foundations were also involved in the "excellence" movement as well. These foundations are often more independent than government agencies, but they too are very much part of the education establishment. Further, there is something of an interlocking directorate of individuals involved with the movement—individuals who have served on more then one commission or who have served as consultants to several agencies.

It is not enough to only understand what the reports state; one must also be aware of those who promulgated the reports, their involvements, and their educational, political, and ideological perspectives. In the case of the reports, the impetus has clearly come from the top of the corporate and educational establishments, from groups that were never committed to the egalitarian thrust of the 1960s. A combination of the changing political mood of the nation, increasing difficulties in obtaining jobs, and the international economic situation made it possible for these groups to press their views and to have considerable influence over both the debates and on the direction of policy.

REFORM DIRECTIONS

The National Commission on Excellence in Education issued its report in April of 1983. The commission was followed by a spate of other reports from different agencies, a few research-based studies written by academic researchers, and a tremendous amount of publicity and discussion. There was a trickle-down factor as well, with discussions taking place at the state and local levels following the lead of the national reports. In New York, for example, the Regent's Action Plan very closely follows the general directions of the National Commission. The reports generally stressed the high schools, which are considered the "weak link" in American education. What is remarkable about the recent documents, and there are about a dozen national bodies that have looked into the "education crisis," is the unity of views and proposals.

The most influential reports generally have common themes and concerns; yet, there is some divergence among the reports. Mortimer Adler and his colleagues argue for a common humanistically oriented curriculum,[3] while Ernest Boyer[4] and John Goodlad[5] are, in general, less harsh on the schools than most of the other reports. Nevertheless, it is possible to summarize some of the more important recommendations of the reports:

- The schools must stress science and math and move away from the "frills" that are seen to have little relevance to preparing America for global economic competition.

- The teaching profession has fallen on hard times. The quality, pay, and autonomy of teachers must be improved. Teacher education programs must be strengthened. "Merit pay" is seen as a means of attracting better teachers and rewarding those who perform well, but there is little guidance concerning how "merit" is to be determined.

- The school curriculum should be more related to the job market and to perceived needs of industry.

- Foreign-language instruction should be started in the elementary schools and should generally receive a high priority.

- Students should spend more time in school, and that time should be used more effectively for instructional purposes.

These are the broad outlines of the recommendations. There are many variations; if all of the detailed proposals were described, it would require a small encyclopedia. But there is unison on the need to improve standards, stress science, and ensure that students are "computer literate." In general, there is a concern for the role of education in equipping America for participation in a cut-throat global economic war.

The College Entrance Examination Board (the people who bring us the SAT and other standardized tests) spent a decade trying to figure out what competencies are necessary for college entrance. The board stresses the links between the school curriculum, the universities, and the labor market.[6] The Education Commission of the States' Task Force on Education and Economic Growth has a focus similar to that of the College Board.[7] The Twentieth Century Fund, a policy-oriented philanthropic foundation, issued *Making the Grade*, which focuses on federal education policy.[8] The substance of its recommendations are similar to the other reports, although it stresses the importance of an active federal government role in education.

Finally, the Business–Higher Education Forum sponsored *America's Competitive Challenge: The Need for a National Response*, a massive document that integrates recommendations concerning education with trade policy, research and development, and even foreign affairs.[9] The Business Forum, an arm of the Council for Economic Development, stresses America's position in global economic competition, and even recommends that the president appoint an adviser on economic competitiveness. The role of education, they say, is to buttress the economy in the "trade wars" of the 1990s.

There are a few dissenters in all of the rhetoric of economic warfare. The Carnegie Foundation's massive *High School* study, which is based on solid research, agrees with many of the major recommendations of the other reports in that it stresses improving school quality and restoring unity to the curriculum, but the schools are not seen as total disaster areas. *High School* offers more understanding of the nuances of educational policy and the difficulties of making massive changes.[10]

Similarly, John Goodlad's *A Place Called School*, a study funded by a number of foundations, gives the high schools passing marks, although pointing to a multitude of problems.[11] It is perhaps significant that those studies that looked most carefully at the schools were most understanding of the complexity of the educational dilemma. Perhaps it's easy to recommend massive changes from a great distance and with a perspective that stresses global economy rather than the realities of public education.

The debate quickly spread from the national to the state and local levels. State education authorities considered the implications of the national reports for their own school systems. Unlike the federal government, the states have the power to impose educational policies, since education is legally a responsibility of the states and localities. Their responses have varied, but many states have raised the qualifications for secondary school graduation, imposed tests for teachers, and have made efforts to increase salaries in the teaching profession. One of the states most active in responding is New York, whose powerful commissioner of education, Gordon Ambach, has been actively involved with education commissions at both the national and the state level. New York also has one of the most centralized educational systems in the country, so it is comparatively easy to implement statewide educational policies quickly. New York's highest policy-making body for education, the regents, issued its own variations on the national education debate in the *Action Plan to Improve Elementary and Secondary Education Results*. Since the regents have the power to order their recommendations implemented, the Action Plan is probably the most important document yet to be published, at least for New Yorkers. The recommendations can be quickly summarized:

Lengthen the school day and the school year.

Institute prekindergarten programs statewide.

Computer literacy.

Raise standards of the regents' competency testing program in science, math, and reading.

Strengthen requirements in math and science and broaden the regents' examinations.

Improve teacher effectiveness and raise teacher salaries.

The cost, as estimated by the regents, is not insignificant: $209 million for the first year and $881 million for the planned five-year implementation period. The debate on the Action Plan has been intense, with many complaining about the cost, the implications for minorities, the narrowing of the curriculum, and other problems. There has been general agreement on the need to improve the schools but many different approaches to achieve improvement. The policy debate, however, has been framed by the Action Plan, and few other specific proposals have been suggested. Reality has also caught up with the Action Plan, and several key elements have already been dropped or postponed, most notably the lengthened school day, which was one of the key elements of the original proposal. This reform proved too costly. Some of the proposals are moving ahead, particularly raising standards and requirements for secondary school, but even these have been scaled down because of fiscal constraints. Others are still under consideration or are moving slowly. Funds for the improvement of teacher education, for example, may be allocated in 1985—in the meantime, very little has changed in this area. The point here is that even in a state that has a centralized education apparatus and a long history of active concern for education, the implementation of reform proposals has been a controversial, costly, and slow process.

THE TEACHING PROFESSION

Without a qualified, committed, and motivated teaching profession, there can be no quality education. Yet, as the commission's report notes, the profession is in trouble. The reports gloss over some important items, however. A key factor is the decline in morale of the profession.

Buffeted by rapidly changing and often contradictory demands, classroom teachers no longer know where they stand. In the 1940s , the teaching community had been attacked from all sides. Much of this criticism is unfair. The schools, and the teachers within them, have been reacting largely to changing societal demands. There is a necessary toll for such rapid changes in policy.

Today's buzzwords for the teaching profession are "burnout," "retrenchment," "retooling," and other terms from the vocabulary of despair. Teaching has always been an uncertain profession in the United States, according teachers lower status and significantly lower salaries than other professions such as law and medicine. Teachers have had only limited autonomy in their classrooms and have never had a great impact on the shaping of educational policy. At least teaching was once considered to be a secure profession that had little chance of layoffs, but this too has changed. Teachers have been fired in large numbers from many school systems. Even those who have kept their jobs are increasingly asked to learn new specialities—to retool—or to take on entirely new responsibilities. While the epidemic of crime in the schools that was evident during the past decade seems to be somewhat abated, teachers must frequently contend with an institutional environment that is less than congenial. Pressures from school boards, from parents, and from administrators contribute to the crisis of morale.

Teachers find themselves in an unenviable situation. Salaries that were rising fairly rapidly a decade ago have not kept pace with inflation. Job mobility, formerly easy, is now very difficult since there are relatively few openings in many fields. This means that a teacher who is dissatisfied in his or her school situation cannot move. While many teachers leave the profession altogether, this is also difficult in today's economy.

Most important, we are losing a generation of teachers because the current teaching population, hired during the 1960s, is not due to retire for another decade, and there are few openings for young teachers. Current incumbents have been battered by the "school wars" of the past decade and there is little fresh blood entering the profession. Further, graduate-level schools of education have cut back on teacher training programs and have not put much effort into reforming or updating them.

Teacher education is in as much a crisis as the educational system, and it is not surprising that the commissions have focused on the schools of education in America's universities.[12] There have been substantial cutbacks in teacher education programs at precisely the same time that a number of analysts are predicting teacher shortages in many fields in less than a decade. Indeed, there is already a shortage in selected fields right now. As enrollments dwindled in the 1970s, many universities cut the programs or phased them out entirely. The programs that remain have been robbed of vitality and have been unable to replace staff. Relatively few new ideas have emerged from the educational community—and implementation has been difficult due to lack of funding and support. If the trainers of teachers are at low ebb, it is unlikely that the profession itself can be much better off. Indeed, schools of education may be hard pressed to meet the demand for trained teachers in the coming decade and there will be yet another crash effort to provide teachers—with a resulting problem of inadequate training. Clearly, policy makers must take a longer view and permit the schools of education to develop new ideas and approaches before the next shortage appears.

It has often been said that the best students do not enter the teaching profession. While it is clear that prospective teachers do not stand at the top of their college classes, neither do they emerge from the lower levels. A recent study of students in the teacher training program at the State University of New York at Buffalo indicated that these future teachers are above the average for the university as a whole. With the rush toward management and computer science, it is surprising that education attracts as many good students as it does. Why should the most able college students enter a profession that has traditionally had only mediocre social status, that today has a poor job market in most areas, and that offers modest and indeed decreasing salaries? At present, a career in education has everything against it—difficult job prospects, poor salaries, and concentrated public criticism. Further, while the market for teachers has already changed for the better in a number of fields and will improve further in most areas, this news has not filtered down to either students or guidance counselors.

The profession is in trouble. It needs new blood and it needs new ideas. It needs incentives and it needs to be assured that the educational enterprise is valued in America. Unfortunately, a "quick fix" is unrealistic. In order to improve teaching, one must work on all aspects of the system, from providing better teacher education in the colleges and universities to improving the working conditions in the schools. At precisely the same time that the commissions call for higher standards, class sizes are increased and basic supplies for many schools are curtailed. School systems are willing to purchase computers for classroom use, but attention also needs to be paid to in-service training for teachers, integrating computers into the broader curriculum, and the like. The lessons of the expensive attempt to revolutionize American education by using instructional television in the 1950s—an effort that yielded few positive results—should be kept in mind. If the computer revolution is to come to the classroom it needs to be carefully integrated into the total curriculum and to have the support of the teaching profession.

The National Commission has seized on the idea of "merit pay" as a quick solution, as if rewarding a few outstanding teachers can solve the deep-seated problems of the educational system. There is considerable disagreement in the teaching community about the concept of merit pay, and there is substantial conflict about how excellence in teaching can be accurately measured. Effective teaching is very difficult to judge, and teachers fear that merit pay will become another means of administrative control. The improvement of teaching depends as much on providing an adequate working environment and good textbooks as it does on rewarding superior teaching. The structural problems of the educational system are much more serious than finding a means of differentiating the performance of teachers.

THE MANIA FOR CHANGE

While the long-term implications of the current "great education debate" are unclear, there will be some significant alterations in current educational policy and practice. Some national trends are already evident: an increased emphasis on science and math; increased standards for graduation from secondary school; more emphasis on foreign languages; decreased stress on "life adjustment" courses and on the school's role as a societal equalizer; and less stress on serving diverse clienteles. The schools are becoming more "academic"—in the narrow sense of that term. Yet, it is equally clear that many of the recommendations presented by the various commissions will not be implemented. Costs tend to be high, and government at all levels is less than anxious to provide the needed funding. Conflicting constituencies within the education community as well as outside of the schools will disagree about many of the proposals. Like everything else, educational policymaking is a matter of political debate and compromise. For better or worse, educational issues are generally decided outside of the classroom and the university.

There has already been significant response to the thrust of the various reports, and particularly to the National Commission on Excellence. In a survey issued in the spring of 1984, a state-by-state listing of new programs and changes in educational policy documents meaningful changes in virtually every state.[13] Larger plans are in various stages of debate and implementation. In New York, the Regents Action Plan lists an impressive number of changes.[14] However, beyond the level of individual schools, the process of change is slow and subject to compromise. Fiscal and political realities intrude on the best-laid plans of reformers. In the 1980s, these are particularly intrusive. In New York, the Action Plan, even prior to implementation, was significantly cut to meet fiscal constraints.

One might also point out the possible negative implications of rapid educational change. The most dramatic example of continuing massive changes in educational policy and practice is the near total collapse of the Chinese educational system during the Cultural Revolution of the 1960s.[15] The system was simply unable to cope with continuous and contradictory policy changes over a period of several decades. On a much smaller scale, the southeast Asian nation of Singapore has continually experimented with its educational system to such an extent that neither teachers nor students can keep track of educational policies from one year to the next. Historically, change in the United States has generally been slower, and the decentralized educational system has meant that implementation has varied somewhat in different parts of the country. Nevertheless, it is possible to discern waves of educational reforms and, to some extent, one current reflects previous changes or even replicates earlier efforts. For example, the current concern with "excellence" is in many respects similar to the educational response to Sputnik and the stress on science in the 1950s.[16]

With the excellence issue, there is a combination of several powerful elements that point to at least some success for current efforts. There has been, in the past few years, a growing public dissatisfaction with the schools. This is indicated in the public opinion polls as well as in the rejection of school budgets in many communities. People feel that the schools have lost a sense of direction and that the educational system, on which millions are spent, is not "producing." There is considerable confusion over what should be produced, and that confusion is part of the problem of the lack of direction of public education. There is also a feeling by the elites that the American economy is in long-term trouble and that the schools, as well as other social institutions, must be changed in order to make the nation more competitive in an increasingly difficult world environment. Demographic changes have caused further problems for the schools. Increased costs combined with decreasing test scores have caused many in government to question the orientation and direction of the schools. Thus, it is not surprising that education should come under scrutiny at this time.

CAUSES AND EFFECTS

The question naturally arises: Why all of this stress on standards in education now? There has been widespread criticism of the schools for a long time, and it has been evident that standards have to some degree deteriorated.

The decline in SAT tests is well known, although the tide may have been stemmed since recent statistics show some improvement. And there has been a backlash in the present, more conservative political environment against some of the educational innovations of the 1960s.

Yet, the combinations of commissions and reports is impressive. The fact is that most of the funding for the commissions comes from the Reagan administration, from prestigious private foundations, or from the top levels of the education establishment.

A preliminary survey shows that a dozen major universities are crucial to the membership of the commissions and to their research staffs. Major corporations, particularly those involved in multinational commerce, are represented strongly as well.

With the members of the commissions and committees coming from a fairly narrow spectrum of opinion, it is not surprising that the recommendations should be fairly uniform and should reflect the interests and concerns of this spectrum. It is always important to look not only at what is being said but also at why it is said and who is saying it.

The current debate on education is stimulated by the Reagan administration, which has its own agenda on education as it does in other areas; by the corporate sector, which is naturally concerned about its competitive position in the coming decades and sees education as an important part of the total technological development of America; and by the elite universities, which have long been concerned about a decline in "standards." It is also possible to point to the presence of people representing engineering, physics, and chemistry on some of the commissions. Their concern for the "hard sciences" and lack of interest in social studies is not surprising.

A consensus for education policy for the coming decade is now being built. The American system, like that of Japan, depends on a broad national agreement for the implementation of major policy changes. The current debate on education is very important in that it will set the national agenda for some time to come. Funding priorities will be established, directions in teacher education and in the curriculum set, and it will be difficult to alter these for some time.

America's schools have traditionally educated for participation in a democratic society. Little is said about social studies, history, or critical thinking in the new proposals. Are we to create a nation of technocrats? What implications will that have for the quality and nature of our political and intellectual life?

Discipline in the schools is fine, but what about creativity? Much is said in the reports about higher teacher salaries but little about the profession of teaching except to stress the need for more control and higher standards. Along with higher salaries come more controls and more accountability to the education bureaucracies. What will that do to a profession that has been under pressure for a long time?

The reports and commissions leave many questions unanswered. Excellence sounds like a good thing, and there is universal agreement that the schools do need some added attention and, perhaps, some significant changes. But the very unity of views of the current reformers should give us pause. Once we look carefully at where the recommendations are coming from as well as their content, it is clear a critical assessment is necessary.

NOTES

1. See A. Harry Passow, *Reforming Schools in the 1980s: A Critical Review of the National Reports* (New York: ERIC Clearinghouse on Urban Education, 1984).
2. National Commission on Excellence in Education, *A Nation at Risk: The Imperative for Educational Reform* (Washington, D.C.: Government Printing Office, 1983).
3. Mortimer Adler, *The Paideia Proposal* (New York: Macmillan, 1982).
4. Ernest L. Boyer, *High School: A Report on Secondary Education in America* (New York: Harper and Row, 1983).
5. John Goodlad, *A Place Called School: Prospects for the Future* (New York: McGraw-Hill, 1983).
6. College Board Educational Equality Project, *Academic Preparation for College: What Students Need to Know and Be Able to Do* (New York: The College Board, 1983).
7. Education Commission of the States Task Force on Education for Economic Growth, *Action for Excellence* (Denver, Colo.: Education Commission of the States, 1983).
8. Twentieth Century Fund Task Force on Federal Elementary and Secondary Education Policy, *Making the Grade* (New York: Twentieth Century Fund, 1983).
9. Business–Higher Education Forum, *America's Competitive Challenge: The Need for a National Response* (Washington, D.C.: Business–Higher Education Forum, 1983).
10. Boyer, *High School.*
11. Goodlad, *A Place Called School.*
12. A recent report, for example, argues that half the nation's teacher education programs should be eliminated. See C. Emily Feistritzer, *The Making of a Teacher: A Report on Teacher Education and Certification* (Washington, D.C.: National Center for Educational Information, 1984).
13. U.S. Department of Education, *The Nation Responds: Recent Efforts to Improve Education* (Washington, D.C.: U.S. Department of Education, 1984).
14. New York State Board of Regents, *Proposed Action Plan to Improve Elementary and Secondary Education Results in New York* (Albany, N.Y.: State Education Department, 1983).
15. See John N. Hawkins, *Education and Social Change in the People's Republic of China* (New York: Praeger, 1983).
16. For a historical overview of educational change in the postwar period, see Diane Ravitch, *The Troubled Crusade: American Education, 1945–1980* (New York: Basic Books, 1983).

Part 1

The Excellence Reports:

An Overview

Setting the Boundaries of
Debate about Education

Gail P. Kelly

In 1983 and 1984 over a dozen major reports on the state of the nation's schools appeared.[1] Each was critical in varying extremes of current practices; each suggested a myriad of changes in school curriculum, standards, instructional methods, the teaching profession, and school administration. All stressed the need for "excellence" in education. The reports emanated from diverse sources:[2] the federal government and its agencies (notably the National Science Foundation and the Terrance Bell-appointed National Commission on Excellence); state governments and their agencies like the Education Commission of the States; diverse private philanthropic organizations like the Carnegie Fund for the Advancement of Teaching and the Twentieth Century Fund; business interests like Dow Chemical Company, AT & T, and Texas Instruments; testing organizations like the College Board; and individuals, like Theodore Sizer and John Goodlad, who were funded by public and private philanthropic foundations and educational organizations like the Association of Secondary School Principals to study American schools. There is much overlap among individuals sitting on the many commissions that produced these reports—for example, Patricia Graham and John Goodlad sat on several. Despite this, there is considerable diversity among the reports about the nature and degree of crisis in America's schools, what reforms are necessary, and how "excellence in education" relates to the country's political, social, and economic life.

This chapter discusses the differences among the reports: their analyses of current educational practices; their prescriptions for change; and what agencies they believe should be responsible for bringing about reform. My purpose here is to show that not only is there little consensus about what reforms are needed to improve the schools, but also that the various reports do not provide a consistent plan for change. Rather, they provide a context for discussing reform and rethinking both the direction of education and the role of government and the courts in this process. The reports reorient policy away from social justice goals that had dominated education in the 1960s and 1970s to new goals of employment, productivity, national defense, and "excellence." They not only focus debate about the role of the courts in educational policy formation, but they also open to question which level of government—federal, state, or local—has responsibility for the schools. The reports discuss whether government should play a major role in education at all, or whether the business market and individual parental demand should determine who goes to what school, for how long, and what kind of education schools should make available.

WHAT'S WRONG WITH THE SCHOOLS?

The federal government's Commission on Excellence labelled the primary and secondary schools of the United States a state of disaster that put the "nation at risk." Another federal agency, the National Science Foundation, decried science and mathematics instruction in the secondary schools. The Education Commission of the States, which was funded by a multitude of industrial and business concerns, faulted the primary and secondary schools for teaching students too little about anything. The College Board blamed the high schools for inadequately preparing youth for college. The Business-Higher Education Forum saw higher education as unable to train skilled managers and technicians that they believed industry needed. These reports claim, in short, that student achievement has declined because schools do not demand enough of their students, do not apply stiff criteria for promotion, do not test students enough, and particularly in high school, provide students with too many choices about what subjects they study. Students do not, according to these reports, take enough courses in mathematics, science, and technology; nor, in the case of the Paideia Proposal and the College Board Reports, do they study enough foreign languages, English, or social studies. The latter two reports claim that colleges have slackened their admissions requirements, letting in a larger proportion of unqualified youth. Many of the reports claim high school and college graduates are at best mediocre—Americans don't know as much as their Japanese peers—and this mediocrity (which is directly produced by the schools) is, according to several reports, responsible for high unemployment rates and America's decline in defense and in world trade.

   This condemnation of the secondary schools, and to a lesser extent primary and college education, is by no means unanimous. While all the reports believe the time has come to reform the schools, a decline in student test scores and achievement in general is not the major impetus for all reform. The reports of the Carnegie Foundation for the Advancement of Teaching, the Twentieth Century Fund, John Goodlad's study, *A Place Called School* (funded by Ford, the NIE, and various other agencies), and Theodore Sizer's study, *Horace's Compromise* (which was prepared for the National Association of Secondary School Principals and The Commission on Educational Issues of the National Association of Secondary Schools), have little nostalgia for the supposed "good old days" when SAT scores were high, American high school students excellent, and the American economy strong. Ernest Boyer, who wrote the Carnegie report, and Paul E. Peterson, who authored the background paper accompanying the Twentieth Century Fund report, *Making the Grade*, both point out that if there is a decline in achievement, it is not all that dramatic if measured by SAT scores, since the population base sitting for the SAT's has broadened considerably. Boyer argues that other measures of student achievement do not show a decline over time at all. The real decline, he emphasizes, is in support for the public schools among the aging white middle class.

In his study Peterson agrees with Boyer that the crisis in American education cannot be attributed to overall decline in student achievement, so much as to the fact that the differences in achievement scores between blacks and whites and between males and females have closed. Drop-out rates among black males have declined while they have risen among white males. Schools have moved toward equalizing educational disparities borne of gender, ethnicity, and race. This trend toward equalization, or fear of it, has contributed to an erosion of total middle class support for public education.

While there is disagreement among the various commissions about whether student achievement, particularly that of white males, signals mediocrity in education, most reports contend that schools do not teach what they ought to teach. Herein lies the crisis of the schools. The National Science Board report, for example, faults the high school for not teaching enough science, mathematics, and technology; so do the Carnegie report, and those of the National Commission on Excellence, the Business–Higher Education Forum, and the Twentieth Century Fund, to name a few. Not only do schools fail to offer an adequate number of courses in these subjects; but students, when given a choice, do not enroll in them. The National Science Board report clearly documents the leveling-off in the number of high school students taking biology, chemistry, and physics and taking advanced placement courses in the hard sciences as well as mathematics. The report claims diffusion of such knowledge in the secondary school is tied directly to America's "competitive edge," currently under challenge by the Japanese in world trade and technology. The association between the American economic recession and secondary school instruction in science, mathematics, technology, and computers characterizes the reports generated by the federal government and the business community.[3]

Not all the reports agree that the secondary school curriculum ought to stress science, mathematics, and technology; rather, the Paideia Proposal, which was funded by the John D. and Catherine T. MacArthur Foundation, as well as the College Board report and Sizer's and Goodlad's studies, which were sponsored by private philanthropic foundations and professional educators' associations, see high schools as places where all students ought to receive a general education reminiscent of the University of Chicago's undergraduate curriculum of the 1950s under Robert Hutchins. The problem, according to these reports, is that American schools do not teach students how to learn or think critically. Rather, American schools have engaged in filling students' heads with fragmented bits of information and have failed to make students conversant with all aspects of knowledge and the interrelationships between knowledge generated by different disciplines. While they agree that the teaching of sciences, mathematics, and technology could be strengthened, the central concern is strengthening the entire curriculum to produce a truly educated person. Specialization, Boyer argues in the Carnegie Report, is for higher education, not the high school. Sizer maintains the schools do not need to introduce more and more courses and greater specialization; they need, rather, to teach the full range of knowledge, including the language arts and social sciences in greater depth. The issue is not whether the schools help the United States compete in a world market, but whether students graduate from high school with a strong general education.

Many of the reports bemoan the fact that students in the secondary school have a range of options available to them. They are critical of the schools for tracking and for giving students choice over what they will learn. Most, but not all of the reports, urge that students be given less latitude and control over their own education. Goodlad's report is an exception. Goodlad sees student alienation as a key reason for mediocrity and faults the schools for giving students too little power over what they will learn and how they will learn it. Goodlad is critical of the "sameness" in American high schools throughout the country.

The considerable disparity in the reports on how far secondary ed ,cation has degenerated, if at all, is not surprising, given the lack of commor. criteria for assessing the schools. Some reports used the American economy as the standard (this is the case, for example, in the American Business–Higher Education Forum report); some attempt to use student performance on standardized tests (for example, the Carnegie report); others, like the report from the Paideia group, start from some idealized conception of what a truly educated person is; while still others, like Goodlad, judge the schools on the basis of whether students, parents, teachers, or the community are "satisfied" with the schools. The National Science Board evaluates the schools by the demand for scientific research and development. As Goodlad aptly pointed out in his report, *A Place Called School*, American society "wants it all"; there are no clearly articulated, agreed-upon goals for American schools; rather, a host of different constituencies make conflicting demands on the schools, leaving no clear direction for schools and providing little consensus for how schools ought to be assessed, much less reformed.[4] As several reports stated, we just don't know how good or bad the schools are; all we really know at this point is that, for a diversity of reasons, most Americans seem to be dissatisfied with the schools and that, in and of itself, makes educational reform a priority.[5]

PRESCRIPTIONS FOR REFORM

The reports all call for changes in school practices, but they vary as to which practices they believe are the key to bringing about "excellence" in education. Many of the reports insist upon changes in curriculum and in the teaching profession—how it is recruited, trained, and rewarded. Several reports stress greater cooperation with industry and business. Few of the reports suggest changes in the ways schools are organized, changes in the way in which knowledge is distributed within them, or changes in the conditions of teaching and learning. Most of the reports, in short, propose reform of content without necessarily proposing reform in the way in which knowledge is presented in schools and the ways schools are organized.

The Curriculum

The reports stand in agreement that the curriculum of the schools needs revision; most insist that "more" be taught. Almost all the reports agree that students should have fewer choices in what they study and that there should be less curricular differentiation between college and noncollege bound students. However, there is little consensus among the reports as to what should be "added" to the curriculum and in what doses. The National Science Board calls for greater emphasis on mathematics, science, and technology, beginning in the kindergarten and extending through the primary and secondary grades. The board specifically calls for one hour a day devoted to mathematics and one half-hour per day devoted to science in kindergarten through sixth grade and full-year courses in mathematics and science in the middle school. It also proposes all high-school students take three years of mathematics and science and one semester of computer science, while the college-bound student should be required to study mathematics and sciences for four years. The National Science Board also recommends that probability and statistics be included in the curriculum.

The National Science Board recommendations, which are mirrored only in part in the other reports, do represent much of the approach the various reports take to curriculum reform: namely, limiting students' options by requiring that more of certain subjects be taken by all; insisting on less differentiation between courses taken by college-bound and noncollege-bound students; and introducing computer science into the high school. While the National Science Board recommends that mathematics and science be given more space in the primary and secondary curriculum, not all of the reports urge that curricular reforms be limited solely to science, mathematics, and technology. Many of the reports urge "more" of all basic subjects—reading, social studies, the arts, communication skills, and writing—as well as mathematics and science. Some urge that more foreign-language instruction be added; othere were mute on the question. The Twentieth Century Fund called for the end of all bilingual programs.[6]

The "add-on" approach to curriculum reform does not characterize all reports; the recommendations generated by Sizer, Goodlad, and the Paideia group call for a radical restructuring of curriculum that places less emphasis on the disciplinary, topical division of knowledge embedded in "add-on" approaches and more on the interconnections of inquiry grounded in diverse subjects. The Paideia group and the Sizer study both propose that schools reorganize knowledge into three areas: 1) language, literature, and the arts; 2) mathematics and science; 3) history and social sciences. The curriculum, they contend, should not focus as much on basic skills as enlargement of understanding. They make no distinciton whatsoever between secondary education for college- and noncollege-bound students. All should receive a general liberal arts education in high school that will help to develop individual creativity. Not only do they call for a restructuring of the knowledge schools teach, but they also urge that teaching methods be altered drastically. Instead of teacher-centered learning, they recommend greater individualization, where coaching becomes the norm rather than the exception in the classroom.[7]

It is interesting to note that only three of the reports see instructional methods related to curricular reform. Most of the reports presume that more knowledge can be imparted through the same methods. They assume higher standards for matriculation and greater emphasis on testing will ensure excellence if taught, as will be explained shortly, by more intelligent teachers. Only the reports written by Mortimer Adler, Theodore Sizer, and John Goodlad associate changes in the knowledge schools teach with how school knowledge is taught.

While the various reports urge the schools to teach "more," new, and perhaps reorganized curricula, few directly address the question to how such new curricula will be generated. Most implicitly place the burden of excellence on the individual teacher. Only the National Science Board dealt specifically with this issue and concluded that the infusion of $1.51 billion would be necessary to develop a first-rate science and technology curriculum for primary and secondary schools.[8] For the board, school reform is not simply a question of urging teachers and schools to teach more.

The question of curriculum development in most of the reports is not touched; nor do most call for greater investment in education. Several commissions believe that business and industry miraculously would come to the rescue, donating their expertise to teach the new curriculum without generating greater costs. The business community, in reports they generated, volunteered little in the way of expertise and assistance: the Business–Higher Education Forum and the Panel on Secondary School Education for the Changing Workplace simply called upon the schools to train skilled labor.

Since most of the reports did not directly deal with how to develop the curriculum they propose, it comes as little surprise to find that the reports tend to focus on individual teachers who, to most of the commissions' way of thinking, were primarily to blame for the perceived crisis in the schools. Reforming teachers is, in many of the reports, the way to revise curriculum, and one that certainly would not entail the expenditure of $1.5 billion that the National Science Board proposes.

Teachers

With rare exceptions, most reports on the schools take an extremely dim view of the nation's primary and secondary teachers and see them, rather than the conditions under which they work, as key to educational quality. Many of the reports have little sympathy for teachers. The Twentieth Century Fund goes as far as to blame teachers' unions for education decline.

The reports all allege that the teaching profession has gone downhill— apparently oblivious to the many reports from the past that have spoken equally as dismally about teachers.[9] The Education Commission for the States claims that those going into teaching are the least intelligent of their collegiate peers. Except for Goodlad's and Sizer's studies, few take issue with this condemnation. The reports further assert that good teachers abandon the profession because of unionization, which prevents school districts from re-warding merit and from firing the incompetent. Teachers' pay, they recognize, is low and there is little wage/status hierarchy in the profession. Excellence in teaching, the Education Commission of the States, the National Commission on Excellence, and the Twentieth Century Fund assert, is a question solely of salary—if teachers are paid better, they will perform better; if there are salary and rank incentives attached to performance, then teachers will strive to improve their instructional behaviors. Without the incentive of merit pay and rank, teachers will be mediocre at best. With the possibility of higher salaries, these reports claim, more intelligent individuals will be attracted to the profession, and the problem of excellence will thereby be resolved.[10]

Out of the reports that recommend salary incentives as a way of bringing excellence to education, only a few deal with teacher training. Those that do enter into an age-old debate on whether teachers should be trained in instructional methods or in subject areas; by schools of education or on the job; by professors of education or by fellow teachers. The reports add little to that debate. The bias of the few reports that deal with teacher education is decidedly against the schools of education that have trained teachers; the tendency is to favor subject area, disciplinary training, although the Carnegie report does point out that currently teachers are trained more in subject areas than in methods and that further grounding in the subject areas may not provide the hoped-for panacea. Only Goodlad's study recommends intensified training of teachers in methods.

While many of the reports roundly condemn the teaching profession for its mediocrity, beyond proposing salary incentives tied to performance and a few changes in their pre-service training, they rarely touch upon changes in the conditions under which teachers work. Only three reports even consider work conditions, and all argue that effective teaching is well-nigh impossible in secondary classrooms. Teachers, Sizer's study points out, have an extremely heavy teaching load. They lack control over their own classrooms: instruction they give is continually interrupted, and they are overburdened with administrative tasks.[11] No provision is made for their keeping current in their teaching fields; often they are assigned classes they are not trained to teach. The reports that consider the conditions of work focus less on creating hierarchy and salary incentives tied to performance than on the ways in which teacher autonomy and professionalism can be restored. For the Goodlad and Sizer studies as well as the Carnegie Commission report, excellence in teaching cannot be brought about solely by material incentives; rather, it depends on restoring to the teacher control over what is taught and how it is taught.

Most reports, however, do not perceive teacher autonomy as particularly important. Like the Education Commission for the States, the emphasis is on evaluating teacher performance. In large part this is because many of the reports do not appear to perceive teachers as a distinct professional group with special training needs, or with needs relating to their work conditions that go beyond those affecting a technician in an industrial plant. In fact, several of the reports, in waxing eloquent about the necessity for a school-business alliance, recommend that technicians from private industry and government be loaned out to the schools to teach a range of courses, from science, technology, and mathematics to social studies.[12] They also recommend that teachers work in industry as a way of improving their teaching skills. By making such recommendations, the reports blur the boundaries of the profession, further proletarianizing teacher labor. In the same way, performance-based material incentives, so prominent in several reports, are seen as a way to get teachers to improve their work, just as cash bonuses serve to improve production in a factory.

If the various reports on excellence are by no means unanimous in their prescriptions for reforming curricula and improving teaching, there is even less unanimity over who should take responsibility for bringing about excellence in education—parents, teachers, school administrators, the states, or the federal government.

WHO IS RESPONSIBLE FOR REFORM

It is indeed telling that the National Commission on Excellence appointed by Ronald Reagan's secretary of education addressed its findings to parents and individual citizens and not to the Congress or the federal government and its agencies. The National Commission on Excellence, if anything, absolved the federal government of any responsibility, beyond a moral one, for educating the nation's young people. Rather, it shifted the responsibility to parents, business, and the local community. In a similar vein, the Twentieth Century Fund questioned federal responsibility for reform. Peterson's lengthy essay accompanying the report addressed but one question: had the federal government's intervention in education caused current mediocrity? The answer was neither yes nor no; what the report opened up was the possibility that the government's shouldering responsibility for excellence was harmful and should be avoided at all costs. These reports reflected a rethinking of not only the federal role in education, but also the role of *any level* of government in education.

While the federal government, in the form of the National Commission on Excellence, seemed willing to divest itself of responsibility for reforming the schools, the National Science Board, also addressing its report to "parents" and the population as a whole, made no attempt to remove the federal government from setting policy for education. The National Science Board recommended the president appoint a national education council to establish national educational policy. It envisioned the federal role as setting educational standards, developing national testing programs, initiating model programs, running summer teacher institutes, etc. In short, the National Science Board suggested the federal government expand its role in education and significantly increase its funding of primary and secondary schooling.

The Twentieth Century Fund, while insinuating that the federal government's intervention in education had been innocuous at best and destructive at worst, was not as willing as the Reagan-appointed National Commission on Excellence to withdraw the responsibility for changing the schools from the federal government. Yet, the commission did not foresee the same role for the federal government as did the National Science Board. The Twentieth Century Fund report saw the federal government intervening only to provide equality in education, not to assure quality or excellence or take active leadership in educational policy, which the fund believed was the province of local communities.

The reports not only vary in their perception of the federal government's role in bringing excellence to the schools; they also are less than clear as to what part state government should play. The National Science Board scarcely mentions the states at all in allocating responsibility for educational reform; the Twentieth Century Fund omits the states entirely, as do the Paideia group and Sizer in writing for the National Association of Secondary Principals and the Commission on Educational Issues of the National Association of Secondary Schools. Goodlad calls upon state government to set educational goals, much like the National Science Board called upon the federal government, but Goodlad clearly argues for decentralization, vesting responsibility in the local district and individual school. Only the governor-chaired Education Commission of the States in its report, *Action for Excellence: Task*

Force on Education for Economic Growth, put the reponsibility for national school reform in the hands of state government. The states were to marshal resources for educational reform, forge links between business and the schools, and set standards for students, teachers, and principals.

Many of the reports put the responsibility for reform on individual schools, teachers, or parents, and not on government at any level. Assuring excellence almost seems a question to be resolved at the classroom or individual school level: teachers are to strive to improve education, or local principals and/or superintendents are to provide necessary leadership for reform while garnering assistance from friendly local business and community leaders. Sizer, for one, in the report of the National Association of Secondary School Principals and the Committee on Educational Issues of the National Association of Secondary Schools, puts the onus of reform on the teacher; Boyer, in the Carnegie report, sees it as the province of the principal; while Goodlad places the responsibility on the district superintendent. Other reports, like that of the Twentieth Century Fund, see parents as key to reform. The fund recommends giving parents greater control over their children's education through a system of educational vouchers. The vouchers would enable parents free reign in choosing their child's schooling; the marketplace of parental demand would therefore ensure quality in education, since schools would have to compete for students much in the same way as supermarkets for customers.

While the reports spend much time urging a business-school partnership, none of the reports, even those deriving from the business community, recommend that business be responsible for or take a leadership role in heralding an era of excellence in the schools. Rather, the role of business appears to be one that sets the goals for the schools, since the schools are to train a capable workforce for companies.[13] But business is not expected to directly contribute to education in exchange. School reform is, in many of the national reports, a matter for individual schools, and not a matter for any level of government or the business community.

THE IDEOLOGICAL ROLE OF THE REPORTS

The preceding pages have demonstrated that there is much disagreement among the many reports on education that have appeared in 1983 and 1984. There is no agreed-upon analysis of what is wrong with American schools, and no clear-cut agenda for reform has emerged beyond numerous exhortations to give students fewer choices in their own education and to provide the secondary schools with a more stringent curriculum. No other clear-cut mandate has arisen from the many commission reports other than that someone should take the initiative for reform and something should be done about teachers. Contrary to what is suggested in the written homilies that purport to interpret the reports for practitioners, the reports do not provide an agreed-upon prescription for reform; rather, they set the terms of a national debate about how we go about defining excellence in education, criteria that might be used to assess the schools, and ways of thinking about reform.[14] The reports raise the question of whether schools should be evaluated in terms of the vagaries of the economy and the job market, or America's position in the world market; by cognitive outcomes like academic achievement, or social outcomes like equality, personal alienation, or creativity.

These reports serve to take discussions about education policymaking out of the arena of the courts and to reopen a debate about the role of government in schooling that had been dormant since the 1960s. In the past two decades, educational goals were defined largely in social justice terms and the courts, by virtue of numerous lawsuits, were charged with the responsibility for the nation's schools in that direction. The emphasis had been on equality of educational opportunity for minorities, women, and the handicapped. The current reports, issued within the first two years of the conservative Reagan administration, have reoriented educational policy away from issues focusing on social justice. Instead, the reports have directed educational policymaking to questions of national defense and the economy, and have reopened discussion regarding the proper role of government in education in relation to that of teachers, parents, and school administrators. The reports have not provided a clear agenda for reform; rather, they question the government's role in reforming schools and open for debate the reponsibilities of parents, teachers, business, and the state in bringing about "excellence."

NOTES

1. The reports discussed in this paper include: Education Commission of the States, *Action for Excellence: Task Force on Education for Economic Growth* (June 1983); *Making the Grade: Report of the Twentieth Century Fund Task Force on Federal Elementary and Secondary Education Policy* (New York: Twentieth Century Fund, 1983); John Goodlad, *A Place Called School: Prospects for the Future* (New York: McGraw-Hill, 1984); National Science Board, Commission on Precollege Education in Mathematics, Science and Technology, *Educating Americans for the 21st Century: A Plan of Action for Improving Mathematics, Science and Technology Education for all American Elementary and Secondary Students So That Their Achievement Is the Best in the World by 1995* (Washington, D.C.: National Science Foundation, September 1983); Theodore Sizer, *Horace's Compromise: The Dilemma of the American High School* (Boston: Houghton-Mifflin, 1984); National Academy of Sciences, National Academy of Engineering, Institute of Medicine, Committee on Science, Engineering and Public Policy, *High Schools and the Changing Workplace: The Employer's View* (Washington: National Academy Press, 1984); The College Board, *Academic Preparation for College: What Students Need to Know and Be Able to Do* (New York: The College Board, 1983); Ernest Boyer, *High School: A Report on Secondary Education in America: The Carnegie Foundation for the Advancement of Teaching* (New York: Harper and Row, 1983); *America's Competitive Challenge: The Need for a National Response: A Report to the President of the*

United States from the Business–Higher Education Forum (Washington, D.C., April 1983); National Commission on Excellence in Education, *A Nation at Risk: The Imperative for Educational Reform* (Washington: U.S. Government Printing Office, 1983); Mortimer J. Adler, *The Paideia Proposal: An Educational Manifesto* (New York: Macmillan, 1982).

2. A useful discussion of the differing groups sponsoring the reports may be found in Sheila S. Slaughter, "The Pedagogy of Profit: National Commissions Report on Education." See also, Frances Kemmerer and Alan Wagner, comps., "Summaries of "Recommendations for the Improvement of School Quality and The Costs of Recommendations for Improving School Quality," Center for Educational Research and Policy Studies, State University of New York at Albany, Fall 1983, mimeo.

3. The reports generated by the federal government include the National Science Board report, *Educating Americans for the 21st Century*; the National Commission on Excellence in Education, *A Nation at Risk*; the National Academy of Sciences report, *High Schools and the Changing Workforce*. Those generated by the business community include the Education Commission of the States, *Action for Excellence*; the Business–Higher Education Forum, *America's Competitive Challenge*.

4. Goodlad, *A Place Called School*, 33.

5. See Goodlad, *A Place Called School*; Boyer, *High School*, and Paul E. Peterson, background paper in *Making the Grade: Report of the Twentieth Century Fund Task Force*.

6. Boyer, *High School*; Adler, *Paideia Proposal*; College Board, *Academic Preparation for College*, all called for foreign-language instruction and stressed general education rather than simply science, technology, and mathematics. Sizer and Goodlad emphasized general education as well, but did not specifically call for greater foreign-language instruction.

7. This is the case as well in Goodlad's report, *A Place Called School*.

8. National Science Board, *Educating Americans for the 21st Century*, p. xiii.

9. See, for example, David Tyack, *The One Best System: A History of American Urban Education* (Cambridge, Mass.: Harvard University Press, 1974).

10. Reports that dwell specifically on hierarchy, career ladders, and merit pay include the National Science Board, *Educating Americans for the 21st Century*; National Commission on Excellence, *A Nation at Risk*; Education Commission of the States, *Action for Excellence*; Twentieth Century Fund, *Making the Grade*. Other reports place less stress upon creating material incentives for teachers, but do urge salary increases as well as greater autonomy and changes in the conditions of work—which are missing in the above-mentioned reports.

11. Sizer, *Horace's Compromise*; Boyer, *High School*; Goodlad, *A Place Called School*.

12. Education Commission of the States, *Action for Excellence*; National Science Board, *Educating Americans for the 21st Century*; National Academy of Sciences, *High Schools and the Changing Workplace*.

13. See note 1.

14. See, for example, J. Lynn Griesemer et al., *Education Excellence under Study: Implications of Recent Major Reports* (Chelmsford, Mass.: Northeast Regional Exchange, 1983); A. Harry Passow, *Reforming Schools in the 1980s: A Critical Review of the National Reports* (New York: ERIC Clearinghouse on Urban Education, 1984); U.S. Department of Education, *The Nation Responds: Recent Efforts to Improve Education* (Washington: U.S. Government Printing Office, 1984); Frances Kemmerer and Alan Wagner, "Summaries of Recommendations for the Improvement of School Quality and the Costs of Recommendations for Improving Schools Quality," Albany: Center for Educational Research and Policy Studies, SUNY/Albany, 1983, mimeo.

Reflections on the Great Debate

Ernest L. Boyer

Twelve months have passed since the National Commission on Excellence in Education issued its report, *A Nation at Risk*. That report struck with megaton force: ". . . the educational foundations of our society are presently being eroded by a rising tide of mediocrity that threatens our very future as a Nation and a people." The report continued, "If an unfriendly foreign power had attempted to impose on America the mediocre educational performance that exists today, we might well have viewed it as an act of war. As it stands, we have allowed this to happen to ourselves."

The National Commission report generated a storm of reaction and response. Some people were horrified: "How could this be?" Others seemed almost gratified: "We told you so!" The resultant national debate was fed not only by the alleged rising tide of mediocrity but also by a flood of other school reports.

Now, a year later, it may be somewhat easier to sort out the issues in this debate, to put things into perspective, and to sketch several tentative conclusions about what the so-called Great Debate has brought us and where we may be headed.

As one participant in the debate, I intend to present what seem to me to be noteworthy achievements that have occurred; to look at some of the disappointments; and, finally, to add a few personal reflections about education, the nation, and the world.

ACHIEVEMENTS

First, the obvious: 1983 was a very special year because, after more than a decade of neglect, education became a top priority again. The schools were nearly everybody's candidate for reform.

President Reagan vowed to keep education high on the national agenda

---

in the forthcoming presidential campaign. All of his rivals for the presidency advanced their own remedies for education's ailments. Thirty governors organized task forces on the schools, as did counties and school districts, superintendents and school boards. Whatever the eventual outcome of all of this upheaval, education in America is not now being ignored, taken for granted, or mindlessly condemned. That alone is an achievement. Education matters once again.

Another achievement worth saluting is the involvement of state political and corporate leaders in the recent push for school improvement. The Task Force on Education for Economic Growth, headed by Governor James Hunt of North Carolina, captured the spirit of the new business/political alliance by focusing on the connection between education and economic growth. Even during the post-Sputnik days, when education reform was the byword, the corporate sector was not so actively involved in education as it is today. Nor were governors then so aggressively committed to reform. (What did occur after Sputnik, but is not so evident now, was a marvelously vital network of citizen committees active at the national and local levels.)

Happily, we do not have in this nation a ministry of education. No education czar sets standards and measures compliance. Instead we have 50 states and 16,000 school districts establishing policies for education and monitoring results. It is here, at the state and local levels, that the battle for excellence will be won or lost. And that is why state and private sector leadership is of special significance to the Great Education Debate of '83.

The contribution of higher education should also be noted. Presidents of our most prestigious universities have been speaking out for public education. Academic leaders have served on national commissions, contributing their time and sharing their influence and ideas. The importance of school/college collaboration has been driven home.

We do not have as many scholars involved in school reform today as was the case after Sputnik—shaping the new English, the new biology, the new math. But school/college connections have been strengthened at the administrative level. In 1981, for example, the first summit meeting between chief state school officers and college and university presidents convened in Colorado. A follow-up conference convened at Yale University in 1983, and, thanks to a grant form the Andrew W. Mellon Foundation, school/college projects are now receiving support in states from coast to coast.

I have been equally impressed by the turnaround in the public attitude toward teachers. For decades teachers have been portrayed as ill-prepared, self-serving people who cared less about students than about salary increments and privileges. Suddenly, teachers are being viewed in a more realistic and more sympathetic light. Although there are certainly inept teachers in U.S. public schools, we are beginning to understand that concentrating only on the weakest teachers misses an essential point. We are beginning to see that whatever is wrong with America's public schools cannot be fixed without the help of those teachers already in the classrooms. Most of them will be there for years to come, and teachers must be viewed as part of the solution, not as part of the problem.

After a brief, unfortunate shoot-out between President Reagan and the National Education Association (NEA) over merit pay, we have settled down to a more thoughtful, constructive discussion about how to improve the working conditions of teachers and how to honor outstanding teachers. I see growing agreement that the time has come to reaffirm the centrality of teaching, to support good teachers and give them the recognition they deserve. This is a real achievement.

Surveys reveal that teachers are deeply troubled not only about salaries but also about their loss of status, the bureaucratic pressures, their negative public image, and the lack of recognition and rewards. To talk about recruiting better students into teaching without first examining the current circumstances that discourage teachers is simply a diversion. In 1983 we discovered that the push for excellence in education must begin by confronting those conditions that drive good teachers from the classroom in the first place.

In our own report, *High School*, we conclude that improving the working conditions of teachers is at the heart of our effort to improve teaching. Teachers cannot be expected to exhibit a high degree of professional competence when they are accorded such a low degree of professional treatment in their workaday world. Nor can we expect to attract the best and the brightest students into teaching when they have had twelve years of opportunity to observe firsthand the daily frustrations and petty humiliations that many teachers must endure.

Teachers' salaries cannot be ignored. A teacher at a midwest high school said, during the Carnegie study, "We are tremendously frustrated with pay. We are college graduates—we are professionals." Another teacher put the problem in very personal terms:

> Utility bills, house notes, and car notes eat up a teacher's paycheck, and you haven't even talked about putting clothes on your back or about doing your grocery shopping or paying doctor bills. So if a lot of us are disenchanted with the teaching profession, it's because we can't live on what we take home. I mean, how can you like what you are doing when it's not taking care of you?

In 1982 the average starting salary for teachers with bachelor's degrees was $12,769. When average starting salaries for teachers are compared to starting salaries of other professionals with bachelor's degrees, the contrast is striking. For engineers, the starting salary is $22,368; for computer scientists, $20,364. The average secondary school teacher's salary in 1981-82 was $19,142. We must do better, and there are signs that some states and communities are moving to do what must be done.

Another significant outcome of the Great Debate of '83 has been the renewed interest in the purposes of education. The Carnegie report declares that "the first essential step is to clarify the goals of education." To be effective, high schools must have a sense of purpose, with teachers, students, administrators, and parents sharing a vision of what they are trying to accomplish. The vision must be larger than a single class on a single day. It must go beyond keeping students in school and out of trouble and be more significant than adding up the Carnegie units that students have completed.

The healthy debate over the curriculum is also encouraging. For the first time in several decades, the curriculum is being thoughtfully examined. Priorities are being established. I see a growing recognition that, to be prepared to live in our interdependent, complex world, students must be well informed. In the end, what is taught is what is learned.

Two different positions characterize the current curriculum discussions. One centers on a humanistic approach to education and its outcomes; the other, on an economic approach, with emphasis on the nation's competitive advantage in the so-called high-tech race. Remarkably, both approaches appear to be primarily concerned with strengthening the core requirements of schooling. But the long-term consequences for education will depend on which approach prevails.

In the Carnegie report we urge the mastery of language, which we define as the "basic of the basics." And in our proposed core curriculum we urge that all students be introduced to those unsequential ideas, experiences, and traditions common to all of us by virtue of our membership in the human family at a particular moment in history. We suggest, in short, that the vision of education should be not only national, but global.

The studies of schooling have also reaffirmed the importance of leadership. For years, studies have pointed to the pivotal role of the principal in bringing about more effective schools. Our own field studies support these findings. In schools characterized by high achievement and a clear sense of community, we invariably found that the principal made the difference. Like a symphony orchestra, the high school must be more than the sum of its parts. If excellence is to be nurtured, strong leadership will be needed to pull together the separate elements in the school and make them work.

At a still deeper level, the Great Debate of '83 revealed some rather remarkable and widely shared assumptions about education. The various reports reaffirmed that education is essential for all students and that it must be lifelong. These themes crop up repeatedly:

> *A Nation at Risk*: [A]t the heart of the Learning Society are educational opportunities extending far beyond the traditional institutions of learning, our schools and colleges. They entered into homes and work places; into libraries, art galleries, museums, and science centers. . . . In our view, formal schooling in youth is the essential formulation for learning throughout one's life. But without life-long learning, one's skills will become rapidly dated.

Action for Excellence: We don't believe a high school graduate in 1985 will retire thirty-five years later from the same job for which he was hired—during that period he will need to be trained and retrained many times. Therefore, it is important for that graduate that the high schools give him the ability to learn and to acquire new skills.

Paideia Proposal: Education is a life-long process of which schooling is only a small but necessary part. The various stages of education reach terminal points. . . . But learning never reaches a terminal point. As long as one remains alive and healthy, learning can go on—and should.

Many of the recent reports on education share one additional assumption: the affirmation that our educational system can offer both *equality of opportunity* and *excellence in achievement*. This is an audacious and courageous goal, and we should be heartened to find that the American people are unwilling to surrender it. Here's how the proposition has been put:

Paideia Proposal: [A] democratic society must provide equal educational opportunity not only by giving to all its children the same quantity of public education—the same number of years in school—but also by making sure to give all of them, all with no exceptions, the same quality of education. [This goal was first stated by John Dewey in *Democracy and Education* and is reaffirmed here.]

Making the Grade: [E]quality of educational opportunity cannot be separated from educational quality. The nation is best served by offering our young people the most rigorous educational experience that we can. The federal government has a responsibility to help overcome the unevenness of state efforts. It will have to provide compensatory assistance, for some time to come, to those who are in need of special help. . . . But that does not mean abandoning a single standard of excellence.

To all of this, we added in *High School* the admonition that the struggle for equity in the schools must not be seen now as a chapter in American history but rather as a continuing part of our unfinished work. To push for excellence today without continuing to push for access for less privileged students is to undermine the crucial but incomplete gains that have been made. Equity and excellence cannot be divided.

Finally, the reports have shown—remarkably, I think—a continuing confidence that "the system" will respond. The American "can-do" spirit has been reaffirmed—this despite dramatic talk of "unilateral disarmament" in education and a feeling conveyed by some reports that the patient was near death. Still, the general mood today can be characterized as upbeat, the message hopeful. Here is one example taken from *A Nation at Risk*: "Despite the obstacles and difficulties that inhibit the pursuit of superior educational attainment, we are confident, with history as our guide, that we can meet our goal." Add to that this quotation from *High School*:

We do not suggest that schools can be society's cure for every social ill. . . . Schools can rise no higher than the communities that support them.

Still, without good schools none of our problems can be solved. . . . It is in the public school that this nation has chosen to pursue enlightened ends for all its people.

One is left with the uneasy feeling, however, that some of these affirmations may have been made to reassure the readers—and the authors, too. Nowhere is the basis for America's hopes for its educational system satisfactorily described. Nonetheless, the fact that this nation at this unsettling time chooses to live by its hopes and its resolve, rather than by its doubts, is in itself a remarkable achievement.

DISAPPOINTMENTS

I must admit that I see a dark lining to the silver cloud.[1] Perhaps the most serious shortcoming of most of the reports is their failure to confront adequately the crisis facing our most disadvantaged students. During our own study I was deeply troubled that some of our public schools seemed to differ from the others not just in *degree*, but in *kind*. The social pathology at these institutions appeared to be so great and the problems so complex that our proposals may not be an adequate response.

The breakup of the home, the community wrenched by crime, the lack of public support, the loss of hope—all of these surround and often seem to overwhelm our most troubled schools. How, I wonder, can the schools appropriately intervene? In *High School*, we discuss the importance of the early mastery of language, the need for more counselors, and the need for more parental participation in the schools. We propose more flexible scheduling arrangements, so that students can work and go to school, so that students can learn at their own pace, so that reinforcement and affirmation will accompany the students' efforts. We propose a reentry school for students who drop out. Yet I am left with an uncomfortable feeling that our proposals fall short of being an adequate response to those schools being drained by debilitating conditions that surround them. However, the strategy is not to set lower standards for students at such institutions (perpetuating the destructive two-track system), but to recognize that the school is a connected institution, to acknowledge that it cannot do the job alone.

I have also been troubled that many of the reforms enacted thus far seem to focus on "the system," not the school. Reports by national and state commissions can highlight problems. State legislators can define teacher requirements and minimum academic requirements. In the end, however, the struggle for quality will be won or lost in thousands of classrooms, in the quality of the relationship between teachers and students. Simply stated, schools have less to do with "standards" than with people, and I am disappointed that teachers and students are not adequately involved in the current push for school reform. And I worry that current strategies may simply add to the powerlessness of teachers.

While listing my disappointments, I must comment on the search for panaceas. Somehow we are still inclined to believe that we can improve schools with a miracle drug or two—a longer school year or merit pay, for example. Do the American people—from legislators and teachers to parents and writers of education reports—understand the scope and intensity of the reform endeavor now under way? And do they have any sense of the effort and the time (as well as the cost) of bringing it to pass?

Frequently I hear that the reports (with few exceptions) are flawed because they do not discuss the financing of education. Viewed from one perspective, however, this is progress. For nearly twenty years almost every debate concerning education began and ended with talk about the budget. We debated more about money than about ideas, and I dreamed of the day when the goals and content of education might be discussed before we focused on the budget. That day arrived. In 1983 audiences—for at least a few fleeting moments—were eager to discuss educational excellence and how it can be achieved, without turning immediately to the costs involved. Placing a detailed price tag on proposed solutions might have dampened the debate before priorities and alternatives could be thoughtfully explored.

Still, I have seen insufficient signals that adequate new financial resources will be unearthed or that the resources we do have will be distributed more equitably. It's true that at least twenty-three states are putting money on the line to launch new school improvement programs. But more money will be needed. And I fear that the monetary responses may not be equal to the challenge, especially if an aging population concerns itself with cutting taxes.

Most disappointing of all have been the confusing, distracting signals from Washington. D.C. Secretary of Education Terrel Bell has supported education, but, at a forum in Indianapolis last December—a kind of grand finale for the National Commission—President Reagan declared that we don't need more money; we need more *discipline* in the public schools. This emphasis is consistent with the programs of the Reagan administration, whose record on publicly funded schools deserves a failing grade. For two consecutive years President Reagan sought to cut federal support for education, while advocating prayer in schools and tax relief for parents with children in privately funded institutions.

No one claims that federal legislation is the only answer, but responsible federal steps can and must be taken to clarify the issues, extend our vision, and serve as a signal for state and local leadership to follow, Presidential distractions are not helpful.

When President Eisenhower proposed the National Defense Education Act in 1958, he declared, "American education faces new responsibilities in the cause of freedom, and, if we are to maintain our leadership, we must see to it that today's young people are prepared to contribute the maximum to our future progress." His leadership by inspiration and example told us that the job could and must be done.

And when President Kennedy announced in the early sixties that America was going to the moon, he was announcing a national project for a decade. Although most people probably did not understand the scope or time or cost of the task, the Kennedy charisma, followed by the Johnson clout (plus the general allure of seeing a man on the moon), carried that monumental project to completion.

Consider this: the cost and time required to achieve the goals of comprehensive school reform are comparable to those of the moon project. It will take five to ten years for the reforms to really transform the schools. Take teacher education, for example: better candidates must be recruited into more substantive undergraduate programs, take a fifth year of training, get a teaching job, serve an apprenticeship, and only then begin to exercise influence. A full decade of patience and persistence will be necessary before results are evident.

Can we hold the attention of legislators, given competing pressures from health services and other serious and compelling social needs? Or the attention of the public, as it sees that the hardest, costliest, and most persistent problems occur among that segment of society with least influence and money? If we're going to give the best education to everyone, it is going to take a sustained commitment. We cannot accomplish such an enormous task without leadership, without a deep commitment by politicians, academics, corporate leaders, and citizens to keep education on the national agenda.

PERSONAL REFLECTIONS

While preparing our report I was struck repeatedly by the difficulty of examining the school in isolation. Education is affected by larger trends— forces beyond the classroom and the campus that determine, inevitably, the destiny of our schools. No debate about the nation's schools can be conducted without reference to the larger context within which each school carries on its work. Let me cite three nagging worries of my own to illustrate this point.

First, most of the studies of schooling—and most of the subsequent discussions of them—ignore or gloss over emerging demographic patterns and their effects on public education. The truth is that, more and more, the students who are going to populate our schools will be precisely those students who have historically been least well served there.

The ethnic and racial composition of young America is changing. While the population as a whole is aging, the proportion of black and Hispanic youths will continue to increase. Minorities now represent 17 percent of the total U.S. population; at the same time, they make up more than 26 percent of the total school-age population.

In 1980 black students made up 16.1 percent of the total enrollment, followed by Hispanics at 8 percent, Asians or Pacific Islanders at 1.9 percent, and American Indians or Alaskan natives at 0.8 percent. By 1990 minorities are expected to constitute between 20 percent and 25 percent of the total U.S. population and more than 30 percent of school enrollment.

Most of the nation's high schools have less than 30 percent minority enrollment. On the other hand, enrollments at many urban schools are more than 50 percent black or Hispanic. In St. Louis and Atlanta, for example, enrollments in city schools are at least 80 percent minority. Only about 10 percent of America's public schools enroll about 2.9 million students—including the vast majority of the students from racial minorities.

By the year 2000 the United States could be home to the world's fifth largest population of persons of Hispanic origin. Our future as a nation will increasingly be linked to our neighbors to the south. For this reason, the Carnegie report suggested that Spanish be taught as a second language in *all* of our schools. Offering all students an opportunity to study English *and* Spanish is one valuable way to demonstrate cultural diversity and to encourage the understanding necessary for national unity, as well. I am certain that the success of our schools, as well as the integrity of the nation, will depend on our capacity to achieve unity with diversity in America. And I am equally confident that, with clear goals, a sensitive climate, and excellent teaching, our children can be well served by public education.

Second, I am left with the nagging feeling that America has a *youth* problem—not just a school problem. Indeed, students were hardly mentioned in *A Nation at Risk*. And yet schools are made up of young people; they must reflect the attitudes of those who walk the corridors and meet in classrooms every day.

Our own school visits revealed a disturbing sense of drift among high school students—a feeling of being unwanted and unneeded. This attitude reflects, in part, a startling shift in American work patterns and family life. The number of children in America affected by divorce has more than doubled since 1960. Nearly one in five families is maintained by a woman who is either divorced, separated, widowed, or has never married. Two-thirds of these mothers work. About half of the children now in first grade will have lived in one-parent homes by the time they graduate from high school. This shift in family life has caused schools to assume burdens and responsibilities of the home.

For many teenagers, school may be the only place to find support and to ease the pain of personal trauma and deep hurt. All too often, schools become crisis centers—helping a pregnant girl, supporting a young student who has had a fight at home, helping a teenager through the trauma of parental separation or divorce. One student said, "When my mom and dad separated I thought I'd die. I couldn't study and I felt like I had to cry all day. My English teacher, who I like a lot, stayed after school one day so we could talk. I would have never made it through without her help." Another student told us, "One reason I like my school is becuase I would rather be at school than at home. I even come to school when I have a cold. The reason is because I get bored at home."

School is home for many students. It is also one institution in our culture where it is all right to be young. Here, teenagers meet each other, share hopes and fears, start love affairs, and experiment with growing up. This role will never appear on the report card of the public school.

Here, then, is the troubling dilemma: can we "fix" the schools without dealing with our larger social problems? Can we have healthy schools if students feel confined and uninvolved?

In *High School*, we urge (inadequately, I fear) more home support for schools. We also suggest that youngsters perform community service. Our aim is to help young people reach beyond themselves to participate in their communities. To formalize this objective, we recommend that every high school student complete a service requirement—a new "Carnegie unit"— involving volunteer work in the community or at school.

The Carnegie unit has historically measured time spent in class—academic contact time. This new unit would put emphasis on time in service. The goal of the new Carnegie unit would be to help students see that they are not just autonomous individuals but also members of a larger community to which they are accountable. The program would tap an enormous source of unused talent and suggest to young people that they are needed. It would help break the isolation of adolescents; bring young people into contact with the elderly, the sick, the poor, and the homeless; and acquaint them with neighborhood and governmental issues.

Here's how the service program would work. During each of their four high school years, students would perform volunteer work in or out of the school. They could tutor younger students; volunteer in the school cafeteria, office, or audiovisual center; maintain sports equipment and playing areas. They might also move beyond the school to libraries, parks, hospitals, museums, local government offices, nursing homes, day-care centers, synagogues, or churches.

The new Carnegie unit would not be bound rigidly by calendar or clock. We suggest that a student invest not less than 30 hours per year or a total of 120 hours over four years, in order to qualify for one Carnegie service unit. The proposed service term should be after school, on weekends, and in the summer. We suggest that students themselves should find their own assignments, supervised perhaps by volunteers.

Are we simply loading one more obligation on the schools—after arguing that schools already have too much to do? Perhaps. Still, promoting excellence in our schools means finding ways to help our children understand that, to be truly human, one must serve. And I have concluded that we cannot have healthy schools if students do not feel good about themselves or about their place in the larger world.

One final thought troubles me as I reflect on the Great Debate of '83: the sense that the scope of this debate may be too narrowly defined. The National Commission on Excellence in Education was quite properly dismayed by America's slippage in the high-tech race. We have lost, or are losing, our competitive advantage. In the words of the commission:

> We live among determined, well-educated, and strongly motivated competitors. We compete with them for international standing and markets, not only with products but also with the ideas of our laboratories and neighborhood workshops. America's position in the world may once have been reasonably secure with only a few exceptionally well-trained men and women. It is no longer. . . .
>
> The risk is not only that the Japanese make automobiles more efficiently than Americans and have government subsidies for development and export. It is not just that the South Koreans recently built the world's most efficient steel mill, or that American machine tools, once the pride of the world, are being displaced by German products. It is also that these developments signify a redistribution of trained capability throughout the globe. Knowledge, learning, information, and skilled intelligence are the new raw materials of international commerce and are today spreading throughout the world as vigorously as miracle drugs, synthetic fertilizers, and blue jeans did earlier. If only to keep and improve on the slim competitive edge we still retain in world markets, we must dedicate ourselves to the reform of our educational system for the benefit of all—old and young alike, affluent and poor, majority and minority. Learning is the indispensable investment required for success in the "information age" we are entering.

No one can argue with this crisp, disturbing analysis. National interests must be served. But I feel a growing need to urge that we enlarge our vision. In fact, the National Commission report might better have been titled, *Nations at Grave Risk*.

In the prologue to *High School*, we say that the world has become "a more crowded, more interconnected place." And we conclude, "If education cannot help students see beyond themselves and better understand the interdependent nature of our world, each new generation will remain ignorant and its capacity to live confidently and responsibly will be dangerously diminished."

It is significant that during 1983, in addition to several celebrated reports on education, three other major statements were released. Two of these—one by the Environmental Protection Agency and the other by the National Research Council of the National Academy of Sciences—spoke with remarkable agreement about the so-called "greenhouse effect." Eminent scientists discussed, cautiously and yet with urgency, the global phenomenon involving a gradual warming of the earth's atmosphere because of an increase in the amount of carbon dioxide in the air around us. This worldwide change, which human beings have brought upon themselves, will—responsible scientists predict—change dramatically the quality of life on earth perhaps for our children's children, certainly for our children's children's children.

In a more recent report, another group of prominent scientists predicts that nuclear holocaust could produce destruction and climatic changes of an even more devastating kind. A worldwide fall of debris and smoke could plunge half of the earth into freezing darkness.

I do not suggest either a doomsday or a Buck Rogers curriculum for U.S. schools. Nor do I suggest that bull sessions about the future should occupy the day. But I must confess that, in the quiet moments before dawn, I wonder how our current push for excellence in education relates to the urgent, deeply disturbing issues our students will confront. Will adding more Carnegie units enrich the quality of their lives or adequately prepare them for the world they will inherit?

I believe that it is possible to build a bridge between 1984 and the year 2000. Through language study, students should learn to communicate effectively and responsibly and learn to evaluate the messages of others. Through science and math, students should confront complicated environmental problems. Through the study of government, history, and western and nonwestern cultures, students should learn about our own heritage, come to respect other cultures, and consider ways to live together on this planet.

Above all, students should learn to move across the disciplines, to think creatively, and to deal thoughtfully with consequential issues, understanding that learning must be measured by the wisdom of its application. For this reason, we recommend in our report that each student complete a Senior Independent Project, a written report that focuses on a significant issue, one that draws on the various fields of academic study that have made up the student's program. If education is effective, every student will be able to meet this challenge. It is not too much to expect of an educated person.

For educators, 1983 was a vintage year. Suddenly, public education moved to the top of the national agenda. Governors, corporate leaders, and college presidents reaffirmed their commitment to public education. Solid progress was made in clarifying goals, shaping the academic core, and giving attention to teachers.

If our progress is to be sustained, we must also increase school budgets, find better ways to educate the most disadvantaged students, and accept into the nation's life a new generation of Americans who can enrich our culture. This nation must also find ways to live more comfortably with its children and to acknowledge that parents and other members of the home should be full partners in the educational process. Above all, we must teach our children not just about the past but about the future, the shadowy lines of which are already beginning to take shape.

Educators are by nature optimistic. And while our push for excellence has just begun, I am confident that great strides have already been made and that, together, we will remain on course. This is a time for renewal and for cautious celebration.

NOTE

1. For a perceptive analysis of progress and problems, see Harold Howe II, "Education Moves to Center Stage: An Overview of Recent Studies," *Phi Delta Kappan* 65 (November 1983): 167–72.

Did the Education Commissions
Say Anthing?

Paul E. Peterson

It is easy to obtain agreement on broad goals for education. Except for Wackford Squeers, the Yorkshire schoolmaster whose perverse pedagogical philosophy was detailed in *Nicholas Nickleby,* we all want students to learn more, to be taught by excellent teachers, and to work in a supportive environment. It is the task of devising ways to *achieve* these goals that poses intellectually challenging and political divisive questions.

One might expect to find some thoughtful answers in the recent spate of national reports on American schools. After all, these studies were carried out under prestigious auspices, many of the country's foremost educators and lay leaders helped to shape their preparation and the products themselves have been extraordinarily well-received. The usually cynical press has given the studies respectful attention; presidential candidates have renewed their commitment to quality schools; and interest groups (such as the National Education Association) have been impelled to rethink (or at least to restate) their positions on educational issues. In every one of the fifty states, public officials have appointed one or more commissions on education. According to the Education Commission of the States, there are currently 184 such entities busily at work.

It seems clear that the outpouring of commission and task force reports has had a profound effect on the national education debate. However, the reports themselves, upon close examination, prove to be disappointing. If we judge them by the standards ordinarily used to evaluate a policy analysis focused statement of the problem to be analyzed, methodical evaluation of existing research, reasoned consideration of options, and presentation of supporting evidence and argumentation for well-specified proposals—they simply do not measure up. With some exceptions, the studies do not address

Reprinted, with permission, from *The Brookings Review,* Winter 1983. Copyright © 1983 by the Brookings Institution. Washington, D.C.

the most difficult conceptual and political issues. Instead, they reassert what is well-known, make exaggerated claims on flimsy evidence, pontificate on matters about which there could scarcely be agreement, and make recommendations that either cost too much, cannot be implemented, or are too general to have any meaning.

The bulk of this essay is devoted to an assessment of the major findings and recommendations of the reports—and to a discussion of some of the issues and topics that they avoid. Then, I shall suggest that the inadequacies of the reports have little to do with the quality of the commissioners who signed them—indeed, one could scarcely find more thoughtful or dedicated public servants—and much to do with the nature of the commission process itself. Broadly representative commissions without responsibility or power, except for whatever influence that media attention may lead to, are ill-equipped for the task of policy analysis. I shall close by observing that even if the various commission reports had never been issued, American schools would be on the mend.

THE COMMISIONS AND WHAT THEY FOUND

The recent studies of American education emanated from both public and private sources. The National Commission on Excellence in Education—chaired by David Gardner, president of the University of Utah—was appointed by the secretary of education and officially had the most exalted status. We shall therefore give special attention to its report. In addition, reports were issued by commissions or task forces convened by the Education Commission of the States; the Business–Higher Education Forum; the Twentieth Century Fund; the Carnegie Foundation for the Advancement of Teaching; and the National Science Board.

The discussion below will focus on these six studies. The list could be expanded, but these are the reports that received the widest public notice, and they are fairly representative of the genre. While the reports differ from one another in certain respects, some of which are mentioned below, they are more notable for the similarities of their analyses and prescriptions.

The Diagnosis: A Nation at Risk

The commissions find, first of all, that the future of the country is at stake. According to the Gardner Commission, "If an unfriendly foreign power had attempted to impose on America the mediocre educational performance that exists today, we might have viewed it as an act of war." The Twentieth Century Fund task force, favorably quoting still another commission, is hardly less apocalyptic: "Continued failure by the schools to perform their traditional role adequately . . . may have disastrous consequences for this nation." The National Science Board panel insists that "alarming numbers of young

Americans are ill-equipped to work in, contribute to, profit from and enjoy our increasingly technological society." The Carnegie Foundation study criticizes the Gardner Commission for blaming schools for the "rising tide of mediocrity," but it, too, asserts that "deep erosion of confidence in our schools, coupled with disturbing evidence that at least some of the skepticism is justified, has made revitalizing the American high school an urgent matter."

These proclamations of crisis are the most arresting portions of the reports. However, the information offered in support of the claims that American schools have failed is patchy, dated, and not nearly as dramatic as the rhetoric employed. For example, the evidence that the reports present on student achievement is at best one-sided. The Gardner Commission cites a number of studies that show the scores of high school students on the Scholastic Aptitude Tests (SATs) and other tests of ability fell during the 1970s. The most comprehensive study of student performance, the National Assessment of Educational Progress, did find that the average mathematics score received by seventeen-year-olds decreased 3.6 percentage points between 1973 and 1980. However, most of the commissions neglect to mention that the National Assessment also found an *increase* of 3.8 percentage points in the reading scores of nine-year-olds over roughly the same period. While the studies emphasize declines in the test scores at the high school level, they ignore the gains that have been made in the elementary schools.

The studies are quick to assume that declining high school test scores can be attributed to shortcomings of the educational system. There are, though, other factors that may be at work here—such as the increased use of drugs and alcohol, a rise in the percentage of students who live in single-parent households, and declining employment opportunities—and no one has been able to establish that changes in the classroom, independent of changes in the larger society, are to blame for drops in test results. In any case, the Gardner Commission relies upon data published several years to a decade ago. According to more recent information, student performance on the SATs has stabilized in the past two or three years and has even turned slightly upward.

Many of the reports also speak of declining public support for public education. The Carnegie study, for example, says that high schools "have been weakened by reduced support, declining public confidence and confusion over goals." While it provides no evidence for this assertion, others have pointed to the results of Gallup polls and to purported declines in support for bond referenda, drops in school expenditures, and increases in private school attendance.

Once again the evidence is mixed. If surveys show that confidence in schools has slipped over the past ten years, the slippage is no greater than the decreases that the polls find in public confidence in Congress, the military, and most other governmental institutions. It may be that as Americans are becoming more informed politically, they are rightly becoming more skeptical of institutions and practices that they once accepted on faith.

However one interprets soft survey data, hard figures on bond votes and expenditures for public education reveal few signs of major decline. It is true that the percentage of school bonds approved in referenda fell from 74.7 percent in 1964 to 47 percent in 1972 and climbed back to only 56 percent by 1977. By 1982, though, the approval level reached 73 percent—virtually the same as the 1964 level.

To be sure, expenditures for education in constant (1979) dollars declined from $93.2 billion in 1978 to an estimated $85.5 billion in 1983, and average teacher salaries in constant (1981-82) dollars fell from $22,261 in 1976 to $20,614 in 1983. But these changes can be attributed in the main to demographic, not political, factors. With fewer children in school (a decline of over four million, or 10 percent, between 1977 and 1983) and a large pool of job-seekers in the teacher labor market, school boards needed to build fewer new classrooms and hire fewer teachers—and they were able to obtain qualified personnel at lower salaries. While this left educators unhappy, the view from the student perspective was not nearly as bad. Per-pupil expenditures (in constant dollars) did decline by 8 percent between 1978 and 1983, but only after a dramatic increase of 45 percent between 1970 and 1978. Schools today are less crowded, pupil-teacher ratios are lower, and expenditures per pupil remain substantially higher than they were just a decade ago.

Perhaps the most persuasive evidence of public school failure would be a flight by families to the private sector. Many have cited the increase in private school enrollment from 9.8 percent in 1974 to 10.9 percent in 1981 as a sign that America's confidence in its public schools is eroding. But even this modest trend in favor of private schools may be partly due to improvements over the last few years in the Department of Education's record-keeping. In any case, the percentage of pupils in private schools was still lower in 1981 than in 1960, when it had been 13.5 percent.

The commissions would have had a sounder basis for proposing reforms if they had limited themselves to the claim that schools were no longer improving as rapidly as in prior decades. Educational expenditures seem to have reached a plateau in the early 1980s, after having climbed steeply for decades, and attendance at private schools had increased perceptibly from its 1974 nadir. But these changes, far from signaling imminent disaster, may have indicated little more than a pause in what has otherwise been a continuous upward spiral in the quantity and quality of American public education. Indeed, as the concluding section of this article will indicate, there is every sign that, even before the commissions reported, schools were beginning to regain much of their earlier momentum.

This is not to say that all is well with every aspect of American education. In fact, my chief complaint about the commission reports is that by exaggerating weaknesses, they fail to pinpoint the real problems. For example, if the evidence is combed more finely, one's attention is drawn to the special troubles of the comprehensive American high school—an institution that most of the commissions pass over without significant comment. It is in the high school that one finds a broad decline in academic performance among black and white students alike--in reading and mathematics, in science and social studies. It is the high school senior taking the SAT whose scores have steadily declined. It is the white sixteen- and seventeen-year-old male who is leaving school at a rate 3 percent higher than in 1970. It is in the high school that adolescent resentment is most evident and the purposes of schooling most difficult to discern. Furthermore, the value of the high school diploma in the marketplace is decreasing; high school grades and teachers' recommendations carry less weight with college admissions officers than do SAT scores; and the comprehensive high school, by attempting to cater to the interests of all, seems to satisfy no one. It is significant that many of the most successful high schools in large central cities are those that have narrowed their scope and purpose—the magnet schools, performing arts schools, and vocational schools. These are increasingly preferred over the once-popular neighborhood schools—where in many cases the dominant force is peer group culture, rather than any well-defined adult purpose.

These commissions do not examine specific institutions such as the comprehensive high school, however. Instead, they survey the educational scene in such a sweeping fashion that only through the selective use of uncertain evidence can they make the case that American schools have declined. By attempting to speak to general problems, they preclude themselves from analyzing particular ones.

B-Level Subhead

Objectives and Recommendations

The goals expressed by the commissions are difficult to dispute. The Gardner Commission insists (against what opposition it is hard to conceive) that "citizens must be able to reach some understanding of complex issues." It also calls for—and then defines—"excellence." For an individual learner, "excellence means performing on the boundary of individual ability," certainly a worthy ideal. For a school, excellence means setting "high expectations and goals for all learners," hardly a controversial observation. An excellent society is, not surprisingly, one that "has adopted these policies."

The Gardner Commission is not the only task force to come out foursquare in favor of excellence. The Business–Higher Education Forum finds that "a citizenry literate in science and math is critical to all sectors of American life; such skills, especially computer-related ones, will be increasingly necessary not only in offices and factories, but in schools and homes as well." The Twentieth Century Fund's task force warns that "disaster can be averted only if there is a national commitment to excellence in our public schools," and that "schools across the nation must . . . . [teach] the basic skills of reading, writing and calculating; technical capability in computers; training in science and foreign languages; and knowledge of civics . . . ." The

Carnegie Foundation report declares that high schools "must have a clear and vital mission," that the content of their "core curriculum must extend beyond the specialities, and focus on more transcendent issues, moving from courses to coherence," and that they "should help all students move with confidence from school to work and further education." The Commission of the States takes as its central thesis that "our national defense, our social stability, and our national prosperity . . . will depend on our ability to improve education and training for millions of individual citizens."

Commissions can hardly be prevented from proclaiming objectives that are so much a part of the accepted wisdom that they are truisms. If the education panels had proceeded forthwith to show us how to get the quality and excellence we all desire, their uninspired prose could surely be tolerated.

But since the proof of the pudding is in the eating, what do the studies serve up? A potluck supper that surpasses any offered by your local PTA. The delectables fall into three categories: wholesome main courses for which no recipe is given; gourmet dishes of extravagant cost; and enticing desserts that, once tasted, turn out to be nothing but sugar and air.

In the category of wholesome entrees fall such recommendations as more homework for students, more time for learning (as a result of improved classroom management), better discipline (through the use of firm but fair codes of student conduct), more leadership by principals and superintendents, and higher educational standards for teachers. Most of the studies are chock-full of this kind of advice. Wherever these recommendations can be put into effect, the benefits will doubtlessly be legion. But educators and parents know this already. The problem is that no one has written any reliable recipes for producing the desired results. Schools are such complex institutions that policy-makers at the national, state, and local levels have been unable to produce, everywhere and anywhere, the management, school discipline, and homework assignments that they want.

The gourmet dishes that are recommended by the commissions include 10 to 20 percent increases in the length of the school year; 15 percent increases in the length of the school day; eleven months, instead of nine months, of pay for teachers (which would require a 22 percent increase in teacher salaries, apart from any cost-of-living or merit increases); reduction in the time spent by teachers on "non-educational" tasks (e.g., hall, lunch, and playground supervision); a 25 percent increase in teacher salaries over and above the rate of inflation; full-tuition scholarships for college students planning to become teachers; awards, grants, and/or special assignments for master teachers; sixty minutes of preparation time a day for every teacher; significant expansion of guidance programs; and higher salary schedules for science and mathematics teachers.

One can hardly quarrel with these recommendations. If teachers were better paid, had more time to prepare for class, were paid over the summer to develop professionally, and had fewer nonteaching responsibilities—and if students were exposed to such teachers for longer periods of time—schools would probably be better places in which to teach and to learn. It may be that some parts of these proposals will be implemented in some places, but it is not practicable to adopt all of them everywhere, given the other demands on society's limited resources. The needs of our schools must always be balanced against other societal concerns, whether these be health care, welfare provision, or military defense. Yet the commissions propose extensive and expensive educational reforms without so much as acknowledging, much less taking into account, the plethora of competing needs and expectations.

The amount of resources devoted to public education in the next decade will depend less on the enthusiam with which the commission reports are received—or on any other political factor, for that matter—than on the state of the economy. Although the reports offer no evidence in support of their claim that better schools are essential for economic growth, one can readily find massive evidence for the reverse proposition: As a country becomes wealthier, it tends to devote more resources—both in absolute amounts and as a percentage of gross national product—to education.

It is this tendency that largely accounts for the massive increases over the past five decades in the resources devoted to our educational system. As our country has prospered during that period, teacher salaries (in 1982–83 dollars) have been boosted from an average of $8,139 in 1930 to an average of $21,259 in 1980. Student-teacher ratios have fallen from 25.2 to 16.6 over this same span of time, and, as shown in Table 1, per-pupil expenditures on education (in constant dollars) have increased by more than *five and a half times.*

Table 1. Current Expenditure per Pupil in Average Daily Attendance in Public Elementary and Secondary Schools, 1929–30 to 1979–80

SCHOOL YEAR	UNADJUSTED DOLLARS	ADJUSTED DOLLARS (1979 PURCHASING POWER)[a]
1929–30	87	$ 373
1939–40	88	458
1949–50	209	630
1959–60	375	919
1969–70	816	1,526
1977–78	2,002	2,227
1979–80	2,272	2,001
1981–82	2,670	2,021
1982–83	2,900	2,115

Source: Department of Education, National Center for Education Statistics, *Digest of Education Statistics* (Washington, D.C.: Government Printing Office, 1980, 1982 eds.).

a. Based on the consumer price index, prepared by the Bureau of Labor Statistics, Department of Labor.

These dramatic improvements have actually been only a few steps ahead of the country's overall gains in prosperity. For example, even though teachers' salaries have increased greatly in the past five decades, and even though their salaries today are further ahead of the earnings of the average employee than they used to be (see Table 2), teachers have never been paid more than 20 percent above the average—and if the past is a guide to the future, it is unlikely that they soon will be.

Table 2, Teacher Salaries as Compared to
Average Employee Earnings in All Industries

Year	Elementary and Secondary Teacher Salaries	Average Earnings of Full-time Employees in All Industries	Percent above Average Received by Teachers
1929–30	$ 1,420	$ 1,386	2.4%
1939–40	1,441	1,282	12.4
1949–50	3,010	2,930	2.7
1959–60	5,174	4,632	11.7
1969–70	8,840	7,334	20.5
1975–76	13,120	11,218	16.9
1980–81	18,409	16,050	14.7

Source: National Center for Education Statistics, *Digest of Education Statistics* (Washington: Government Printing Office, 1982), p. 57.

If the gourmet dishes on the menu are delicious but unaffordable, the desserts that the commissions serve are less tasty. What are we to make of the noble sentiment that "the teaching of English in high school should equip graduates to comprehend, interpret, evaluate, and use what they read"? Or of the proposition that "the teaching of mathematics in high school should equip graduates to understand geometric and algebraic concepts . . . [and] apply mathematics in everyday situations"? How can we take advantage of the suggestion that "the teaching of social studies in high school should be designed to enable students to fix their places and possibilities within the larger social and cultural structure"? These recommendations look beautiful, but in fact they are mere puff. Why urge educators to do what they already want to do without telling them anything other than that they should spend more time doing it?

Two commission recommendations that seem exempt from these criticisms—merit pay for teachers and a de-emphasis of bilingual education—have received a good deal of attention. The press, eager to find a bit of grain in so much chaff, sifted through the reports until it found these two kernels worthy of notice.

As to merit pay, the Gardner Commission urges that the salaries of teachers "be professionally competitive, market-sensitive, and performance-based." The Twentieth Century Fund report proposes "reconsideration of merit-based personnel systems for teachers." Thus, both commissions directly challenge the longstanding practice of paying teachers on the basis of education and seniority. President Reagan has endorsed the merit pay proposal, and his Democratic challengers have given the idea at least qualified support. Even teacher organizations have indicated a willingness to discuss the concept. Here, at last, is a central policy issue on which two of the commissions give the public clear guidance.

Or do they? One would expect any policy analyst offering a recommendation on such a key issue to set forth the arguments in favor of that recommendation; consider the counterarguments and explain why they are unpersuasive; assess the costs and benefits of merit pay in countries, states, or cities where it has been practiced; and provide specific suggestions regarding the ways in which the proposed policy might be implemented. Not a single word on any of these topics is to be found in any of the reports. The Gardner Commission says feebly that merit pay "should be tied to an effective evaluation system that includes peer review," but this, its comment on implementation, raises more questions than it answers. What sort of evaluation system would be "effective"? How can we have peer review without mutual back-slapping? For its part, the Twentieth Century Fund asserts that "merit-based systems and collective bargaining are not incompatible." We are relieved to hear the news, but what is the evidence? How do the two arrangements complement one another? Specifically, how can teachers unite to promote and defend their common interests through collective bargaining while fine distinctions in quality are continuously being made among them? On these and other tough questions, the commissions maintain a Sphinx-like silence.

Three commissions discuss the role of foreign languages in American schools. The United States has traditionally been rigidly monolingual in its public education. It now has a growing population of Hispanic immigrants who are more likely to maintain their separate linguistic capacities than the members of any previous immigrant group—the reasons being geographic proximity to the homeland, frequency of return visits, and the continuing flow of in-migration. Thus, language instruction is certainly an especially timely issue and one well worth considered attention.

Indeed, the question has become so urgent that most of the commissions simply duck it. Only the Twentieth Century Fund task force is bold enough to address the issue of bilingualism directly. In a passage given extensive media attention, the panel recommends that "federal funds now going to bilingual programs be used to teach non-English speaking children how to speak, read, and write English." While this statement seems to place the task force squarely in opposition to current national policy, in fact the group's report does not take on the central point of controversy in the debate about bilingual education: Does a child learn English more quickly if taught only in the English language? Or does the child master English more quickly and acquire greater self-confidence if, while learning English, he or she is taught other subject matters in his or her native tongue? On this crucial question, the task force offers no insights.

WHAT THE COMMISSIONS DID NOT SAY

It is conceivable that most of the commissions regarded bilingual education as too peripheral an issue to be worthy of their attention. But it is difficult to imagine a rationale for their evasion of central organizational and governmental questions. If in fact there is a crisis in American education—if in fact we know what we want and we know how to do it—then surely either those in charge have been derelict in their duties or current institutional arrangements preclude effective action.

There were plenty of organizational options that the commission could have considered. Deregulationists have insisted that the federal government remove itself from educational policy-making. Educational interest groups, notably the National Education Association, have said that schools will not be adequately funded unless and until the federal government finances one-third of their total budgets. Many state legislators have insisted that states mandate specific performance standards for individual schools. Decentralizers have called for fewer state mandates and more flexibility for local school principals.

Perhaps the most innovative type of reform that the commissions might have suggested is a reorganization of secondary schooling. As noted earlier, it is in the last years of high school that student attainment has fallen most precipitously and that student dissatisfaction has been expressed most clearly. If the commissions actually believed that the nation was at risk, they should have shouldered the responsibility of proposing fundamental reforms in the last years of secondary schooling.

For example, they might have recommended granting a two- to four-year tuition voucher to every sixteen-year-old, for use at any accredited institution at any time before the recipient reaches the age of twenty-five. A plan of this sort would take advantage of the current administration's interest in non-public schools and focus it on the stage in the educational process at which it makes the most educational sense. It would also exploit the fact that sharp declines over the rest of this decade in the number of adolescents—between 1985 and 1990 the population of fourteen- to seventeen-year-olds will fall by 11.3 percent—will mean that the supply of secondary school facilities will exceed the demand for their use. Shrinkage of the supply will inevitably occur over the next few years. Which schools disappear can be determined either by political considerations or by the choices that students make.

Choice is already the hallmark of postsecondary institutions. At the age of seventeen or eighteen, young people are given a plethora of options that range from private college to state university, from junior college to vocational training center. Even at the secondary level, alternatives to daytime public schools attracted 21 percent of those receiving a high school diploma or its equivalent in 1980. Just over 13 percent received degrees by earning a high school equivalency certificate or by attending evening schools, while nearly another 8 percent received their degrees from private schools. At a time when teenagers are becoming more mobile and independent, they need to be given a greater sense of autonomy in their schooling. A growing number of students now attend schools without walls (high school programs that draw on resources throughout a city instead of limiting themselves to what is available in any one school building), participate in career training programs, and travel long distances from home to attend schools of their choice. If a tuition voucher arrangement facilitated still more choice and differentiation in secondary education, schools might become more repsonsive to the social, educational, and vocational needs of young adults. Those students who wanted to "stop out" could postpone their education until they were ready to make best use of it.

I have described the tuition voucher option not because I believe it will resolve the "crisis" in education, but because it is an example of the kind of far-reaching but still practicable proposals the commissions might have put forward. A committee appointed by the National Academy of Sciences to examine vocational education in depressed areas did recommend vouchers for low-achieving high school students, but none of the high-visibility commissions with broader mandates even comes close to proposing a major organizational innovation. All of them seem to want to keep the basic organizational arrangements now in place—although they do not say that with any conviction either. A crisis is discovered and various reforms are proposed, but in the end no institutional change is deemed necessary to push back the "rising tide of mediocrity."

On governance matters—as on most others—the Gardner Commission takes the clearest nonposition; it says only that "state and local officials . . . have the primary responsibility for financing and governing the schools," while "the Federal Government has the primary responsibility to identify the national interest in education." The task force of the Education Commission of the States weighs in with this observation: "It is our strong conviction that the states and local communities must have the chief responsibility for supporting the schools and for making educational policy. . . . But . . . this is no time for the federal government . . . to shrink suddenly from the issue of education as a national priority."

The Carnegie report, which took the American high school as its central focus, could have been expected to address forthrightly the problems of the comprehensive high school. But that phrase does not even appear in its chapter of recommendations. In fact, the possibilities for organizational reform are virtually ignored, save for the peculiar suggestion that the federal government fund residential academies for gifted students—an undertaking that either would be extraordinarily expensive or would serve so few students that it could hardly address the larger issues at stake. Otherwise, the Carnegie study limits its recommended governance reforms to the following shibboleths: "The States should recognize that their overriding responsibility to the schools is to establish standards and to provide fiscal support, but not to meddle . . . To achieve excellence in education the federal government also must be a partner in the process."

Some minor adjustments in the organization of our school system are suggested—the Twentieth Century Fund, for example, proposes a Master Teachers Program and special federal fellowships for failing students—but the overwhelming, if latent, message in all the reports is that *very little needs to be done differently*. Despite their claims that school systems have deteriorated, the commissions evidently believe that with only the slightest organizational modifications these systems can correct themselves. All that is needed is more money, more public confidence, and more exhortation from on high.

WHY COMMISSIONS SAY WHAT THEY DO

As we have seen, at least six separate educational commissions operating independently of one another all produced policy analyses of dubious value. Why? It could hardly have been the fault of the people involved. Most of the commission members were distinguished Americans with able minds and broad experience. While I was not privy to the deliberations of all of these commissions (and, therefore, the following thoughts are somewhat speculative), I am convinced that their difficulties probably lay in the organizational and political realities of commission decision-making.

As institutions, most commissions are ill-equipped to perform the tasks assigned to them. Commissions are usually asked to address broad public problems that in principle are not susceptible to easy solutions. They typically consist of distinguished citizens who are expected to produce reports expeditiously and with near unanimity. Commissions ordinarily have no power or authority except for whatever they can derive from their own accumulated prestige. To have an impact, their findings must be widely discussed and disseminated. Given these organizational and political restraints, a "successful" commission report is likely to have several not altogether satisfactory characteristics.

1. *The report is almost certain to exaggerate the problem it addresses.* If a commission explores a topic and finds that little is wrong or that not much can be done about what is wrong, the report will never reach the threshold of public attention. The major exception to this rule of thumb occurs when a commission is asked to investigate a great disaster or tragedy in order to insure that it will not be repeated. Under those circumstances, a commission may be tempted to stress the idiosyncratic and unpredictable (e.g., it was one maniac acting alone who shot the president). But when the public's attention

is not already riveted on the topic at hand, a commission (or its staff) is tempted to dramatize its subject matter. This usually requires selective use of evidence and a profusion of strong rhetoric. Careful reasoning, balanced assessment of available information, and cautious interpretations are unlikely to survive the commission's need for public attention.

2. *The report will state only broad, general objectives.* Although commissions tend to be bold in finding serious problems, they are less adventurous in stating their own goals. A representative commission is likely to have within it diverse views on such matters as what schools should do and how they should do it. Agreement is more likely on generalities like excellence and quality, less likely on such hypothetical recommendations as "no more than twenty minutes of physical education, because it has no redeeming academic value."

This sort of outcome is especially probable when the charge to a commission is as broad and general as that given to the education panels. The secretary of education asked the Gardner Commission "to make practical recommendations for action to be taken by educators, public officials, governing boards, parents, and others having a vital interest in American education." At a similar level of specificity, the Business–Higher Education Forum was asked by the president to prepare recommendations designed "to strengthen the ability of this nation to compete more effectively in the world marketplace."

In this regard, the education commissions differed from the National Commission on Social Security Reform, whose charge was quite specific. The social security system was on the verge of bankruptcy, and the commission was asked to review a range of already developed proposals for tax increases and expenditure reductions. Even though the commission's work was complicated by the fact that it could only make imperfect estimates of future social and economic trends, it nonetheless had a well-defined goal— fiscal solvency—that disciplined its considerations.

Education commissions worked within a much more nebulous framework, and they lacked the internal capacity to define more narrow objectives that could be addressed concretely.

3. *The report will recommend changes that are beyond current technology and resources.* The education commissions had no authority, and therefore they had no responsibility. They could insist upon better classroom management, because no one could hold them responsible if it did not materialize. They could call for a 25 percent salary increase, because they did not need to collect the revenue to pay for it.

By contrast, the social security commission had great power and therefore inordinate responsibility. Since its membership was appointed in equal numbers by the president, the Senate, and the House, and since it included representatives of the leaders of both political parties, the commission had all but the formal capacity to enact its recommendations into law. No one expected the social security commission to recommend vacuous or impractical reforms; the participants bore too much responsibility for their actions for that to occur. Instead, the issue was whether any agreement at all could be reached, given the diversity of ideological perspectives at the table and the extraordinary political interests at stake.

Commissions lacking such power and responsibility reach consensus by including every member's favorite proposal in the list of recommended solutions. As long as a proposal does not offend any represented interest except that of the poor taxpayer, then it can be added to the collection. Members spend much of their time at commission meetings becoming acquainted with one another. Since members are not paid for their participation, the activity is expected to be enjoyable and intrinsically satisfying. Harsh disagreements, rigorous cross-questioning, and hard-nosed analysis of proposed solutions are more the exception than the rule. Only when a commission member perceives a vital interest at stake does he or she employ the kind of rigorous analysis that this same person might routinely undertake in other spheres of activity.

4. *The report will not spell out the details of its proposed innovations.* The more detailed a recommendation, the less likely the commission is to agree on its virtue. Differences of opinion can be smoothed over by leaving crucial questions of implementation to someone else. Since the commission does not know whether even the general concept will win wide acceptance, struggling over the details does not seem worth the effort.

5. *The report will seldom call for institutional reorganization.* The most controversial proposals are those that call for a rearrangement of institutional responsibilities. Broadly representative commissions in education typically include a school board member, a superintendent, a representative from a state department of education, a dean of a school of education, a teacher, a representative from the business community, a trade unionist, and minority representation. (Commissions lacking such breadth will be accused of being narrow, partisan, and self-serving; their recommendations will not have the prestige required to win wide publicity and general applause).

Such a group is unlikely to agree on organizational reforms expressed even in the most general terms. While substantive policy proposals such as merit pay may be stated vaguely enough to gain general consent, reorganization proposals have too discernible a set of political consequences to be easily compromised. As a result, the "hot potatoes" are simply set to one side (after a half-day or so of heated discussions).

6. *The report will poorly document the value of the solutions it proposes.* Documentation is a painstaking, time-consuming, boring activity. It requires days of reading, gathering, and assessing information, followed by hours of careful writing and editing. It is staff work!

The reasons the staff does not do the work are legion. Understaffing is one factor. Commissions are expected to be cost-effective, to deliver a large bang for few bucks. One full-time staff member, with overhead, may cost nearly as much as all the other commission expenses combined. That staff member spends inordinate amounts of his or her time planning meetings, handling expense vouchers, preparing minutes, drafting versions of the report, and handling internal and external communications.

But even if staff were ample, the necessary documentation work would probably not be done. While a good staff can document the problem, it cannot gather evidence to assess proposed recommendations until these are agreed on by the commission. Unfortunately, the commission typically agrees on its proposals only at the end of its term of office—which in all probability has already been extended beyond the originally anticipated terminus. In the first months of a commission's life, members become acquainted, listen to experts discuss the problem, receive testimony from interested groups, and explore alternatives. By the time agreement is reached, it is too late to look at the evidence. Moreover, staff-produced analyses in the final stages of manuscript preparation might even sabotage the commission process. Detailed assessment of a proposal would uncover unanticipated difficulties that, if brought vigorously to the commission's attention, would be perceived as a staff attempt to circumvent the commission's policies. In the end, the staff, no matter how knowledgeable and industrious, concludes that it is better to leave certain problems unmentioned than to spell out and justify proposed recommendations in detail.

Commissions do have their functions in American politics, but fact-finding, rigorous analysis, and policy development are usually not among them. Commissions are more appropriate for dramatizing an issue, resolving political differences, and reassuring the public that questions are being thoughtfully considered. Oscar Wilde said it the best: "On matters of grave importance, style, not sincerity, is the vital thing."

THE COMMISSIONS MAY SEEM TO SUCCEED

Although the commission reports have limited value, they may, as luck would have it, come to be seen as having had a major impact. Not only have the reports been given widespread publicity and not only have they spawned new activity in many state legislatures, but it would not be surprising to find that in the next few years test scores improve, public confidence returns, and fiscal support for public education increases.

Several factors point in this direction. First, student performance has already begun to improve, especially among pupils now at the elementary school level and, most recently, at the junior high school level. As these students proceed through the educational system, the test scores of high school students, including those taking the SATs, can be expected to increase. Secondly, many of the changes wrought by school desegregation have now been absorbed by public schools. Periods of social transition are likely to affect adversely the particular generation that undergoes the change and disruption. Those who follow enjoy the benefits of the new regime without having the costs of transition. Thirdly, there is some reason to believe that the United States is now entering a period of sustained economic growth. To be sure, fiscal deficits, third-world debts, and possible oil interruptions remain potential threats to a sustained recovery. But if the current economic resurgence continues, schools will be among the beneficiaries. Even if federal aid does not increase, state and local governments, which currently finance 90 percent of the cost of public education, can be expected to commit to education substantial portions of any new resources that a more productive economy generates.

States and localities may be even more prepared to move in this direction because a number of national commissions have urged them to do so. But the commissions seem more to have reflected than to have spawned a widespread revival of interest in schools. Commission reports appear to have been well-received in spite of their contents, because Americans had already become interested in school quality. Even before the reports were issued, bond referenda were being approved with increasing frequency; candidates for state office were already finding educational issues to be a key component of a winning campaign strategy; and Democratic presidential hopefuls, calling for renewed attention to the nation's human capital, had identified education as a major campaign theme.

In the United States, one seldom knows whether leaders are shaping or following public opinion. In the case of the commissions, I suspect it has been mainly a matter of following. But by running fast to the head of the pack and shouting loudly en route, the commissions may have made an impression after all.

Part 2

The Social, Political, and Economic Context

Political and Economic Analysis

Joel Spring

The economic and political origins of the excellence movement in education in the 1980s can be understood by a close study of three of the movement's influential educational reports. The political origins of these reports have had a determining effect on their interpretations of the relationship between the schools and the economic system, and their prescriptions for educational reform. I will first discuss the political context of these three reports and the current economic conditions to which these reports are reacting. It will then be shown how the political base of each report has shaped reactions to economic conditions and influenced proposals for educational change in the excellence movement.

The first report to be considered is that of the Reagan administration's The National Commission on Excellence in Education. This report was given the ominous title of *A Nation at Risk* and was compiled by a group primarily composed of representatives from the educational community.[1] It is important to understand that the commission was appointed by the Reagan administration and worked within the context of administration concerns with educational policy. These concerns, since the time of the 1980 election, have focused on reducing the federal role in education, supporting school prayer, and seeking aid for private education through tuition tax credits. In the 1980 election Reagan was not supported by the major educational organizations like the National Education Association (NEA) and, at least on education issues, had to turn to a different constituency composed of critics of public schooling, moral reformers, and the Christian school movement.[2] This constituency, of course, shared many values with the membership of the Moral Majority. Reagan offered the critics of public schooling and moral reformers a promise of less federal intervention and school prayer. To the Christian school movement he offered tuition tax credits.

By 1983 Reagan's educational program had achieved mixed results. There was some reduction in federal control, particularly with the passage of the Educational Consolidation Act, but proposals to abolish the Department of Education, create a system of tuition tax credits, and legislate school prayer did not pass Congress. Therefore, with the impending 1984 election, Reagan's educational program was being criticized by his original supporters for being ineffective, and by the public school establishment for its apparent lack of support for public education. As will be discussed later, the *A Nation at Risk* report provided Reagan with a politically safe method of trying to project an image of friendship toward public education without alienating his original educational constituency.

The second report to be considered is that of the Task Force on Education for Economic Growth of the Education Commission of the States. The report, *Action for Excellence,* was put together by a group primarily composed of state governors and the leadership of some of the most powerful corporations in the United States. The task force consisted in part of twelve governors, three state legislators, one representative of organized labor, six educators, and four organizational leaders. Certainly the most impressive part of the membership were fourteen business leaders. The co-chairs of the task force were Frank Cary, chairman of the Executive Committee of the IBM Corporation, and Honorable Pierre S. du Pont IV, governor of Delaware and an heir to the DuPont chemical fortune. Also on the task force were the chief executive officers of Texas Instruments, the RCA Corporation, Ford Motor Company, the Xerox Corporation, Dow Chemical Company, Control Data Corporation, Johnson Publishing Company, Time-Life Inc. and SFN Companies. In addition, business membership included the vice-chairman, board of directors, of the American Telephone and Telegraph Company, and the chairman of the National Association of Manufacturers.[3]

As will be discussed later, the important place of major corporations on this task force determined its reaction to economic conditions and educational proposals. In addition to economic concerns, individual members had particular educational interests. DuPont had been instrumental in organizing and served as chairman of a national program called Jobs for America's Graduates (JAG). JAG trains selected youth in basic employment skills for entry-level positions.[4] The vice-chairman of JAG, Governor Lamar Alexander of Tennessee, was another important member of the Task Force on Education for Economic Growth. In the last several years Governor Alexander has attempted to build his political fortunes in Tennessee on an educational reform package that has as its main element a career ladder for teachers.[5] The major opposition to the career ladder has come from the state affiliate of the National Educational Association. The use of career ladders, along with master teacher plans and merit pay, has become the central focus of discussion in proposals to improve the quality of American teachers.

The third report to be considered, *High School: A Report on Secondary Education in America,* sponsored by the Carnegie Foundation for the Advancement of Teaching, has yet a different political base. Foundations have played an important role in shaping the intellectual life of the United States by the types of projects, scholarship, and reports they fund. They have also had a major influence in the promotion of welfare capitalism. The basic tenet of welfare capitalism is that to avoid serious social discontent in a capitalist society, some intervention to aid those in dire economic-social need is necessary. The general attitude of the foundation movement in the United States was best expressed by Alan Pifer in his last report in 1982 after serving eighteen years as president of the Carnegie Corporation of New York. Pifer warned that without welfare capitalism

> there lies nothing but increasing hardship for ever-growing numbers, a mounting possibility of severe social unrest, and the consequent development among the upper classes and the business community of sufficient fear for the survival of our capitalist economic system to bring about an abrupt change of course. Just as we built the general welfare state in the 1930's and expanded it in the 1960's as a safety valve for the easing of social tension, so will we do it again in the 1980's. Any other path is simply too risky.[6]

The report of the Carnegie Foundation for the Advancement of Learning was authored by its president, Ernest L. Boyer. Boyer relied upon consultants and observers for the collection of data. The overwhelming majority of observers, sixteen out of twenty-three, were university faculty members. The other six were associated with school systems, foundations, and educational research organizations. The seventeen consultants were almost evenly divided between academics and leaders of other foundations. The ideological background of the foundation and those associated with the report made it less likely than the other two to serve immediate political and economic interests.[7]

Therefore, we have under consideration three reports serving different sets of interests. *A Nation at Risk* is being used to serve the political aspirations of an incumbent president; *Action for Excellence* serves the economic interests of major corporations and the political interests of governors; and *High School* serves the interests of those seeking long-term social stability.

These three political perspectives are reflected in the reports' responses to current economic problems. Both *A Nation at Risk* and *Action for Excellence* use the public schools as a scapegoat for current economic problems and argue that reforming education is essential for economic improvement. On the other hand, the *High School* criticizes those that use the schools as a scapegoat for economic failures and argues that there are other important educational concerns beside national economic development.

To understand the arguments of these reports one must examine aspects of the economic development of the United States since the early 1970s. During the decade of the 1970s and into the 1980s there was relatively high unemployment, particularly among youth, declining productivity, and dwindling capital investment by American industry. The high unemployment figures during this period were caused by the large number of youth from the "baby boom" entering the labor market. This baby boom did not affect West

Germany and Japan. There was no increase in labor demand during this period. In other words, unemployment was not caused by a decline in available jobs but by an increase in the number of persons seeking employment. This flooding of the labor market, or cohort overcrowding, resulted in a decline in wages, particularly for entry-level occupations. In the 1970s and into the early 1980s American youth has had a difficult time finding employment at wages comparable to those of the previous decade. The response of American business to a labor surplus and declining wages was to become more labor intensive and decrease capital outlays. For instance, a company might choose to add work shifts to increase production, as opposed to investing in new equipment.[8]

These changes in labor use and capital investment contributed to a slow growth in productivity in American industry. Productivity is simply defined as the level of output divided by the amount of labor used to produce it within a certain period of time. The increased use of labor naturally led to a productivity problem within the boundaries of this formula. Between 1960 and 1978 the rate of average annual percent increase in labor productivity in the United States was 1.7 and in Japan it was 7.5.[9]

What is happening in the 1980s is almost the exact opposite of the trends of the 1970s. With the bust of the baby boom there are now fewer youth entering the labor market. One set of figures shows that the average number of new workers entering the labor force in the 1970s was approximately 2.5 million; by the late 1980s this number will decline to approximately 1.5 million workers. Another estimate has set the figures for the decade of the 1980s at a 14 percent decline in the number of persons between fourteen and twenty-four-years-old and a 20 percent decline in high school enrollments.[10]

What is important to understand about these economic changes is that the poor position of the United States in world markets has not been caused by the public schools, but by the decisions of business management. Even to suggest that the schools were responsible would be to stretch any existing economic argument.

A Nation at Risk has allowed the probusiness Reagan administration to shift the blame for declining American productivity and resulting problems of foreign trade from the decisions of business management to the public schools. The issue of public schools served a very useful political purpose. President Reagan was able to support a plan to increase productivity without pointing a finger at American businesses in that if the schools were to blame, educational reform could at the same time be seen as an economic cure. This projected an image of an active reformer without offending the traditional business constituency of the Republican party.

Our nation is at risk. Our once unchallenged preeminence in commerce, industry, science, and technological innovation is being overtaken by competitors throughout the world. This report is concerned with only one of the many causes and dimensions of the problem, but it is the one that undergirds American prosperity, security, civility. We report to the American people that while we can take justifiable pride in what our schools and colleges have historically accomplished and contributed to the United States and the well-being of its people, the educational foundations of our society are presently eing eroded by a rising tide of mediocrity that threatens our very future as a Nation and a people.[11]

These are the opening lines and the central theme of *A Nation at Risk,* which is primarily concerned with how the failure of the public schools has supposedly caused a weakening of technological development and a decline of America's position in world trade. The report specifically warns of Japan's efficient production of automobiles, South Korea's steel production, and West German products. It directly links international trade with economic development and proclaims, "If only to keep and improve on the slim competitive edge we still retain in world markets, we must dedicate ourselves to the reform of our educational system for the benefit of all—old and young alike, affluent and poor, majority and minority." `

The business-dominated Task Force on Education for Economic Growth's report, *Action for Excellence,* uses the schools as a scapegoat for economic problems, but also addresses immediate labor problems faced by American business.

Like *A Nation at Risk,* the report opens with a description of America's declining productivity as compared with other countries. Again, without suggesting that it was the decisions of business management that caused the problem and that the cure might also be in the hands of business, the task force writes, "It is the thesis of this report that our future success as a nation—our national defense, our social stability and well-being and our national prosperity—will depend on our ability to improve education and training for millions of individual citizens."

The report also reflects how business id dealing with labor problems. As mentioned previously, the baby-boom bust has resulted in fewer new workers entering the labor market. Business's response to this situation has been to work increasingly with the school to maximize the size of this labor pool by improving the education of those students who would have been marginal and unemployed in the 1970s.

There are many examples of the increasing number of school and business partnerships; here we will briefly examine five programs. The Boston Compact, signed by the city school system and the Boston business community as represented by the TriLateral Council and the Private Industry Council, specifically focuses on the preparation of students for the local labor market. The compact argues that Boston's recent period of prosperous growth has not benefited local poor and minority residents because of their lack of skill in reading, writing, math, and self-discipline. The school system has agreed to prepare students for local labor market needs, and the business community has agreed to give hiring priority to Boston school graduates.

Another example is the Atlanta Partnership of Business & Education, Inc., chartered by the state of Georgia with the goal "To enhance the Economic Development Potential of Atlanta And To Improve The Standard Of Living Of Its People By Raising the Educational Achievement Of Its Citizenry." The Atlanta Partnership has made direct links between developing magnet schools and local labor market needs. The advisory committee of the Atlanta Partnership provides continual council to each magnet school, "so that the curriculum and its delivery stay attuned to developments within the industry"[15]

Chicago United has also taken the approach of linking the schools to the needs of the local labor market. It has taken a major role in changing the administrative organization of the schools. One result is that businesses have opened their own alternative educational centers where students are brought during school hours. This gives business direct control over the training and socialization of students. The Continental Bank and Harris Bank of Chicago have organized two centers for economics and business studies. The Holiday Inn has two centers for hotel/motel careers and Montgomery Ward operates a center for marketing and retail.[16]

Adopt-a-School programs are taking place in most urban centers in the United States. The idea of the program is for individual businesses to work cooperatively with a particular school to help improve and enrich the school program. This plan allows a business to be identified with a particular school. For instance, in Denver twenty-nine different organizations, including the Central Bank of Denver, the Samsonite Corporation, the Lions Club, and the Denver Broncos, have adopted schools.[17]

Another national program to provide increased business involvement in schools as a means of enhancing the employability of students is Jobs for America's Graduates (JAG). The presence of JAG officers on the Task Force on Education for Economic Growth was mentioned earlier. The JAG program emphasizes helping youth who are identified as potentially unemployable to find and hold an entry-level job. The program stresses an orientation to the real world of work and basic employment skills. It reflects corporate interest in the proper socialization of youth to work and in the expansion of the labor pool.[18]

These current trends in partnerships between business and education received added support in the 1982 Job Training Partnership Act that guarantees that business will be the predominant force in these relationships. The stated purpose of the legislation is "to establish programs to prepare youth and unskilled for entry into the labor force and to afford training to those economically disadvantaged individuals . . . . facing serious barriers to employment." The legislation requires that business hold a majority on the local administrative unit governing the program.[19]

Urban employers are now reporting difficulties in finding qualified employees for entry-level positions. Increasing the pool of potential employees means renewed attention to the urban poor and minority groups. To a large extent business either abandoned or neglected urban school systems during the school desegregation crisis of the 1970s, but with the possibility of a shrinking labor pool driving up wages, business has shown an expanding interest in the education of the disadvantaged.

The developing cooperative links between business and the schools can be considered to serve two purposes. On the one hand, business wants to assure that the more able students receive the type of education needed to serve the technological and research needs of corporations; on the other hand, less able students must be properly prepared and socialized for work. To accomplish these two objectives, the business community has decided it is necessary to tighten their linkages to the schools so that they can influence the curriculum for their benefit and assure that any socialization occurring in the schools conforms to their needs.

The *Action for Excellence* report stresses in several places the necessity of building these links between the schools and American business. In this introduction to the report it is stated, "We believe especially that businesses, in their role as employers, should be much more deeply involved in the process of setting goals for education in America and in helping our schools to reach those goals." As one of the "action recommenations," the report states, "Business leaders should establish partnerships with schools." And in bold type in the section on "Education and Growth" it is proclaimed, "If the business community gets more involved in both the design and the delivery of education, we are going to become more competitive as an economy."[20]

The Carnegie Foundation report, *High School*, provides an interesting contrast in tone to the other two reports. First, it rejects the use of the public schools as a scapegoat for problems in the American economy. As the report states, "And to blame schools for the 'rising tide of mediocrity' is to confuse symptoms with the disease." Secondly, it tempers its concern with economic productivity with a recognition of other important educational goals: "Clearly, education and the security of the nation are interlocked. National intersts must be served. But where in all of this are students? Where is the recognition that education is to enrich the living of individuals? Where is the love of learning and where is the commitment to achieve equality and opportunity for all?"[21]

High School reflects a greater concern than do the other reports discussed here with maintaining institutions that assure social stability. It does not reject linkages between schools and the economy, nor does it reject the idea of greater business involvement in the schools. In fact, an entire chapter is devoted to lauding those relationshps. But it differs in its emphasis on the idea that the public high school, and by inference all levels of public schools, must be saved to maintain the school's role in assuring the safety of the present organization of social and political institutions. The mandate is clear: "A deep erosion of confidence in our schools, coupled with disturbing evidence that at least some of the skepticism is justified, has made revitalizing the American high school an urgent matter."[22] This attitude of saving the high school is not new in Carnegie thought; Conant's 1959 report, *The American High School Today*, also attempted to save high schools after a decade of criticism that they were the weakest link in national defense and were anti-intellectual.[23]

The Carnegie Foundation report does not reject the idea of linking national economic goals with public schooling nor the idea of greater business involvement. Its concern is that the criticism of the high school might destroy public faith in that institution, and that the broader goals of supporting an ideology of equality of opportunity might be lost as schools are made to serve primarily economic ends. In other words, the preoccupation with immediate economic goals might destroy the role of the school as a mechanism of welfare capitalism.

With regard to proposals for reform, all three reports share a concern with increased academic requirements. There are variations in these proposals for increased academic requirements and, in general, they reflect actual changes that are taking place in states throughout the country. It is interesting, however, that these proposals have not received as much public attention as the proposals related to teachers. To understand why this has occurred, one must place the proposals within their political context.

It is clear that the Reagan administration's *A Nation at Risk* had to walk a very narrow political tightrope. Obviously, there could be no proposal for increased federal involvement in education. More importantly, President Reagan could not stress increased state academic requirements because of the possible alienation of his original educational supporters. Over the last ten years, the Christian school movement has fought in the courts to eliminate all state minimum standards because they believe that these standards interfere with the free exercise of religion. In many of the court cases, Christian schools have stressed their belief that state standards impose the teaching of secular humanism. In general, the private school movement has been more interested in fewer, not more, state-mandated requirements.[24]

This presented a political problem: which parts of the *A Nation at Risk* report support Reagan's effort to project an image of concern with social issues and the public schools? The solution was to focus on that section of the report dealing with teachers and, for very specific ideological and political reasons, to concentrate on the issue of merit pay. Reagan's attempt to shine the public spotlight on this issue made 1983 into what I call the "Year of the Teacher."

Although merit pay for teachers became the central focus of the Reagan administration's rhetoric, it was not the only proposal regarding teachers in the report. The report also called for increasing educational standards in teacher education, a demonstration of competence of teacher education graduates, and the use of nonschool personnel to ease the shortage of mathematics and science teachers. These subjects might have appeared to the Reagan administration as too complex for the simple purpose of image-building.

On the other hand, the merit pay proposal was simple and fit into the general tone of Republican rhetoric. Merit pay connotes an image of an efficiently run business where hard work receives its just reward. But more importantly, merit pay provided Reagan with an opportunity to try to divide the two teachers' unions. Traditionally, both teachers' unions have been strongly opposed to merit pay proposals because of the difficulty of determining merit.

When Reagan announced support of some form of merit pay plan in the spring of 1983, there was a mild display of sympathy for the proposal from Albert Shanker, president of the American Federation of Teachers. It is not clear why Shanker took this position. In June 1983 Shanker invited Governor Lamar Alexander of Tennessee, who has been previously discussed in regard to the *Action for Excellence* report, to explain his plan to the national convention of the AFT. Union politics probably played a role; the Tennessee affiliate of the AFT's rival union, the NEA, was leading the state battle against Alexander's plan. In one sense, the invitation was like a slap in the face to the NEA.[25]

Shanker's initial show of sympathy and willingness to discuss the issue provided Reagan with an ideal political opportunity to try to divide the educational community and to win support from some members of the public school establishment. During the week of June 15, 1983, Reagan invited Albert Shanker and education officials representing school boards, state superintendents of education, and school administrators to the White House to discuss merit pay and master teacher plans. The NEA was not invited.

Education Week described this meeting in the following manner:

> Mr. Reagan, according to other sources, was also commencing a "divide-and-conquer" strategy to gain the support of most of the education community as the 1984 Presidential campaign begins, while excluding the N.E.A. The strategy, the sources said, involves generating education and public support for teacher-pay reforms, while portraying the N.E.A. and the Democratic candidates seeking its endorsement as being "on the wrong side of the issue." "It is clear that one of the things the Administration is thinking about is how merit pay divides our community," said one education lobbyist.[26]

In the end, Reagan's attempt to divide and conquer garnered few political gains from the educational community. The AFT continued to attack Reagan administration policies and back Democratic candidates. By December 1983, at a meeting staged by the administration's National Commission on Excellence in Education, Reagan was emphasizing school discipline and stressing that the federal government should not provide more money for education. This speech indicated that Reagan was less confident of his ability to win notes from the educational community and was instead appealing to the general public.

One of the things that Reagan did accomplish in his 1983 attempt to win support from the educational community was to make teacher pay plans a central issue of educational reform discussions. In addition to the actions of President Reagan, Governor Lamar Alexander worked vigorously to get the Task Force on Education for Economic Growth to recommend his career ladder plan for teachers. As a result career ladders became one of the important recommendations in *Action for Excellence*. The report stated, "We strongly recommend that each state create a 'career ladder' for teachers that will help attract and keep outstanding teachers." In the wording of the report, the career ladder concept was given a "strong recommendation" while proposals for improved in-service training, recruiting, and training were given a simple recommendation.[27]

An important difference between the National Commission on Excellence in Education and the Task Force on Education for Economic Growth is one of emphasis on public communications. Although Reagan jumped on the teacher issue, the governors and corporate leaders who put together *Action for Excellence* did not make it the central focus in its publicity. For this group the important issue has continued to be building close ties between the schools and business.

In striking contrast to *A Nation at Risk* and *Action for Excellence* is the *High School*'s treatment of the teacher issue. Both *A Nation at Risk* and *Action for Excellence* place the blame for the quality of teaching in public schools on the shoulders of teachers. Teachers are told that they are of poor academic quality, that they received inadequate training in colleges of education, and that they lack initiative and creativity on the job. In essence, what these reports do is blame the victim! The solutions center around tighter technocratic control and increased monetary incentives.

The Carnegie Foundation's *High School*, on the other hand, provides a more sympathetic view of the plight of the modern teacher. The blame is placed not on the teacher but on the conditions under which the teacher works. In *High School* we learn that teachers suffer from the intrusion of a hierarchical administrative structure, an overburden of administrative details, overcrowded classrooms, and too large of a classroom load.[28]

High School makes recommendations that are more supportive of changes in the working conditions of teachers. Along with a call for increased rewards and improved training and recruiting, the Carnegie Foundation recommends a reduction of the high school teaching load to four daily classes, with one period for small seminars, a minimum of sixty minutes for class preparation, and exemption from monitoring and clerical activities. To stimulate the intellectual life of the school the report recommends, based on Robert Schaefer's 1967 book *School as the Center of Inquiry*, that schools be organized as centers of inquiry that would allow teachers to explore "the nature of what and how they are teaching."[29]

The differences between the content and uses of these three reports regarding teachers illustrates the impact of politics on education. Merit pay, career ladders, and competency tests for teachers are relatively easily understood by the public and therefore are politically useful. They present a public image of getting tough on the teacher issue; and they are political solutions, in the sense that they represent legislative ways of exerting more control.

On the other hand, the working conditions of teachers do not make a good political issue. Too messy and difficult to define to the general public, this concern also tends to focus attention on the structure of schools and not the individuals within the schools. There is no easy legislative solution that can be neatly packaged and presented to the public. A solution might also suggest a reduction of legislative control, not an increase in control. For these reasons, improving the working conditions of teachers, thereby reducing teacher burnout, is not a popular political topic.

What this means is that as federal and state politics have become increasingly tied to education over the last three decades, the nature of political life has come to define the solutions to many educational problems. The political style requires solutions that are simple and can be understood by the public, that project a good image for the politician, and that involve increasing political control. This has meant increasing technocratic solutions involving the manipulation of pay plans and increased testing. Issues such as working conditions, intellectual climate, and the humaneness of schooling find little place in the rhetoric of image-building political candidates.

What have been the consequences of these three reports? First, President Reagan dropped the teacher issue as his major educational concern in the 1984 election. This obviously occurred because of his inability to win the support of the teachers' unions. Secondly, the major thrust of the Task Force on Education for Economic Growth is now taking place. States have enacted or are proposing legislation to increase academic standards and to change teacher pay plans and recruitment. But, more importantly, the partnerships between schools and business are increasing at a rapid rate. The schools are becoming more concerned with meeting the needs of the labor market as defined by business. The Carnegie Foundation's report, however, appears to have had little direct political impact, except for those working within the educational establishment.

All of this activity over the last year raises some very serious questions about the political and economic nature of American schooling. Since the 1950s the schools have been linked to national policy objectives. In the 1950s the public schools were called on to win the cold war against the Soviet Union by providing more mathematicians and scientists. The parallels between the 1950s and present rhetoric should be noted. In the 1960s Presidents Kennedy and Johnson called upon the public schools to end poverty and improve the economic conditions of minority groups. In the 1970s Presidents Nixon and Ford tried to use expanded career and vocational education programs to solve problems of unemployment. In none of these eras did the public schools win the military arms race, end poverty, or cure unemployment.[30]

What we are discussing here is the linking of education to national policy objectives, which should not be confused with equal educational opportunity. Also, an important issue over the last decades, increasing equal opportunity, has primarily been a result of judicial actions, with political institutions and politicians responding to court actions.

Linking education to national policy objectives assumes that something called a "national interest" actually exists. The problem with the concept of a national interest is that it requires someone or some group of people to define it. In other words, the national interest is a political decision. In reality a group of people with power define their interests and then declare them to be national interests. Presently, the national interest is being defined as increased technological development to improve international trade. As has been discussed, education has become the scapegoat and solution in the debate over this newly defined national interest.

What are the consequences of this continual linking of education to national policy objectives? First, it has caused confusion and financial strain within the public schools. Every decade has its new policy objective, which has meant the withdrawal of funding and programs established in the previous decade. Many educators have watched newly established programs collapse with shifting political winds.

Second, academic changes might serve the interests of business but not of individuals. Corporate and political leaders want schools to produce increased numbers of workers in certain areas to depress wages or maintain already depressed wages. The push for more scientists and engineers in the 1950s and early 1960s resulted in a flooded labor market and unemployed scientists and engineers in the early 1970s. Presently, wage scales for scientists and engineers are moving upward, and companies are seeking to flood the market with new graduates. At the other end of the spectrum, business is concerned about the decrease in numbers of those entering the labor market and wants the schools to concentrate on socialization for specific occupations.[31]

Federal and state politics have allowed for the shaping of American education to meet the needs of some supposed national interest. Often, this national interest is defined by those with the most power. If we are to save our schools from the turmoil of political use, we must deal with the question of who should decide what knowledge is of most worth. This is the fundamental question.

Relating educational change to economic needs has resulted in a continued shaping of the curriculum to meet the needs of the workplace. This is most evident in the increased demands for more mathematics and science in the curriculum. It is openly admitted that the goal is to produce more scientists and engineers. But is this what is needed in a democratic society?

One could argue that America's economic problems have been primarily political in origin. For instance, America's economic problems could be related to the high deficits and inflation caused by the Viet Nam war or to the federal government's handling of the energy crisis of the 1970s. If this were true, then one might argue for more political education in the schools. The point, of course, is that it is wrong to bias public school curricula in one direction when there is no proof that the most important social, economic, and political problems have been adequately defined.

This issue can more clearly be understood by considering other possible alternatives to secondary school requirements. Maybe America's problems stem from an inability of the population to think clearly through important issues. If this were true, why not have all secondary schools require three years of philosophy? Maybe the problem is the inability of the population to understand and act on political, social, and economic issues. One might then replace the meaningless hodgepodge of social studies with a requirement that all secondary students have three years of sociology, three years of economics, and three years of political science. Perhaps society has been ruined by too much technology and not enough appreciation of the arts and humanities. If this were true, why not require three years of music, three years of art, and three years of literature? All of these curricula could be argued for in terms of some national need and purpose. The real question regarding the curriculum is, what knowledge is of most worth?

Another fundamental issue is what the excellence movement means without adequate funding, and with a lack of support and proposals for compensatory education. What seems to be clearly emerging is a new form of elitism of the worst type. Certainly, elitism is not contradictory to equality of opportunity as long as everyone has an equal opportunity to join the elite. In the present situation the elites will be those able to complete the new academic requirements and go on to college. But without increased funding for central city schools, improved compensatory education programs, and increased support for college students, it will only be the children of the affluent who will participate in this new technological elite.

In other words, without more economic support for the above types of programs, there will be an increasing tendency for school systems to divide students according to the income of their parents, and into those who will be trained to be the leaders of the new technology and those who will be socialized to fill other occupations. Present reforms might be the final step in making the public schools the central reproductive mechanism of class society.

I argue that education has been a political football and has been made to serve special economic interests. As a result we will probably see public school systems increasingly separate students according to the needs of the labor market. And, without adequate funding for compensatory education and central city schools, this division will increasingly follow social class lines.

Second, we will see the development of a curriculum designed to prepare students to solve technocratic problems and to serve corporations. In other words, students will be trained to be servants of power and not thinking participants in a democratic society. Lastly, teachers will probably experience some increase in pay along with an increase in work. Additional controls will be exerted over the profession. None of these changes will guarantee better teachers unless there is an improvement in working conditions and in the intellectual atmosphere of the schools.

NOTES

1. The commission membership included four college administrators, two college faculty members, one member of a state school board, one member of a local school board, a representative from the National School Boards Association, one state school administrator, three local school administrators, one former governor, a head of a foundation, a retired corporate executive, one teacher, and one private citizen.

2. In the 1980 election Republicans essentially dismissed the possibility of support from the two teachers' unions. Both the National Education Association (NEA) and the American Federation of Teachers (AFT) stood squarely in the Democratic camp in the 1976 and 1980 elections. The role of the NEA in national politics has become extremely important in the last two national elections. In 1976 the NEA endorsed its first presidential candidate, Jimmy Carter, on the strength of his promise to establish a separate Department of Education. In 1980, it was claimed that the NEA was responsible for Carter's defeat of Edward Kennedy in the Democratic primary. A more complete discussion of federal politics of education can be found in Joel Spring, *American Education*, 2nd ed. (New York: Longman, 1982): 171–97.

3. Task Force on Education for Economic Growth, *Action for Excellence* (Denver, Colo.: Education Commission of the States, 1983): 6–7.

4. "JAG: Jobs for America's Graduates, Inc.," undated pamphlet distributed by JAG; "Synopsis: Jobs for America's Graduates," fact sheet distributed by JAG; and "Initial Research Results," in *Crossroads* 1 (March 1982):3.

5. See "Final Passage of Tennessee Plan Likely," *Education Week*, 22 February 1984, 1.

6. Alan Pifer, "When Fashionable Rhetoric Fails," *Education Week*, 23 February 1983, 24.

7. Ernest Boyer, *High School: A Report on Secondary Education in America* (New York: Harper & Row, 1983): 325–26.

8. See Daniel Quinn Mills, "Decisions About Employment in the 1980s: Overview and Underpinning"; and Michael Wachter, "Economic Challenges Posed by Demographic Changes" in Eli Ginzburg et al., *Work Decisions in the 1980s* (Boston: Auburn House, 1982).

9. Mills, "Decisions About Employment," 8–9.

10. Wachter, "Economic Challenges," 35–42; and Michael Timpane, *Corporations and Public Education* (New York: Carnegie Corporation, 1982): 8–9.

11. National Commission on Excellence in Education, *A Nation at Risk: The Imperative for Educational Reform* (Washington, D.C.: United States Department of Education, 1983): 5.

12. National Commission on Excellence, *A Nation at Risk*, 7.

13. Task Force on Education for Economic Growth, *Action for Excellence*, 14.

14. *The Boston Compact: An Operational Plan for Expanded Partnerships with the Boston Public Schools,* September 1982, booklet distributed by the Boston Public Schools.

15. *The Atlanta Partnership of Business & Education, Inc. Second Anniversary Report,* undated booklet distributed by the Atlanta Partnership of Business & Education, Inc.

16. *Chicago United and the Chicago Board of Education: Partners in Change* (March 1, 1983), booklet distributed by the Chicago Public Schools. "Chicago: 404 Businesses Support Career Education Drive in Schools," in *You & Youth* 2 (November 1980), published by Vocational Foundation, Inc.

17. "Adopt-A-School 1981–1982," pamphlet distributed by the Denver Public Schools.

18. See note 4.

19. Public Law 97-300 Job Training Partnership Act (October 13, 1982).

20. Task Force on Education for Economic Growth, *Action for Excellence,* 3, 18.

21. Boyer, *High School,* 5–6.

22. Boyer, *High School,* 6.

23. James B. Conant, *The American High School Today* (New York: McGraw-Hill, 1959).

24. See Spring, *American Education,* 248–51.

25. "Invites Tennessee Governor to Speak at AFT Meeting," *Education Week,* 8 June 1983, 2.

26. "Meets with Education Officials on Teachers, NEA Left Out," *Education Week,* 15 June 1983, 1.

27. Task Force on Education for Economic Growth, *Action for Excellence,* 37.

28. Boyer, *High School,* 154–86.

29. Boyer, *High School,* 159–60.

30. For a history of this period see Joel Spring, *The Sorting Machine—National Educational Policy Since 1945* (New York: David McKay, 1976).

31. For a study of educational inflation see Richard Freeman, *The Overeducated American* (New York: Academic Press, 1976).

Educational Reports
and Economic Realities

Michael W. Apple

THE POLITICS OF CONTROL

Perhaps it was inevitable, but it still seems odd at first to find so much attention to educational issues in the eighties. For a decade or more, schools have tended to languish on the sidelines of official political discourse. Then within the space of a very short time, our formal institutions of education have come center stage. Elementary, secondary, technical, college, and university education, coupled with the special attention being paid to the training and evaluation of teachers, is no longer a topic for politicians, government officials, pressure groups, business, union members, columnists, academics, parents, and others to talk about when the "important" things are over. Instead of being the functional equivalent of conversation about the weather, discussions about education have again become deadly serious matters.

The last time education as a national issue received so much attention occurred at the very height of the cold war. Then, the federal government and business saw education as part of a larger battle with the Soviet Union and its allies over the production of technical expertise and knowledge, defense, "manpower" planning, and industrial might. The National Defense Education Act and similar legislative mandates and policies provide examples of the government's (the "state's") earlier concern with these issues.[1] The similarities between then and now are striking. Educators today live with the legacy of these concerns and policies that engendered large-scale changes in curriculum and teaching. Elsewhere I have discussed these alterations, including the de-skilling (and partial re-skilling) of teachers, the creation of an expensive and capital-intensive curriculum in our schools, and the connections between these attempts at transforming the educational system into an overt agent of state military and industrial policy and gender and class relations.[2] I shall point to them again later in this chapter. But the fact is that both the pressure education is under today and the proposed solutions to the educational dilemma have a history; the fact that such pressures and solutions are connected to these larger political, economic, and ideological forces makes them quite consequential. Education talk *is* and must be serious talk, but perhaps not in the way we are used to thinking about it.

At both the local and federal levels, movements for accountability, competency-based teacher education and testing, systems management, mandated "basics," academic standards, and so on, are clear and growing. This is not occurring in the United States alone. A number of countries are experiencing similar movements, in part because similar structural problems beset their economies, and in part because the United States exports both its crisis and its management techniques and procedures throughout the capitalist world.[3] (These countries often see these techniques as having the imprimatur of science and efficiency and, hence, tend to employ them, even to the detriment of their own situations.) The many reports being produced currently did not start these movements. They are themselves, in many ways, products of these tendencies.

I shall not review here all the content of the multitude of reports and reform proposals that have crossed our desks and gained so much media attention in the past few years. These have been described in detail in numerous places. In fact, it is quite possible that the specific content of each of these proposals is less consequential than the overall tendencies they represent and, especially, how they will be used by various contending groups. In a chapter of this size, I can only paint a picture of these tendencies in rather broad strokes; but, though broad, the outline of what seems to be happening in education will be quite visible.

It is important to begin with the realization that the reports are as much political as they are educational documents. First, all discussions of educational policy, to the extent that they deal with the issue of changes in content, are political. The knowledge that is taught is always someone's knowledge: debates over it sponsor certain groups' visions of legitimate culture and disenfranchise others.[4] Second, the reports are attempts at rebuilding a consensus over education that has been partly fractured during the past decade. Thus, they will be couched in a language of the "common good," a language that seeks to have something in it for everybody so that as many powerful people as possible can fit under its linguistic umbrella. And the documents are calls for action, calls to use scarce resources and political power for specific ends; therefore, the language of these many reports needs to be analyzed not necessarily for its truth value (though as we shall see later, this is not unimportant), but for its rhetorical use.

Others have noted the political nature of this discourse as well. Stedman and Smith's comments are illustrative here:

At the outset, it should be recognized that these reports are political documents;

the case they make takes the form of a polemic, not a reasoned treatise. Rather than carefully marshalling facts to prove their case, they present a litany of charges without examining the veracity of their evidence or its sources. By presenting their material starkly, and often eloquently, the commissions hoped to jar the public into action, and to a great extent they have been successful. Caveats and detailed analysis might have lessened the reports' impact.[5]

Lastly, and very importantly for my points about looking for the meaning of the documents in their specific uses, the various reports are decidedly political in terms of the context in which they are to be read. They do not spring out of untilled soil. They arrive at a specific time, a time in which rightist reaction is a considerable force in the government and society at large, and when western economies are less than fully healthy. This is important in terms of the uses to which the documents may be put.

BETWEEN PROPERTY RIGHTS AND SUBSISTANCE RIGHTS

What is the nature of the crisis that the reports are responding to? It is first and foremost an economic crisis, but it is much more than that. Behind it is a crisis in authority relations and ideology as well. At the outset, let me focus primarily on economic issues. School policies and the curricular, teaching, and evaluative practices they entail have historically had important connections to economic pressures. The various reports continue this history. It is clear that for a large majority of them it is not only the internal problems within the school that are so worrisome, but also, in a major way, the relationship between the school and what is happening to the country's national and international industrial "might." We need, of course, to be careful of being too reductive here. Schools and educational reports and policies do have relative autonomy. They cannot be read directly from the needs of the state or the economy. Educational institutions and personnel in general, and curriculum and teaching policies and practices in particular, have their own internal histories, their own discourses, and their own interest in protecting themselves from external forces. Yet since the reports *are* so self-consciously directed at current economic conditions, it is crucially important to place these documents within these conditions.

What are the elements of what is happening economically? In broad outline, the context is provided by the following:

The powers of the American state are now deployed in a massive business offensive. Its basic elements are painfully clear. Drastic cutbacks in social spending. Rampant environmental destruction. Regressive revisions of the tax system. [Looming trade wars and high unemployment now considered "normal."] Loosened constraints on corporate power. Ubiquitous assaults on organized labor. Sharply increased weapons spending. Escalating threats of intervention abroad.[6]

We are currently witnessing, in the words of Piven and Cloward, "nothing less than the recurring conflict between property rights and subsistence rights, which originated with the emergence of capitalism itself."[7] In short, the economy of the United States is in the midst of one of the most powerful structural crises it has experienced since the depression. In order to solve it on terms acceptable to dominant interests, as many aspects of the society as possible need to be pressured to conform to the requirements of international competition, reindustrialization, "rearmament" (in the words of the National Commission on Excellence in Education), and, in general, the needs of capital accumulation. The gains made by working men and women, minority and poor groups, and others in employment, health and safety, welfare programs, affirmative action, legal rights, and education in government, in the economy, in local communities, and elsewhere must be rescinded since they are "too expensive," both economically and ideologically. Both of these latter words are important. Not only are fiscal resources scarce (in part because current policies transfer them to the military), but people must be convinced that their belief that personal rights come first is simply wrong or outmoded, given current "realities." Thus, the power of the state—through legislation, persuasion, administrative, legal, and ideological pressure, and so on—must be employed to create the conditions believed necessary to meet these requirements.[8]

Though Theodore Roosevelt's dictum that "We must decide that it is a good deal better that some people should prosper too much than no one should prosper enough" may be behind these assaults and pressures from capital and the right, the reality is something else again. There is prosperity and there is prosperity. Given the fact that 80 percent of the benefits of most past social programs have gone to the top 20 percent of the population, we should want to ask "who benefits?" from any proposals coming from current government bodies, commissions, and from affiliated organizations.[9] The benefits of proposed education reforms are not immune to this question.

Perhaps some figures will be helpful in enabling us to focus this question. It is estimated that by 1985 a poor family will be least 5 percent less well off than in 1981, while a middle class family will be 14 percent better off. A rich family will show a 30 percent gain in its already large advantage. These figures, even if taken by themselves, indicate a marked redistribution of income and benefits from the poor to the rich.[10] They are made even more significant by the fact that the middle class is actually shrinking as the numbers at the extremes grow. We have an increasingly "double-peaked" economic distribution as the number of well-to-do and poor increase.

These inequalities—though growing—have been around for quite some time. In the United States, the bottom 20 percent of the population receives a smaller percentage of total after-tax income than the comparable group in Japan, Sweden, Australia, the Netherlands, West Germany, Norway, France, and a number of other nations. This gap is not being reduced at all within the

United States. In fact, in the past three decades, the gap between the bottom 20 percent of U.S. families and the top 5 percent has nearly doubled. The percentage of families that received less than one-half of the median national income actually increased between 1950 and 1977. Again taking the early 1950s as our starting point, in 1951 the top 20 percent of the population received 41.6 percent of the gross national income while the bottom quintile received only 5.0 percent. When we look at more current 1981 figures the bottom 20 percent still receives the very same 5.0 percent, but the top 20 percent has "captured a 41.9 percent share."[11] While these changes do not seem overwhelming, the amount of money this entails is very large and is certainly indicative of a trend favoring the top 20 percent.

Yet this is not all. One out of every seven Americans lives in poverty, as does one out of every five children under the age of six. More than one-quarter of all Hispanics and more than one-third of all Afro-Americans live below the poverty line. "In 1981, even before the major Reagan cuts, more than 40 percent of families living below the poverty line received no food stamps, medicaid, housing subsidies, or low price school lunches." Even the government has estimated that the diet of those living (subsisting?) at the official poverty level is so deficient "that it is suitable only for 'temporary or emergency use.'"[12]

Gender, race, and age inequalities as well are so pervasive as to be almost painful to recount. Women working fulltime outside the home earn less than 60 percent of male full-time wages. Black women working fulltime earn only 53 percent and Hispanic women only 40 percent of what men earn. In 1980, one in three women working fulltime outside the home earned less than $7,000 a year. In the same year, women with college degrees averaged only 56.5 percent of the earnings of men with equivalent education and only 81.4 percent of the income men with high school diplomas earned. In 1981, nearly 53 percent of the families headed by black women and over 27 percent of those headed by white women were officially poor. If we consider the elderly poor, 72 percent are women and, in 1980, of the elderly black women living alone, 82 percent were near or below poverty.[13]

Men of color earn 80 percent of the earnings of white men with comparable levels of education and of similar age. Access to comparable jobs is virtually blocked and, in fact, may be worsening, given current policies. Thus, "more than 60 percent of black men and 50 percent of all Hispanic men are clustered in low-paying job classifications."[14]

Finally, examining unemployment makes the picture of this part of our economy even more graphic. Some econometric measures indicate that the unequal cumulative impact of unemployment on minorities and women has actually doubled between 1951 and 1981. The data on unemployment rates tell a similar story. Though current figures are slightly lower than the nearly 21 percent for blacks and 9.7 percent for whites in 1982, the differential has not lessened. For white teenagers, the unemployment rate was approximately

25 percent; for black youth it was a staggering 50 percent, with an even higher unemployment rate in many urban areas. For these reasons and others, "the income gap between white and black families has actually widened slightly since 1970, as black median income dropped from 66 percent to 65 percent of white median family income."[15]

I could go on at greater length; in fact, it is very tempting to do so since many Americans do not ordinarily have to confront the immense inequalities in our society, especially since it no longer seems fashionable for the media to present anything else but the official statistics generated out of Washington. What is important here is to inquire into how the proposals take these data into account.

As we have just seen, for many of the American people, even when educational levels and "skills" are equalized, the economy has *not* been as responsive as the theory behind the reports would have it. Education is not the solution to the bulk of these problems. Existing and quite widespread conditions of discrimination, exploitation, and inequality—that is, structural conditions generated by the economy and the dual labor market, and by governmental policies that largely reproduce these conditions—are among the root causes.[16]

To be fair, the reports do not totally ignore the problems these data signify. Most of the authors of these documents undoubtedly care about such inequalities, and they certainly care about what is happening to our economy, though perhaps not in a way that might lead to more democratic economic and cultural arrangements. Yet, they construct their responses largely upon a vision of the future economy that is wrong and upon educational solutions that are largely inappropriate.

A HIGH-TECH SOLUTION?

One major response of the reports is to blame our economic problems on our educational system and on our lack of high-technology industries. For these authors, however, only the economic problems as defined by industry are significant enough to cause a crisis. Thus, a large part of the solution lies in making our schools and their curricula more responsive to industrial and technological needs. However, a sense of the effectiveness of this high-tech "solution" can be seen from recent data on employment trends. Let us look at this just a bit more closely.

The reports recognize that we are becoming what has been called a "service economy." Because of this, certain kinds of jobs will be created, while others are lost. The largest increase in the number of jobs will be in relatively smaller firms. They will also be in business services, health care, and the wholesale/retail trades. This transformation is readily visible in the fact that the number of people working in health care is already double that of people employed in construction. McDonald's employs three times as many workers as does U.S. Steel.[17] Yet these expanding positions are generally low-paying and have little autonomy. Even the expansion of business services, with its focus on a high-tech, computer-driven future, needs to be examined carefully since it is estimated that the widespread computerization of the business world will create a net *loss*, not a net gain in jobs, especially among women.[18] This last figure is quite telling: women constitute the fastest growing segment of labor and already hold the largest share of working class positions in the economy. The almost total neglect of gender specificities, the blindness to the sexual (and racial) division of labor and "women's work" in general, when coupled with the romanticism of their high-technology vision, weakens the economic position of the reports in the extreme and obscures their redefinition of the legitimate knowledge needed by industry and the military.[19]

Given the fact that in our economy there has been a major expansion of positions with little autonomy and control while those jobs with high levels of autonomy have declined, one has to raise questions about such a high-tech vision. The further fact that these "proletarianized" positions are increasingly being filled by women is made even more important by the realization that women make up a clear majority (54 percent) of working class positions. This percentage is increasing. Women, minorities, and youth—the lowest paid and least autonomous workers—now constitute 70 percent of all such positions.[20] Since a high-tech solution will not have a totally beneficial impact on this group, to say the least, the reports' envisioned economic future cannot but ignore the bulk of the data I have brought together in these last two sections of my analysis.

One of the major social functions of the reports lies in the implications of this neglect. They will actually make it harder for us to recognize these gender, race, and class inequalities as truly structural, as long-lasting and anything but accidental. Not only are these inequalities insolvable by small increments of educational reform, but a large part of their "solution" may also in fact exacerbate the problem. If structural conditions within a corporate society constantly generate these lamentable conditions, is giving more of the school over to the needs of capital the solution? Must we accept corporate notions of what counts as important knowledge, and corporate definitions of necessary "skills" and "work habits" as the limits of our response?

It is quite possible to claim that the corporate sector, a sector that dominates our economy and has enabled the logic of the commodification process relentlessly to enter nearly all aspects of our cultural and personal lives, bears a significant portion of the blame for our social and educational crisis. "Adam Smith notwithstanding, profit maximization by large, economically powerful, private corporations has not maximized the public good." The investment and employment decisions that business has made have in large part generated "dislocation, discrimination, declining real wages, high unemployment, pollution, poor transportation systems, and run down crime-ridden cities."[21] These are not "costed-out" when the corporate sector makes these decisions, but these social costs *are* born by the public. The effects on communities, the health and welfare of the bulk of the population, and on our cultural lives and education have been enormous.

Thus, by employing the language of the "public good" and yet bringing the educational system more closely into line with the needs of the corporate sector, what counts as the public good and what counts as the knowledge and skills that are required to be taught in schools to fulfill these needs of the "public" are severly truncated. Such truncated discourse may help dominant groups, but it is open to question whether such benefits will be shared by the rest of us.

CLASSROOMS AND TEACHERS

If the reports in general mistake effects for causes and misconstrue the emerging tendencies within the economy, are they more accurate at the level of classroom dynamics and their proposals for curriculum and teaching?

In responding to the economics that lies behind the reports, we should not assume that everything is fine in the classrooms of America. All of these documents are responding to some very real problems in classrooms. If one enters many classrooms, one is not immediately struck by the power of existing curriculum content and teaching.

What is the empirical status of curriculum and teaching practice in classrooms? While perhaps not totally generalizable and despite the possibility of some flaws in the research design, the findings from the study conducted by John Goodlad and his associates do enable us to gain a much better glimpse of what happens inside classrooms.[22] The "modal classroom" exhibits the following characteristics: "A lot of teacher talk and a lot of student listening, unless students are responding to teachers' questions or working on written assignments; almost invariably closed and factual questions; little corrective feedback and no guidance; and predominantly total class instructional configurations around traditional activities—all in a virtually affectless environment."[23]

This differential curricular emphasis is quite visible in the elementary school; the overwhelming emphasis is placed on the teaching of English, reading, and language arts. Next in importance, though still receiving less stress, is mathemtics. Finally, science, social studies, and the arts account for a relatively small portion of classroom time. At the lower elementary grade levels, these differences are even greater.[24]

My own research, as well as that of Gitlin and others, documents how many newer curriculum models and materials tend to reduce the actual content down to atomistic units. Their effects on teaching as a labor process and on curricular quality are profound, often resulting in the de-skilling of teaching and a neglect of all but the most superficial and reductive knowledge.[25]

At the high school level, McNeil's interesting ethnographic work has revealed similar patterns.[26] In history classes, for instance, nearly all topics to be studied "were reduced to simplistic teacher-controlled information." Aside from a relatively small amount of text material, little or no reading was required on the part of the students. Serious class discussions on the material were few and far between. And even when schools possessed extensive resources that could have been used to enhance the study of these topics, little use was made of them.

This gives one side of the coin, the structures of both time and curriculum in classrooms. Yet what about the experiences of teachers? (It is remarkable, by the way, that given the emphasis placed on merit plans and "upgrading" teaching, for example, in the reports that so little time is actually spent on the real conditions teachers experience.) Since all too often educational research tends to ignore what teachers themselves think, it is not surprising that in most of these documents the real lives of teachers—their hopes, fears, frustrations, and sense of success—are largely absent. Interviews done by the Boston Women's Teachers' Group, however, have partially overcome this lacuna by pointing to some of the reasons, though not all, why classrooms look the way they do. For many committed teachers, existing structures within the educational system—including its characteristic overadministration, its differential power in decision making, the lack of interpersonal contact among teachers, and so on—seem to inexorably produce what has been called "teacher burnout,"[27] especially in our more urban school systems. As they put it:

> The conditions elementary school teachers encounter in their day-to-day school lives—conditions such as the overwhelming emphasis on quantification (both in scoring children and keeping records), the growing lack of control over curriculum (separating conception from execution) and over other aspects of their work, the isolation from their peers, the condescending treatment by administrators, and the massive lay-offs of veteran teachers—underlie teachers' frustration and anger, as well as their feelings that there are no realistic alternatives to the current institutional structure.[28]

Based on these interviews and on their own experiences, the question is put quite bluntly by the Boston Women's Teachers' Group: "Can we expect schools to educate, encourage, and expand the horizons of our children if these same institutions serve to restrict and retard the growth of teachers?"[29] The fact that at the elementary school level it is primarily *women* who make up the teaching force—"given" the sexual division of labor—and that it is women who are experiencing this loss of control and overadministration points to an issue that should be of great concern to us. It documents once again the close relationship over time between the control of curriculum and teaching and the control of women's work. The proposals to rationalize and standardize the work of teachers that are now so quickly being taken up and that are so evident in the reports need to be seen as exactly that: one more instance in a much larger history of attempts to control the labor process of women workers.[30] For we cannot ignore the fact that 87 percent of elementary school teachers and 67 percent of teachers overall *are* women.[31]

I want to stress this point. Not only do the reports have a problematic view of the labor market external to the school, but they also have a seriously deficient perspective on the internal labor market as well. Only by linking the attempts to rationalize teaching and knowledge to the question of *who* is doing the teaching can a complete picture of the effects of such standardization and external control be gained. What is happening is actually a repetition of an older strategy. When larger economic and governmental crises erupt, export the crises outside the economy and government to other groups.[32] Like the earlier period when schools were blamed in the fifties and sixties, the crisis is exported to the "problems" of (women) teachers.

With this said though, it still must recognized that problems do exist in schools. But do they warrant the kind of "solutions" generally advocated by the reports? Our overall answer to that question must again be no. Many of the reasons for that answer appear in the work of two policy analysts who engaged in a thorough examination of the educational content of the documents. Stedman and Smith, in what is perhaps one of the very best analyses of the strengths and weaknesses of the reports, conclude their discussion in the following way.

The commissions used weak arguments and poor data to make their case. Neither the decline in test scores, the international comparisons nor the growth of hi-tech employment provided a clear rationale for reform. By ignoring their background reports and carelessly handling data, their reports further lost credibility. In particular, the commissions made simplistic recommendations and failed to consider their ramifications. They proposed increasing time without altering pedagogy, instituting merit schemes without describing procedures, and adopting the "new basics" without changing old definitions. They ignored numerous problems—teenage unemployment, teacher burnout, and high dropout rates—that must be solved before American education can be considered sound. They did not address the special needs of the poor and minorities. A blind acceptance of these recommendations could lead to little improvement. Worse, a rapid adoption in the hopes of a speedy improvement could lead to a disenchantment with reform. There is a crucial dilemma facing educational policy. On the one hand, there appears to be a legitimate desire to impose new and more rigorous standards on our nation's schools. On the other hand recent studies of school effectiveness indicate the need to rest considerable responsibility for a school's instructional program on the shoulders of the staff of a school. Over and over we find that without the commitment of the school staff, top down mandates will fail. Local school systems and state governments, therefore, should examine these reports carefully before adopting any of their recommendations.[33]

In short, the reports often misuse their data, data that are technically problematic in the first place. They have an inaccurate view of the labor market and of the future of high-tech jobs, and they drastically oversimplify what might be necessary to make lasting alterations in schools. They elevate to a privileged positon that knowledge needed by industry and cloak it in the language of democracy,[34] in the process ignoring many persistent social problems faced by poor people, people of color, and women and men workers. Furthermore, their proposals for the most part never get to the level of the teaching act itself, except to take an ideological position that favors restructuring the labor of a largely female work force. Finally, they are tacitly elitist in major ways in that reform comes from the top, not from the participants themselves.[35] Their ultimate effects, then, will not necessarily be to make schools more interesting places or to change for the better the conditions of curriculum and teaching I described. Instead, they will continue trends that have already had a number of negative effects. Let us examine this in somewhat more detail.

What has been called the "commodification of education" is evident behind the logic of the proposals currently under review. One indication of this is the rapid advance of the process of rationalization, a process that is expanding to nearly all areas of the educational process. Changes in curriculum content and form bear witness to these transformations, as do major changes in what counts as good teaching.[36]

For example, at this writing thirty-eight of the fifty states now have some form of minimal competency testing for their students. "The tests represent and reinforce a redefinition of the content of education as specific skill learning, where skills are defined narrowly." Thus, the language of competency, performance, and effectiveness replaces broader language systems centered around knowedge, understanding, and personal development. In the process, learning and teaching are redefined. Time on task and the management of instruction become the arbiters of value.[37] Good teaching is only that which is demonstrated on competency tests for teachers. Good curricula are only those that have immediately available and easily testable results. Good learning is merely the accumulation of atomistic skills and facts and answering the questions on standardized achievement tests. Both of these approaches to curriculum and teaching are really aspects of what might best be thought of as de-skilling and both signify as well a restructuring of many of our cultural institutions by a technicist logic that in times of rightist resurgency can do little more than turn our schools over to the ethos and needs of that top 5 percent I identified earlier.[38]

In its most general terms, Wexler and Grabiner put it this way:

Taken together, these various processes of student and teacher deskilling and expansion of methods of measurable organization and administrative surveillance constitute the commodifying aspect of a larger historic process of educational reorganization. They empty the content of curriculum and teaching of any cultural history that is not reducible to narrowly defined technical skill. The technical skill, by virtue of its method of acquisition and evaluation, is not the kind of generative capacity which engages the imagination.[39]

Thus, technique wins out over substance and education is turned into nearly a parody of itself. Rationality is redefined to signify not thoughtfulness but meeting bureaucratic needs and conforming to the requirements of "our" economy. Education should be something more than this in a democracy you say? Sorry, it's too expensive.

CONCLUSION

Even if the concrete proposals made in the various commission documents are not instituted—and few of them are actually specific enough to be easily implemented at a school level—it is in these tendencies that we shall see the reports' lasting effects. Inequalities will increase. Teachers and the curriculum will be blamed for a large portion of our social dislocations and economic and ideological problems. The knowledge we need to engage in the democratic discussion of the ends and means of our dominant institution will be severely limited, for what will be taught in schools will be disembodied technical skills and workplace dispositions. The skills and knowledge associated with political debate and deliberation over the ends and means of our institutions, hence, will continue to atrophy. The labor process of the employees who now work in these schools will continue to look more and more similar to the rationalized and tightly controlled labor of all too many of their colleagues in the stores, factories, and offices of America.[40] In the guise of the public good, a public consisting of the powerful will be "rearmed."

Profits may indeed rise for a time. Students may indeed learn a portion of our reindustrialized "basics." But at what cost to their own futures and those of their teachers? Surely it is a cost that is too high for those on the "lower peak" of that double-peaked economy. Progressive educators in concert with politically sensitive community and women's groups, labor unions, people of color, and others have had a long history of fighting against the dominance of property rights over human needs. This fight is now occurring in our schools. To ignore our schools, to give the curriculum and teaching that goes on in them over to one limited but powerful segment of our society, would be a disaster. Obviously, schools are but a limited part of the larger society. Action in them cannot take the place of action in the economy and the state to insist that persons are more important than property. Yet fighting the battles to maintain and expand the substance of democracy in education *is* critical. It may be an essential precondition to creating a knowledgeable citizenry that will understand its own conditions. Winning some victories over the education of our children, hence, may not be sufficient, but it certainly is necessary.

NOTES

I would like to thank Rima D. Apple and Lois Weis for their comments on the substance of this chapter. Additional assistance was provided by Michael Olneck and Sheldon Danziger.

1. See Joel Spring, *The Sorting Machine* (New York: David McKay, 1976) for a history of such federal policies and some of the conditions out of which they arose.

2. Michael W. Apple, *Education and Power* (Boston: Routledge and Kegan Paul, 1982), and Michael W. Apple, "Work, Gender and Teaching," *Teachers College Record* 84 (Spring 1983): 611-28.

3. See Michael W. Apple, "Common Curriculum and State Control," *Discourse* 2, no. 2 (1982): 1-10.

4. For further discussion of these issues, see Michael W. Apple, *Ideology and Curriculum* (Boston: Routledge and Kegan Paul, 1979), and Michael W. Apple and Lois Weis, eds., *Ideology and Practice in Schooling* (Philadelphia: Temple University Press, 1983).

5. Lawrence C. Stedman and Marshall S. Smith, "Recent Reform Proposals for American Education," *Contemporary Education Review* 2 (Fall 1983): 87. Along with Stedman and Smith, I shall focus largely on committee reports, not on, say, the work of Sizer and Boyer. The latter two are interesting but may actually have little power other than "moral suasion."

6. Joshua Cohen and Joel Rogers, *On Democracy: Toward a Transformation of Amercian Society* (New York: Penguin Books, 1983): 15.

7. Frances Fox Piven and Richard A. Cloward, *The New Class War* (New York: Pantheon Books, 1982): 41.

8. The role of the state in times of economic crisis is discussed further in Manuel Castells, *The Economic Crisis and American Society* (Princeton: Princeton University Press, 1980). See also Erik Olin Wright, *Class, Crisis and the State* (London: New Left Books, 1978). For a more general overview of theories of the state, see the nicely written volume by Martin Carnoy, *The State and Political Theory* (Princeton: Princeton University Press, 1984).

9. I have reviewed these data at greater length in Apple, *Education and Power,* especially chapter 1.

10. Martin Carnoy, Derek Shearer, and Russell Rumberger, *A New Social Contract* (New York: Harper and Row, 1983): 22-23.

11. Cohen and Rogers, *On Democracy,* 30.

12. Cohen and Rogers, *On Democracy,* 31. The official poverty income level and rate fluctuate, of course, and are manipulated for political purposes. For a family of four, the official level is currently $10,178. Recent figures show an increase in the percentage of people living in poverty from 14 percent to over 15 percent of the total U.S. population.

13. Cohen and Rogers, *On Democracy,* 31-32.

14. Cohen and Rogers, *On Democracy,* 32.

15. Cohen and Rogers, *On Democracy,* 32.

16. For a clear historical treatment of the growth of dual labor markets and segmented work in the United States, see Gordon, David M., Richard Edwards, and Michael Reich, *Segmented Work, Divided Workers* (New York: Cambridge University Press, 1982).

17. Carnoy, Shearer, and Rumberger, *A New Social Contract,* 71.

18. Carnoy, Shearer, and Rumberger, *A New Social Contract,* 88.

19. This neglect of women's labor is a serious problem in most educational proposals. It often nearly destroys the credibility of their economic claims and of the

educational policies that emerge from them. See Michael W. Apple, "Old Humanists and New Curricula: Power and Culture in *The Paideia Proposal*," *Curriculum Inquiry*, in press.

20. See Erik Olin Wright et. al., "The American Class Structure," *American Sociological Review* 47 (December 1982): 709-26.

21. Carnoy, Shearer, and Rumberger, *A New Social Contract*, 61.

22. John Goodlad, *A Place Called School* (New York: McGraw Hill, 1983).

23. Kenneth A. Sirotnik, "What You See Is What You Get: Consistency, Persistency, and Mediocrity in Classrooms," *Harvard Educational Review* 53 (February 1983): 29.

24. Sirotnik, "What You See Is What You Get," 23.

25. See Apple, *Education and Power*, chapter 5; Apple, "Work, Gender and Teaching "; Andrew Gitlin, "School Structure and Teachers Work," in Michael W. Apple and Lois Weis, eds., *Ideology and Practice in Schooling* (Philadelphia: Temple University Press, 1983): 193-212; and Thomas Popkewitz, B. Robert Tabachnick, and Gary Wehlage, *The Myth of Educational Reform* (Madison: University of Wisconsin Press, 1982).

26. Linda McNeil, "Defensive Teaching and Classroom Control," in Michael W. Apple and Lois Weis, eds., *Ideology and Practice in Schooling* (Philadelphia: Temple University Press, 1983): 116.

27. It is unfortunate that phrases such as "burn-out" have such currency. They tend to reduce the phenomenon to the level of the individual, thereby removing from serious scrutiny the structural issues concerning the control of one's labor and skills. See Michael W. Apple, "Teaching and 'Women's Work': A Comparative Historical and Ideological Analysis," *Teachers College Record*, in press, and Apple, "Work, Gender and Teaching."

28. Marilyn Frankenstein and Lois Kampf, "Preface to 'The Other End of the Corridor,'" *Radical Teacher* 23 (Spring 1983): 2.

29. Boston Women's Teachers' Group, "The Other End of the Corridor: The Effects of Teaching on Teachers," *Radical Teacher* 23 (Spring 1983): 3.

30. Apple, "Teaching and 'Women's Work.'"

31. For further discussion of these points and for criticisms of the reports' proposals for merit pay plans and the like, see Sara Freedman, "Master Teacher/Merit Pay—Weeding Out Women from 'Women's True Profession': A Critique of the Commissions on Education," *Radical Teacher* 25 (November 1983): 24-28.

32. I have discussed how powerful elements within the state and economy export their crisis in Apple, *Education and Power*, especially chapter 4.

33. Stedman and Smith, "Recent Reform Proposals for American Education," 102-103.

34. Technically speaking, the writers of the reports actually attempt to create a *compromise* between the cultural capital of what could be called the "academy"—with its academic standards and visions of high-status culture centered around the disciplines of knowledge—and the needs of the industry. Thus, we should not see the authors of the reports or the reports themselves as being only mere "tools" of industry. In the present political and economic context, however, what will be seized upon and highlighted within the reports will not be the requirements of the academy, especially since universities themselves are currently faced with declining revenues, a situation that forces them to increasingly act in the interests of business and industry. For further discussion of this, see Apple, *Education and Power*, chapter 2.

35. This cannot be said of all aspects of the reports. For example, they could have overtly proposed "extensive adoption of gifted and talented programs, the resurrection of systematic tracking by early test scores, or the introduction of specialized math and science programs for the academic high achievers." Instead most of them

chose to focus on "the basics" and had as their overt goal raising the achievement of the "average student." See Stedman and Smith, "Recent Reform Proposals for American Education," 94.

36. Philip Wexler and Gene Grabiner, "The Education Question: America During the Crisis," unpublished paper, University of Rochester, p. 31.

37. For an excellent analysis of problems with the time-on-task orientation of the reports, see Henry M. Levin, "About Time for Education Reform," *Educational Evaluation and Policy Analysis* 6 (Summer 1984): 151-63.

38. Levin, "About Time for Education Reform," 151-63. I have discussed the transformation of learning and the process of de-skilling in much greater detail in Apple, *Education and Power.*

39. Wexler and Grabiner, "The Education Question." For further analysis of the restructuring of education, see Henry Giroux, "Public Philosophy and the Crisis in Education," *Harvard Educational Review* 54 (May 1984): 186-94.

40. Compare here to Richard Edwards, *Contested Terrain* (New York: Basic Books, 1979).

Main-Traveled Road or Fast Track:
The Liberal and Technical in
Higher Education Reform

Sheila Slaughter

The many recent reports on education have focused almost exclusively on the secondary school. However, the researchers and policy makers involved in preparing these reports and making recommendations for reform do not always see secondary school as an end in itself. Instead, many of the reports on secondary education make explicit recommendations about how to better prepare students for college. Implicit in these recommendations are concepts of what the higher learning of the future should look like. In this paper, we will briefly analyze selected reports so the educational community can carefully inspect their implications for higher education. The reports are as follows: *Academic Preparation for College, Action for Excellence, High School, Making the Grade, A Nation at Risk, The Paideia Proposal,* and *A Place Called School.*[1] We will look at these reports from a social justice perspective, to see which groups gain and which lose educational ground on the basis of the proposed reforms. The dimensions of the reports with which we will be especially concerned are: access, excellence, curricula, career preparation and distribution of social rewards, research agendas, resources for change, and values.

Although higher education has not received as much attention as secondary, reports on the postsecondary sector are starting to emerge, especially as Congress begins deliberations over revision of the 1965 Higher Education Act. A review and analysis of selected reports on postsecondary education will allow us to compare the implications for higher learning contained in the secondary school reports with concrete proposals for higher educational reform. Such a comparison will enable us to see if there is a convergence of recommendations, an emerging consensus about reform of higher education. The reports reviewed are the series issued by the Business–Higher Education

Forum, *America's Competitive Challenge, Corporate and Campus Coopera-tion,* and *The New Manufacturing,* as well as the recently released National Institute of Education's *Involvement in Learning.*[2] In considering these re-ports, we will focus on the same concerns and dimensions as in the secondary school reports.

SECONDARY SCHOOL REPORTS: THE LIBERAL AND THE TECHNICAL

Although there is great variation among these reports, for analytical purposes they can be roughly grouped along a continuum that runs from the liberal to the technical.[3] Those reports at the liberal end of the continuum tend to see secondary education as an end in itself and address themselves as best they can to the general welfare of all students. Among the more liberal reports are *High School, The Paideia Proposal,* and *A Place Called School.*

The reports at the technical end of the spectrum tend to see secondary education primarily as an institution where students learn skills to be used in other settings. A general education in and of itself is not a sufficient end; the welfare of individual students is not so important as the skills they offer society. Thus, secondary school readies students for job placement or pre-pares them for college. The remainder of the secondary school reports dis-cussed come closer to the technical than the liberal end of the spectrum.

Again, we want to emphasize that these distinctions—the liberal and the technical—represent different ends of a continuum, not hard and fast cate-gories. Indeed, in some instances these distinctions seem to blur: for example, a few of the liberal reports are somewhat concerned with job placement and college preparation; some of the technical reports advocate curricular reform long associated with liberal education. However, the distinction is important with regard to education's impact on social mobility and rewards. On the one hand, the more technical reports see highly competitive educational and economic systems as tightly linked, and emphasize the importance of select-ing only those few students able to master complex, specialized skills for ever higher levels of education and, ultimately, social rewards. On the other hand, the more liberal reports are in the main silent on the articulation of education and economy. While this silence is somewhat evasive, the refusal to tie early educational performance to preferential placement at least temporarily holds open the possibility that economic stratification is not the only outcome of schooling.

The Liberal Reports

On the question of access, the liberal reports are quite clear. All high school students should have an education that prepares them for college. They are vehemently opposed to any vestige of tracking.[4] Since such an approach to pupil grouping is designed to benefit the poor and minority students who, as a category or class, are most likely to suffer from tracking, it implies that a broader and more heterogeneous population will be prepared for higher education.[5]

Although the liberal reports are concerned with broadening the educational base for postsecondary education, they do not see increased access as compromising excellence or quality in any way. Each of these reports speaks out for a democratic elitism, founded on the belief that all students are capable of first-class work. Basics are stressed, be these in a "common core," "three columns," or "five fingers."[6] As the *Paideia Proposal* puts it: "There are no unteachable children. There are only schools and teachers who fail to teach them."[7] The logical implication of this position is that all students will be adequately prepared for college so the pursuit of higher learning will become a matter of personal predeliction.

The research agendas for higher education proposed in these reports focus primarily on the educational process. They are concerned with finding ways to use the knowledge we have to train and revitalize the performance of principals and teachers, with discovering a variety of pedagogies for a varied student body, with identifying and replicating effective teaching and learning. They are also concerned with discovering means to solve problems at the local school level through long-term planning, curriculum development, monitoring and evaluation of teacher and student performance. Thus, the research agenda for higher education focuses on the education process itself, across many disciplines and all levels of learning.

The values espoused by the liberal reports are in keeping with their recommendations for increased access, higher standards, a core or common curriculum, and humanistic education together with a systematic exploration of the teaching-learning process. The moral values stressed are cooperation, commitment to the common good, and discovery of ethical principles that guide one's life. The political values are democracy, pluralism, and the rights of citizenship put forth in the Constitution. Little attention is given to economic values.

Although these values are presented and upheld for their own sake, they are also translated into educational practice. They animate the schoolroom with a belief in the educability of all students; with a commitment to a common educational experience shared across lines of color, class, creed, and even ability levels; and through a militant defense of equal educational opportunity. For higher education, adherence to such values probably means expanded enrollment, greater emphasis on liberal and interdisciplinary education or humanizing professional and technical study, as well as a lifetime commitment to inquiry.

The liberal reports have two outstanding weaknesses: they are somewhat vague about the mechanism for improving student scholarship, and they do not address the question of resources for reform. There is some commonality of mechanisms for improving scholarship across the reports—localized decision making, strong leadership on the part of the principal, more careful selection and training of teachers, better classroom organization, an improved core curriculum—but none of these seem sufficient to deal with the pervasive and immediate problem of low achievement and high dropout rates. Over time and accompanied by significant redistribution of educational resources, these mechanisms might transform education. But they do not adequately address the difficulties faced by students already in the system who are unable to reach standards set by district or state. Indeed, the continued failure of such students to perform well during a transitional period might become an argument against the sorts of reform proposed in these reports.

With regard to resources, the more liberal reports do not address the question: who shall pay for the proposed reforms? Yet, if this question is not asked and answered in ways that mobilize political support for educational reform, such reform is unlikely. However, these reports give scant attention to education's articulation of the economy, whether in terms of resources, values, or preparation for job, college, and career. This oversight may be costly in terms of resources. Over time, the raison d'être for public support of American education seems to have shifted from a political rationale, which emphasized the need for an informed citizenry, to an economic one. The economic rationale for education stresses the relationship of education to the economy, usually in terms of greater productivity and the orderly distribution of career opportunities; more recently, this relationship has been stressed in terms of increasing America's competitiveness in the global market place. Failure to present reform proposals in ways that address the articulation of education and economy may mean these reports are not treated seriously.

The Technical Reports

By and large the technical reports see education as an institution that prepares students for a job or for college. The technical reports claim to seek ways to improve discipline and achievement by more rigorous application of standards. Education becomes a product rather than a process. Techniques for improving product quality, standards, reliability, and market competitiveness are explored. This language obscures proposals for changes in national education policy that have far-reaching social and economic implications, as well as implications for higher education. Let us consider these implications in more detail, using the analytical categories earlier identified: access, excellence, curriculum, career preparation and distribution of social rewards, research agendas, resources, and values.

Although all students attend secondary school, the technical reports see only some students as being steered into curricula that lead to college.[8] In contrast to the liberal reports, these advocate differentiated curricula. Access to these curricula will, by and large, be determined by testing. The many studies demonstrating that standardized achievement tests discriminate against poor and minority students are ignored, as are studies that show that such test performance bears little relation to job performance.[9] Instead, the technical reports advocate increased student testing, especially at transitional points, such as entry to high school or college. The students who test well will receive special treatment, although the word "tracking" is not used. For higher education, such a policy means fewer students, especially low-income and minority students, but those who enter will rank high on the tests that colleges have long identified with "quality."[10]

The concept of excellence advanced in these reports honors nineteenth-century notions of moral and mental discipline, together with "high tech" furniture of the mind. Like the liberal reports, the technical reports ask for more time on tasks, a longer school day and school year, more homeowrk, and no social promotions. Unlike the liberal reports, the technical also explore what sanctions are best used to control unruly, disruptive, or uneducable children. In the main, they emphasize evaluation, either from classroom or school, or from access to high-reward curricula.[11]

The technical reports display a high degree of consensus about curriculum. As in the liberal reports, all students are supposed to master the same no-nonsense "new basics": English, the arts, math, science, social science, computers, and foreign languages. However, the technical reports imply differentiated treatment of these subject matters based on student ability. The two levels at which students proceed are fairly clear. Those who test well will learn to master literature as the language of upper-class discourse, to appreciate and consume the arts, to prepare for work in engineering, management, and high-technology fields where a second language facilitates overseas assignments. Students who do not pass the required tests learn standard English appropriate for office and service jobs; they come to recognize the legitimacy of high culture, master computers through key punching, and engage in on-the-job training. As *A Nation at Risk* notes, one of the functions of the social studies curriculum is to "enable students to fix their places and possibilities within the large social and cultural structure."[12]

The implications for higher education are clear. We see them in the detailed elaboration of the advanced or enriched curriculum proposed for college entrants. Students pursuing these curricula will enter college with a high level of technical preparation, especially in math, science, and computers. They will be knowlegeable about the mechanics of these subjects, but also well versed in principles, theories, and programming. While conversant with the humanities and able to communicate with clarity and authority, they will probably select a postsecondary curriculum that will allow them to begin building and serving the new technology.

Job placement and career preparation follow curriculum. All students are prepared for work in the dynamic sector of the economy, but some are prepared through high-tech college curricula for high-level management or research positions in the new technology; the rest are prepared to take jobs immediately upon graduation from high school, performing de-skilled, low-reward labor in service to the machines and systems that constitute the high technology.

For higher education, the career preparation advocated in the technical reports will probably call for long-term, substantial reallocation of resources. To deal with the skills of students from high-tech high schools, universities will have to develop fields that cater to meeting the problems of corporations engaged in "technological change and global competition."[13] The humanitites and social science, along with professional fields that serve the state—such as social work and education—will contract, while fields connected with the development of high-tech, high-service areas will expand. Preparation of teachers in the growth areas will probably occur in these new fields rather than in schools of education. The very shape of higher education will change so it becomes less responsive to a variety of economic and professional constituencies and more closely aligned with the multinational sector of the economy that is currently concerned with developing high technology. While the research agenda for the sort of higher education implicit in the technical reports is not clearly spelled out, there is enough talk of partnerships between education and industry to infer that the bulk of funded inquiry will serve the research and development (R & D) needs of internationally competitive corporations.

The values in these reports are largely negative. They translate the worst middle-class values—competitiveness, acquisitiveness, individualism—from a domestic situation where they are constrained by custom, tradition, and law, to an international arena where the U.S. makes unbridled demands for global supremacy, a continued and highly disproportionate share of world resources, and the power to determine the destiny of other nations. In the words of *A Nation at Risk*, education must become a tool to reclaim "our once unchallenged pre-eminence in commerce, industry, science and technical innovation."[14] These values are designed to appeal to the heavily voting middle class through their highly charged emotional logic, a logic shaped by a politics of scarcity and fear.

The emotional logic goes as follows. The U.S. economic plight stems from an ill-considered, sentimental domestic policy, and also from external threats. The nation is at risk not only from lack of discipline, but also from the "economic miracle" wrought by the Japanese and the engineering savy of the West Germans. Their gains are always America's loss. The U.S. is also presented as threatened by the military prowess of unnamed but undoubtedly Soviet bloc countries. In a world so filled with menace, the only response is competition so rigorous that finally U.S. global dominance is achieved in both trade and arms. As *America's Competitive Challenge* warns, without strong economic and educational systems, "the United States will find it difficult, if not impossible, to achieve other important national goals—from maintaining a strong national defense to improving the quality of life for all American citizens."[15] To preserve a satisfying standard of living for the future, then, the U.S. citizenry is asked to sacrifice for the system, giving up chimeras of social conscience, such as full employment, educational equity, affirmative action.

What makes the emotional logic the least bit convincing is fear: fear that too much has already been given to others. The way such fears are played upon is perhaps best illustrated by the juxtaposition of "excellence" and "equality" throughout the technical reports. While all maintain that striving for excellence does not mean giving up equality. there is a strong suggestion that enough has been done for minorities, and that further efforts will pull everyone downward. For example, *Action for Excellence* says the U.S. has made "substantial progress" in aiding students "put at a disadvantage by poverty, minority status, or both," and it is now time to "take on another task . . . building quality." The Twentieth Century Fund Task Force is more direct, saying "emphasis on promoting equality in the schools has meant a slighting of commitment to educational quality."[16]

The educational practice that stems from these values and this logic is obvious. These reports turn their backs on the education reforms of the 1960s, from affirmative action to remedial programs, and refuse to pursue quality of education energetically. Instead, the reports use the rubric of excellence and quality to call for a greatly tightened U.S. educational stratification system, one that revalues the college degree and reempowers the middle class.

The technical and liberal reports imply very different futures for higher education. Were the liberal reforms enacted, there would be greater access to higher learning, probably accompanied by a very gradual expansion of postsecondary education, together with the continued maintenance of a curriculum that contained arts and science, education and social science, new technologies, and the professions. Since the great majority of students of the reformed high school would be able to pursue postsecondary credentials successfully, higher education would probably be less tightly tied to career preparation and distribution of social rewards. Instead, preparation for careers and allocation of rewards might move directly to the professions and corporations, freeing higher learning to concentrate on education. So too, the research agenda for the liberal university would focus on the educational process, preparing students to learn in any site.

Were the technical reforms enacted, access to higher education would be constrained; the sector as a whole would be cut back, with certain fields— perhaps the humanities, education, and the social sciences—severely pruned. However, the same or even a greater amount of resources would probably be consumed as costly high-tech, high-service programs were expanded. Higher education would be closely tied to career preparation, with well-specified credentials providing entry to richly rewarded and highly specialized technical or managerial occupations. The research agenda for the technical university would promote national economic growth and international dominance through close cooperation with multinational corporations.

HIGHER EDUCATION REPORTS: THE FAST TRACK AND THE MAIN-TRAVELED ROAD

Some of the recently issued higher education reports make the visions of higher education implicit in the secondary reports more concrete. The reports we have selected for analysis reveal some of the same policy cleavages as do the secondary reports. One group of reports, put out by the Business–Higher Education Forum, elaborates the "fast track" that would be created from a close collaboration between powerful corporations, great research universities, the enlightened public, and cooperative elements among union leadership. The other report, issued by the National Institute of Education, moves beyond the fast track and tries to point the way to a reformed higher education that would accommodate the more peripatetic as well.

The Business–Higher Education Forum "was created for the express purpose of promoting discourse and acting on issues shared jointly by America's business and the nation's higher education institutions."[17] However, the forty-seven corporations and forty-one academic members are hardly typical of most of America's business or the majority of higher educators. The corporations are among the nation's most wealthy and powerful; many appear in the Fortune 500 and in Dye's list of dominant corporations.[18] The great majority of the universities represented are prestigious research institutions, often with a technical emphasis. They are about evenly balanced between private and public, and there is also a sprinkling of prestigious private colleges concerned primarily with undergraduate education. The Forum is housed by the American Council on Education, and its activities are funded by foundations and government.

The Forum consists of chief executive officers of great corporations and great universities. The Forum report, *America's Competitive Challenge,* was a response to President Reagan's request for a position paper on education. Among the signatories are John F. Burlingame of General Electric, Philip Caldwell of Ford, Robert Anderson of Rockwell International, James E. Olson of AT&T, together with Derek Bok of Harvard, David Saxon of the University of California, Richard Cyert of Carnegie-Mellon and Matina Horner of Radcliffe. The succeeding reports, *Corporate and Campus Cooperation* and *The New Manufacturing,* are elaborations on the inital report and form part of an ongoing series. The next report, scheduled to be released in spring of 1985, will deal with business school curricula.[19] These reports, then, can be treated as an ongoing effort of corporate and university leaders to address mutual problems, and the three reports will be treated as a whole.

Although access to higher education is not directly dealt with, the reports quite explicitly address themselves to the best and the brightest: those few most likely to succeed in the global race to make the U.S. the most industrially competitive nation on earth. Thus, the reports are not concerned with mass higher education or with most institutions of higher education. Instead, they focus on those few research institutions on the "fast track," those universities in a position to advance the frontiers of research in the dynamic sector of the economy.

Excellence is defined in terms of economic success. The Forum begins by clearly stating that the function of the educational system, as well as all other social systems, is service to the economy. Indeed, *America's Competitive Challenge* makes only a single recommendation, one that is worth quoting in full:

> As a nation, we must develop a consensus that industrial competitiveness is crucial to our social and economic well being. Such a consensus will require a shift in public attitudes about national priorities, as well as changes in public perceptions about the nature of our economic malaise.[20]

The conception of academic excellence as enhancing economic competition is elaborated in subsequent reports. In *Corporate and Campus Cooperation,* the Forum tells us investment of R&D dollars in the university pays off when "American industry can successfully commercialize the results."[21] *The New Manufacturing* seeks research universities able to participate in developing and accelerating investment in the "advanced automation manufacturing processes . . . . imperative if American producers are to survive into the next century."[22]

As in other technical reports, curricula for economic growth are stressed, in high-technology industries—"aircraft, computers, office equipment, synthetic materials, drug and scientific instruments"—and "high growth *service industries . . .*—insurance, financing, aviation, shipping and engineering."[23]

Again, as in other technical reports, the Forum envisions a two-track educational curriculum. The fast truck has two lanes. First, universities are expected to develop a curriculum for multinational executives, one that would teach foreign management pratices, foreign language and culture, as well as offer an international studies program designed to "strengthen programs and data bases in the areas of industrial, commercial, legal and financial practices and institutions."[24] This executive curriculum also has provision for government-and corporation-sponsored midcareer changes for scientists, engineers, and managers. Second, research universities are to engage in high-tech R&D that can be quickly commercialized, especially in communications and computer technology.

For the many citizens unable or unprepared to enter the fast track, the Forum offers an alternative adult education, one that is especially concerned with the needs of "displaced workers" regularly de-skilled by technological innovation. They will be able to participate in a self-financing national program that offers them "Individual Training Accounts (ITAs)." These accounts are analogous to Individual Retirement Accounts (IRAs) and will enable workers to pay for their own training and retraining needs across a lifetime.

The research agenda for industry-university partnerships proposed by the Forum is clearly articulated in *The New Manufacturing*. Corporations and higher education must move beyond traditional modes of manufacturing— batch and mass—to flexibly automated plants that will use computer and communicatons technology to integrate all manufacturing functions: design, engineering, materials handling, fabrication, assembly, inspection/testing, and sales/distribution. These decentralized computer-controlled factories will produce high-quality, specialized products around the clock for specific demand, with a labor pool at least one-third smaller and at unit cost of 30-50 percent less than in traditional manufacturing facilities.[25] Executives and researchers have to get these factories out of industrial and university laboratories and into production.

Given the thrust of these reports, the only career for which students on the fast track should be prepared is business. With the advent of flexibly automated manufacturing, high-tech, high-reward career lines seem to converge. Since management will operate in automated plants organized without many workers, they will need to know less about supervising large groups of people, more about relations between machines and humans, and a great deal more about production processes. In order for R&D partnerships and technology transfers to work, university researchers will have to be in close contact with corporations. Independent professions, too, whether doctors, lawyers, or engineers, will have to monitor the new technology closely to exploit its discoveries, protect intellectual property, and serve as consultants to the new systems.

While career preparation and social rewards for students on the fast track are quite clear, the lot of the ordinary students is less certain. If the manufacturing processes envisioned in these reports are successfully introduced, the work force as we have known it over the last hundred years will change drastically, with as extreme a social dislocation as in the first industrial revolution. By its own estimates, the Forum believes that the new manufacturing is likely to result in the loss of anywhere from four to ten million jobs.[26] Since the new manufacturing jobs that will be provided by flexibly automated factories will probably be filled by highly educated and skilled workers, the Forum hopes the slack for displaced workers will be taken up by growth in industries that develop services for the new technologies. Even if service industries expand, the Forum warns that workers will have to compete with machines for jobs and should be retrained to develop strengths that machines do not have. In sum, the Forum hopes to mitigate the social dislocation caused by the introduction of the new manufacturing through education and retraining, but beyond suggesting that as a nation we have a moral obligation to provide fiscal mechanisms (like ITAs) for such education and retraining over a lifetime, the Forum has little to say about where and how reeducation will occur, what jobs students and workers will be trained for, what salaries will go with them.

The Forum addresses the question of resources explicitly and straight-forwardly. The American citizenry will pay the lion's share of the cost of global supremacy in the new manufacturing. They will pay by bearing the costs of retraining displaced workers, through allowing industry elaborate and clearly specified tax breaks to "write off" large portions of the cost of industrial R&D and upgrading universities with state-of-the-art equipment. Although corporations will supply few resources, they will benefit dispropor-tionately from direct and indirect subsidy via government-financed industrial and academic research and university programs that train corporate execu-tives, scientists, and engineers.

Throughout its reports, the Forum asserts the primacy of private enter-prise. If the U.S. is to be internationally successful in its high-cost, high-tech, high-service, high-return fields, then all restraints on competition should be abolished: tariffs, antitrust laws, environmental guidelines, specifically, and federal regulations, generally. Explicitly rejected as "counter productive" and un-American are alternatives such as "protectionism, national economic planning, income redistribution and plant closing restrictions." Instead, the Forum offers its own version of planning. It recommends establishing a quasi-public planning mechanism, designed to be dominated by the multi-national sector and able to appropriate large sums of public monies to en-hance U.S. corporations' global economic position. The role of the state is secondary and supportive: it is to "create an environment in which the in-dividual and collective talents of the private sector can be focused to meet the competitive challenge."[27]

What these reports present is a pedagogy of profit, one so deeply rooted in capitalism as to be blind to any other possibilities. The private sector is paramount and all available social energy and resources are di-rected toward its well-being. The needs of U.S. corporations are unabashedly put before the needs of people, and this is justified by claiming corporate well-being is a prerequisite for economic health. The greatly increased claims corporations make on public resources are justified by greatly in-tensified international competition. In essence, the U.S. citizenry is being asked to pay very dearly for the triumph of American-based multinationals in a world market. As the U.S. populace is asked in the name of the economic crisis to devote more educational resources to students already blessed, so too they are asked to tighten their belts in order that already powerful corporations can come to dominate the world.

Somewhat surprising is the apparent readiness of the presidents of great American universities to support the economic and pedagogic logic of these reports. A 19 percent increase in the federal basic research budget somehow does not seem enough for endorsing a rapacious national

economic development scheme that repudiates a decade of liberal education. However, university presidents may support the Forum because it
holds out the promise that research universities, as institutions, will share
in efforts at national planning and will receive the "physical capital (plant
and equipment)" to accomplish a task in which they take pride: adding
value to "human capital" through a "commitment to improved technological
innovation."[28] As the president of Rockwell International, Robert Anderson,
and the president of the University of California, David Saxon, cochairs of
the Forum Task Force, put it in a letter transmitting their report to President
Reagan, the task of revitalizing the American economy "will call for institutional change as well as technological innovation. We must operate from a
new worldwide perspective. We must find new approaches and forge new
partnerships for coordinated action."[29]

Perhaps the academic presidents' participation and support in developing
multinational corporate policy initiatives means the research university will
be party to these partnerships.

The values embodied in the reports are the survival of the fittest abroad,
mitigated by corporate paternalism at home, corporate sector dominance of
the state, albeit with provision for consultation by concerned groups, and
an uncompromising commitment to capitalism. As *Corporate and Campus
Cooperation* notes, quoting Clifton C. Garvin, Jr., chairman of the Exxon
Corporation, on management responsibilities, "It is up to us at the senior
level to see that the job gets done . . . . Given a clear signal from the top,
things will happen."[30] The corporate stewards of our economy are ready to
consult with government, education, labor, and the general public on policy
development, but only if they share a consensus about three basic premises:
the need to increase U.S. economic competitiveness in global markets, to
enhance the vitality of U.S. manufacturing industries, and to increase automation. Moreover, corporate and education leaders seem to be convinced
that business and education exist in symbiosis with capitalism. The Forum
quotes Milton Eisenhower, former president of Johns Hopkins, on this point:
"Higher education and business are basically interdependent. One needs money
to produce educated people, and the other needs educated people to produce
money."[31] The educational practice that follows from these values is quite
explicit in the several reports: it puts intellect to work in service to the
achievement of global economic dominance by U.S.-based multinational
corporations.

The Main-Traveled Road

Involvement in Learning was sponsored by the National Institute of Educa-
tion and presented to the secretary of education and the director of the NIE.
It is concerned primarily with undergraduate education at four-year schools.
As the liberal reports on secondary education present a sharp contrast to the

technical, so this report contrasts sharply with the Forum papers. *Involvement in Learning* closely echoes many of the refrains heard in the liberal reports. On the whole, these reports go farther down the road taken by American educational reformers since the Civil War, asking for increased access, more schooling, and a common education experience that creates community.

Involvement in Learning also shares some of the weaknesses of the liberal secondary reports. The mechanisms of a reformed and successful pedagogy are somewhat vague. We get no clear sense of what resources are needed to realize reforms, especially in a transitional period. Again, as in the case of the liberal secondary reports, *Involvement* does not address the articulation of higher education with the economy. At the postsecondary level, this is a serious omission since higher education, unlike high school, awards students the credentials to negotiate entry into professional occupations or professional schools. To overlook this function of undergraduate education is to ignore its student-drawing power, as well as the problems created by the distribution of social rewards via college curricula. This report, then, leads us down the main-traveled reform road, with its emphasis on access and educational entitlement, but does not take us all the way through a full consideration of what truly open access at the postsecondary level might mean.

Let us briefly consider *Involvement* in terms of the analytic categories suggested earlier: access, excellence, curricula, career preparation and distribution of social rewards, research agendas, resources for change, and values.

Involvement calls for including an ever-increasing proportion of the population in higher education, regardless of age. The report further argues that access and excellence are not incompatible, indeed, that access without excellence robs students of educational opportunity. In contrast to the Forum reports, excellence is defined in educational rather than economic terms. Excellence is to be measured by educational outcome—increased knowledge, intellectual capacities, and skills—rather than by the input measures traditionally used: institutional endowment and expenditures, intellectual attainment of faculty, test scores of entering students.

The curriculum proposed calls for at least two full years of liberal education with an emphasis on cognitive development, stressing problem solving, analysis, synthesis, and interdisciplinary work. These two years are supposed to check rampant vocationalism. As with the liberal reports, the research agenda advanced here stresses exploration of the educational process. The specific research proposals brought to the attention of the higher education community focus on enhancing students' learning and growth, faculty's development and teaching capability. Moreover, the report suggests that publications that push back the frontiers of knowledge should not be required from all faculty at four-year institutions. Instead, faculty should concentrate on scholarship that enriches teaching.

The values expressed in *Involvement in Learning* are close to those in the liberal reports. There is a strong belief in the educability of the general population, a conviction that every citizen has the right to a higher education, and commitment to realizing individual, intellectual, and human potential through education. Education is seen as the key to social and political equity, as providing a guide "for intelligent action beyond the campus."[32]

Clearly, more public resources would have to be devoted to higher education if the reforms proposed in this report are to be realized. The authors of the report try to bridge the gap between their reform recommendations and available resources by calling for "excellence without extravagance."[33] They propose to raise the level of quality in American higher education by using what we know about the conditions under which growth and learning can be maximized. Thus, the report argues, systematic attention to educational research, learning theory, and pedagogical techniques can increase quality without radically increasing cost. While this formulation of the resource question might be adequate if higher education were to remain in "steady state," it may be insufficient in the face of the new demands made on higher education resources by groups like the Business–Higher Education Forum.

Involvement in Learning is a strong defense of the liberal aspect of higher education, but it virtually ignores the technical. To ignore the technical is perilous for at least three reasons. First, it is unrealistic. At present, technical curricula draw a much greater proportion of the student body than the liberal. We do not know if two years of liberal education will be meaningful to students unless such a curriculum addresses the needs and anxieties about career, security, and status that brought students to college in the first place. Indeed, it might be more realistic to try to liberalize the technical than to insist that career-minded students take conventional liberal arts courses.

Second, the report emphasizes access to college, but does not speak about access to curricula that confer social rewards, nor about the criteria that should guide selection of such curricula. Even if the report is read as encouraging each college to set its own standards for access to high-reward curricula, this is not enough. For intelligent public discourse, we need to know who gains and who loses and on what grounds. To say everyone gains begs the question. College becomes like high school; selection is moved to the graduate level; and criteria for selection are still uncertain. If other sites for selection or credentialing—corporations or professional associations, for example—are contemplated, this needs to be made clear.

Third, the report makes no connection between higher education and national policy. In an era characterized by intense debate over the generation and use of public resources, it speaks of further educational entitlement without contexting educational rights in a responsible, concrete scheme or plan for the more democratic collection and distribution of public monies.

It may fail to command attention because it does not tell us how higher education should articulate with the economy. In sum, this report defends the liberal aspects of higher education, but in a way that makes mobilizing widespread support difficult. In contrast to the technical reports, it does not address the economic and status anxieties of the heavily voting middle class. Neither does it place higher education's training function in the context of the debate over national planning now occurring. Nor does it point to a nationally realizable plan for economic recovery that would create meaningful careers for those who gain access to higher education.

CONCLUSION

The reports we have reviewed have very different educational and economic implications. And, in the final analysis, the economic may be more important than the educational. The liberal reports follow the main-traveled road mapped out by reform politicians since the Second World War. They ask for increased access and higher levels of educational entitlement. However, their educational program does not address the changed environment postsecondary education now faces. One of the central rationales for further funding can no longer be automatically invoked: presently, higher levels of education do not necessarily mean higher levels of economic prosperity and productivity. Unless proponents of liberal education reform suggest new ways in which education might articulate with the economy and demonstrate the uses of a liberal education by suggesting new solutions to our current economic problems, we are unlikely to go further down the main-traveled road to reform.

The technical reports are more firmly grounded in conservative economic fantasies than in educational practice. Yet they appeal to the laissez-faire "social" superego to which so many of us respond, however reluctantly. But laissez-faire economic policies are probably even more unlikely than liberal ones to meet the educational and economic problems created by the internationalization of capital, the development of high technology, and the dislocation and de-skilling of large portions of the labor force. Before committing ourselves to an educational policy that rests on nineteenth-century economics, we would do well to look to the future and consider alternative interpretations of our economic difficulties.[34]

NOTES

1. The College Board, *Academic Preparation for College: What Students Need to Know and Be Able to Do* (New York: The College Board, 1983); Education Commission of the States, *Action for Excellence: A Comprehensive Plan to Improve Our Nation's Schools* (Denver: Education Commission of the States, 1983); Ernest Boyer, *High School* (New York: Macmillan, 1983); Twentieth Century Fund, *Making the Grade: Report of the Twentieth Century Fund Task Force on Federal Elemen-*

tary and Secondary Education Policy (New York: Twentieth Century Fund, 1983); National Commission on Excellence in Education, *A Nation at Risk: The Imperative for Educational Reform* (Washington, D.C.: US Government Printing Office, 1983); Mortimer J. Adler, *The Paideia Proposal: An Educational Manifesto* (New York: Macmillian, 1982); John I. Goodlad, *A Place Called School: Prospects for the Future* (New York: McGraw-Hill, 1984).

2. Business–Higher Education Forum, *America's Competitive Challenge: The Need for A National Response* (Washington, D.C., The Business–Higher Education Forum, April 1983); Business–Higher Education Forum, *Corporate and Campus Cooperation: An Action Agenda* (Washington, D.C.: The Business–Higher Education Forum, May 1984); The Business–Higher Education Forum, *The New Manufacturing: America's Race to Automate* (Washington, D.C.: The Business–Higher Education Forum, June 1984); Study Group on the Conditions of Excellence in American Higher Education, *Involvement in Learning: Realizing the Potential of American Higher Education* (Washington, D.C.: National Institute of Education, October 1984).

3. These categories are borrowed from Merle L. Borrowman, *The Liberal and Technical in Teacher Education; A Historical Survey of American Thought* (New York: Teachers College, Columbia University, 1956).

4. *The Paideia Proposal* and *A Place Called School* are also against even limited ability grouping, whether for gifted or high-risk students. While this position is laudable for its egalitarianism, it creates some problems, especially for students who have trouble with school. *High School* is somewhat more realistic in developing programs for these students, although the programs proposed run the risk of becoming another form of tracking.

5. James S. Coleman et. al., *Equality of Educational Opportunity,* 2 vols. (Washington, D.C.: Office of Education, U.S. Department of Health, Education and Welfare, Washington, D.C., USGPO, 1966); Samuel Bowles and Herbert Gintis, *Schooling in Capitalist America: Educational Reform and the Contradictions of Economic Life* (New York: Basic Books, 1976); Christopher Jencks, *Inequality: Reassessment of the Effect of Family and Schooling in America* (New York: Harper and Row, 1972).

6. Boyer, *High School,* 127; Adler, *Paideia,* 23; Goodlad, *A Place Called School,* 286.

7. Adler, *The Paideia Proposal,* 8.

8. The technical reports are as follows: *Academic Preparation for College; Action for Excellence; Making the Grade;* and *A Nation at Risk.* For full citations see note 1.

9. Ken Richardson and David Spears, eds., *Race and Intelligence: The Fallacies behind the Race-IQ Controversy* (Baltimore, Md.: Penguin, 1972); Randall Collins, *The Credential Society: An Historical Sociology of Education and Stratification* (New York: Academic Press,1979).

10. Judith K. Lawrence and Kenneth C. Green, *A Question of Quality: The Higher Education Ratings Game.* (Washington, D.C.: Association for Higher Education, 1980), research report.

11. See, for example, Twentieth Century Fund, *Making the Grade,* 20.

12. National Commission on Excellence, *A Nation at Risk,* 25–26.

13. Education Commission of the States, *Action for Excellence,* 35.

14. National Commission on Excellence, *Nation at Risk,* 16.

15. Business–Higher Education Forum, *America's Competitive Challenge,* 1.

16. Education Commission of the States, *Action for Excellence,* 44; Twentieth Century Fund, *Making the Grade,* 6.

17. Business–Higher Education Forum, *America's Competitive Challenge,* 51.

18. Thomas Dye, *Who's Running America?—The Reagan Years* (Englewood

Cliffs, N.J.: Prentice-Hall, 1983).

19. Interview with Alan H. Magazine, Forum director, November 19, 1984, Business–Higher Education Forum, Washington, D.C.

20. Business–Higher Education Forum, *America's Competitive Challenge,* 2.

21. Business–Higher Education Forum, *Corporate and Campus Cooperation,* 6.

22. Business–Higher Education Forum, *The New Manufacturing,* 8.

23. Business–Higher Education Forum, *America's Competitive Challenge,* 16.

24. Business–Higher Education Forum, *America's Competitive Challenge,* 14.

25. Business–Higher Education Forum, *The New Manufacturing,* 1–2.

26. Business–Higher Education Forum, *The New Manufacturing,* 24–25.

27. Business–Higher Education Forum, *America's Competitive Challenge,* 1.

28. Business–Higher Education Forum, *Competitive Challenge,* iii.

29. Business–Higher Education Forum, *America's Competitive Challenge,* iv.

30. Business–Higher Education Forum, *Corporate and Campus Cooperation,* 27.

31. Business–Higher Education Forum, *Corporate and Campus Cooperation,* 25.

32. Study Group on Conditions of Excellence, *Involvement in Learning,* 3.

33. Study Group on Conditions of Excellence, *Involvement in Learning,* 3.

34. See, for example, Irving Howe, ed., *Alternatives: Proposals for America from the Democratic Left* (New York: Pantheon Books, 1984).

Part 3

Current Reforms and the
Legacy of the Sixties

The Struggle for Excellence
in Urban Education

Richard C. Hunter

INTRODUCTION

The question of excellence in urban education during the 1980s has accelerated. Significant demographic changes that have altered the makeup of city schools in America point up the challenges our nation faces. The hidden truth is that the United States has been faced with progressive deterioration of a whole series of great urban institutions in the postwar era. The whites had been fleeing to suburban housing areas and the blacks had been concentrating in the central cities. In 1958–59, for the first time, the schools in Richmond, Virginia, had a black majority (51 percent).

City schools in America have changed dramatically during the past decade. In city after city, the so-called "minority" students are now the "majority." In the past two years a national thrust has been initiated to make up for past inadequacies. According to Fantini and Weinstein, urban schools today are subjected to persistent stress. Further, this stress is affected by the social realities of the community in which the school is situated.[1]

Political and fiscal anomalies in urban government have made it enormously difficult for some urban schools to obtain the support necessary to carry out even their traditional instructional tasks, much less assume responsibility for various social ills. Yet, both their traditional tasks and their new social responsiblities are ineluctable.[2] Urban schools are charged with the responsibility to deal effectively with both. City and school problems are usually treated separately, but, in fact, changes in one affect the other. Schools are as much the victim of urban decay as they are its cause. Central-city schools have become dominated by racial minorities and children of low-income households. Student achievement is often low, and the teaching staff sometimes has a poor reputation.

According to statistics recently published by the Joint Center for Political Studies, the schools in twenty-three of the twenty-five largest cities in the United States have predominantly minority enrollments, with blacks, Hispanics, and Asians the largest groups. In these same city schools in 1950, one student in ten was a minority student. In 1960, this figure rose to one in three and in 1970 it reached one in two. Evidence indicates that racial imbalance operates both among and within school districts. In reference to demographic changes in cities in the United States, Berry states:

> If whole states are either majority, minority or close to it, then we must change the record that too often in the past meant quality education is not equated with minority education. The nation is going to have to change this image with commitment to equity and excellence at the same time.[3]

THE EFFECTIVE SCHOOL MOVEMENT

Today, many urban school districts are in transition to effectiveness and achievement. Ruffin summarized the attitudes of the late 1960s and early 1970s with respect to the matter of accountability in education as follows:

> Code words such as "the school has a different population," "ghetto," "inner city," and "disadvantaged" are no longer being accepted as excuses for not having sound teaching methods and reasonable achievement standards, and for not promoting scholarship.[4]

During the late 1960s and the early 1970s the pessimistic view of many critics of urban schools diminished with the effective school-reform movement. Urban education is moving back into the educational mainstream. The transition to effectiveness takes years before sustained maintenance of gains can be observed; however, the second-class status assigned urban schools by partially informed critics is being eradicated.

According to Edmonds, educators have become increasingly convinced that the characteristics of schools are important determinants of academic achievement. Researchers who have found that parts of the schooling program make a difference in effective schools are becoming more and more numerous. Edmonds concluded the following:

> Several school effects researchers have independently concluded that effective schools share certain essential characteristics. However, two important caveats exist: researchers do not yet know whether those characteristics are the cause of instructional effectiveness; nor have the characteristics been ranked. We must conclude that to advance school effectiveness, a school must implement all of the characteristics at once.[5]

Edmonds concluded that the characteristics of an effective school would be as follows:

- Strong educational leadership by the principal.

- Clear and widely understood instructional goals.

- Safe and orderly school climate conducive to teaching and learning.

- Teachers with high expectations for student success.

- Frequent monitoring of pupil achievement as the basis for program evaluation.

Urban school districts are beginning to remove barriers to effectiveness, and many ineffective schools are being transformed into effective schools. The pendulum has swung to rebuilding a strong academic structure, based on a higher quality of scholastic achievement. Significant progress in urban school districts will depend on the success the superintendent has in focusing on clearly enunciated goals and the programs that make their attainment possible.

RECENT REFORM MOVEMENTS

In 1983 the National Commission on Excellence in Education presented their assessment of American education:

> Our Nation is at risk. The educational foundations of our society are presently eroded by a rising tide of mediocrity that threatens our very future as a nation and a people . . . . Some 23 million American adults are functionally illiterate.
> . . . achievement of high school students on most standardized tests is now lower than 26 years ago when sputnik was launched.[6]

The report made a loud and clear call to improve public school performance and made a number of suggestions that deserve consideration by urban educators. They also recognized that schools are only one element in the education of children; the impact of social changes on the education of children must also be considered. The National Commission on Excellence recognized the priority of rebuilding a strong academic structure, based on a higher standardized system of scholastic achievement, and has initiated steps to address the problems of educating our children.

The Task Force on Education for Economic Growth echoed a similar call for tougher standards, more homework, longer school days and school years, and merit pay for teachers. The report states that the federal government should not neglect its responsibilities and financial commitment to education, but it also addresses what states and local communities can do to improve their schools. It urged deeper involvement by the business community in setting goals for American schools and attaining those goals.

In an eight-point action plan, the task force adopted the following recommendations:

- "Drastic" improvements in methods of recruiting, training, and paying teachers;

- Making school "more intense and more productive," with basic skills curriculum and precise standards;

- Provisions for "quality assurance in education," including ways to measure teacher effectiveness and reward excellence.

- Better utilization of existing school funds;

- Developing in each state plans to improve public schools in kindergarten through grade twelve;

- Establishing partnerships between businesses and schools;

- Improved leadership and management in the schools with the principals setting the academic pace;

- Increased efforts to serve students at the top of the academic ladder as well as those at the bottom.[7]

The task force for economic growth shared the conviction that a real emergency is upon us and issued a challenge for excellence in public schools:

> Technological changes and global competition makes it imperative to equip students in public school with skills that go beyond the basics . . . The challenge is not simply to better educate our elite but to raise both the floor and ceiling of achievement in America. Our future success as a nation—our national defense, our social stability and well-being and our national prosperity—will depend on our ability to improve education and training for millions of individual citizens.[8]

The next section will focus on the response of the Richmond, Virginia, public school system to the problems and opportunities identified in the effective school movement and in the task force reports. Results of the efforts to improve standardized test scores indicate that urban schools can take action to increase student achievement.

THE FIVE-YEAR PLAN FOR UNPARALLELED ACHIEVEMENT

Successful schooling is essential for all in modern America. Schooling must be more demanding because so much more will be demanded of our youth. To assure quality education in the Richmond Public School System with its 86 percent black enrollment, the school board has worked diligently to establish a unique set of goals. An integral component of this goal-setting process was the school board's participation in a series of seminars and work sessions sponsored by the Danforth Foundation.

The Richmond school board has developed and adopted six general goals (and enabling objectives) to guide its work on behalf of the students enrolled in the Richmond Public Schools. Members of the school board are of the opinion that these goals will bring focus to their work as well as to the efforts of teachers, administrators, other staff members, students, and parents in the division. The board recognizes that other goals and objectives already exist within the Richmond schools; thus the goals included in the board's goal statement are to be considered not only as general and overarching, but the board's priorities for the future. The six goals are expected to bring coherence and concentration to the work of everyone in the division.

The Goals

- To continue the present pattern of increased student achievement.

- To prepare each pupil to assume a productive role in a technological society.

- To attract and retain personnel of the highest professional and personal qualities and compensate them commensurate with superior performance.

- To improve the leadership effectiveness of the Richmond school board, administrators, and staff toward the fulfillment of their respective duties and responsibilities within the division.

- Establish a systematic process and procedure for general oversight of the achievement of the division's goals and objectives.

- Elevate and enhance community confidence in the Richmond Public Schools.

Goal One: To Continue the Present Pattern of Increased Student Achievement

The Richmond school board believes that continued improvement of student achievement across the school division calls for strengthening of current approaches to student evaluation, diagnosis, and prescriptions for learning. Nationally recognized experts will be retained to review and recommend procedures that more fully evaluate urban pupil performance. Diagnostic resources will be expanded to include greater reliance upon current research, computer technology, and information drawn from other relevant disciplines, with particular attention given to visual and other physical and emotional conditions that adversely affect learning. Prescriptive learning plans based on more complete sets of information are to be made for those pupils who are not performing at reasonable levels established for urban students. In addition, the theme of "unparalleled achievement" is expected to permeate life in every Richmond school.

More specifically, the board intends that

- Programs and other assistance for less-motivated students will be reviewed and recommendations made for improvement.

- The middle school program will be strengthened.

- Academic offerings for the average student will be reviewed and recommendations made for strengthening such offerings.

- A "relentless reading program" will be developed and implemented to give greater reading skills to all students.

- A comprehensive computer-assisted instructional program will be developed to enhance classroom instruction, and computer literacy will be addressed to increase student knowledge about computer programming.

- By the spring of 1989, elementary school students will attain the seventy-fifth percentile as measured by the SRA composite reading and mathematics mean score, computed against the national sample average.

- By the spring of 1989, secondary students will attain the sixtieth percentile as measured by the SRA composite reading and mathematics mean score, and computed against the national sample average.

Goal Two: To Prepare Each Pupil to Assume a
Productive Role in a Technological Society

The board believes that vocational and academic programs, both in philosophy and practice, must be linked, and calls for coordinated vocational and academic programming. Mutual understanding and shared objectives among the district's educators will reduce the polarization and/or conflict between vocational and academic pursuits.

More specifically, the board intends that:

- A review and strengthening of vocational and academic career counseling programs will be conducted.

- More consistency and coordination between vocational and academic courses will be achieved.

- The number of pretechnological and vocational courses for students will be expanded.

- All high school students will be required to take vocational courses.

- More flexible school schedules will be arranged to allow greater opportunity for student employment.

Goal Three: To Attract and Retain Personnel of the Highest
Professional and Personal Qualities and Compensate Them
Commensurate with Superior Performance

Professionals in education render significant public service that warrants compensation and respect equivalent to their contribution to the public good. In recent national studies of American education, the relationship of the quality of teachers and administrators to the nation's interest is clearly established. Thus the board intends to link the quality of performance to compensation in the interest of children and youth of the community.

More specifically, the board and adminstration will:

- Strengthen recruitment and training programs, especially those designed to meet critical employment needs: e.g., teachers of emotionally disturbed pupils.

- Review and improve all staff performance appraisal and compensation procedures.

- Expand the employee merit program to employees not working in schools.

- Review and expand employee recognition programs.

- Implement a program that highlights the importance of employees serving as positive community role models for all students, reflecting superior levels of citizenship and propriety.

- Compensate personnel for the quality they contribute through a superior pay scale that leads all school districts in Virginia and that compares favorably to salaries in other professions.

Goal Four: To Improve the Leadership Effectiveness of the Richmond School Board, Administrators, and Staff toward the Fulfillment of Their Respective Duties and Responsibilities within the Divison

The board believes that effective leadership is indispensable to the achievement of all other goals and objectives within the division. Moreover, excellence in leadership must be exhibited at all levels and in discrete areas of responsibility such as teaching, administration, and policy making.
　More specifically the board intends that:

- More efficient ways will be found to conduct the business of the school board and the school division.

- Time will be allocated to the improvement of leadership effectiveness.

- Special training (with consultative support) will be provided when necessary to carry out specific leadership and adminsitrative functions.

- Staff development efforts will be intensified for all personnel, especially principals.

- Programs will be developed to inspire and equip teachers to teach to "student possibilities."

- The concept of "unparalleled achievement" will exemplify the behavior of both students and professionals in the Richmond public schools.

- Continuous review of goals of the school system will be achieved and progress reports will be made to the community.

Goal Five: To Establish a Systematic Process and Procedure for General Oversight of the Achievement of the Division's Goals and Objectives

The Richmond school board takes seriously its oversight responsibility and understands that it is an essential governance task requiring both time and resources. Furthermore, the oversight function is dependent upon administrative support and cooperation, accompanied by a clear delineation of the areas to be monitored.
　More specifically, the board intends that:

- For the short range, the superintendent will organize and conduct an assessment of the school division's instructional supervisory structure and will recommend modifications for the board's review.

- Organizational efficiency studies will be utilized periodically.

- The board's own performance as a policy body will be self-appraised in terms of criteria to be developed for that purpose.

- For the long range, the board and the superintendent will develop a comprehensive plan for fulfilling the oversight function, including periodic reports to the staff, parents, and the community at large.

Goal Six: To Elevate and Enhance Community Confidence in the Richmond Public Schools

In regard to goal six, the board believes that confidence in a school system flows from the community's knowledge about its schools. Citizen attitudes and beliefs about public education are based upon the competence of school people to educate youth, satisfaction with the fiscal management of the schools, and an understanding of what schools are trying to accomplish and how they go about that work. Confidence builds pride; pride encourages support of schools; support by the community encourages staff and students; and the cycle inspires an upward spiral of educational achievement. There is a need for parents, the community, and the board to embrace all of the division's goals.

More specifically, the board intends that:

- Community dialogue regarding education and special pilot projects designed to strengthen the commitment to the Richmond public schools will be expanded.

- Current efforts to enhance the school division's public-relations program will be expanded.

- Periodic in-depth assessment of community sentiment and knowledge about school matter will be conducted.

- Information from community polls will be utilized to improve educational activities in the schools and to share information with the community.

The goals presented herein reflect the school board's commitment to channel long-overdue resources into all components of the instructional program. Effective schools must have explicit, clearly stated goals and objectives.

BUILDING ON ACHIEVEMENT

Standardized test scores in Richmond public schools suffered during the early 1970s, ranging in 1974–75 between the twentieth and thirtieth percentiles for fourth, eighth, and eleventh grade students. Expectations for student achievement were low. Ignoring the cynicism of skeptics, in 1976 the Richmond School board established the goal that achievement levels would reach the national average by 1980–81. Five years later, this goal was met and exceeded at all elementary grade levels. By 1981–82, eighth grade scores had risen from the twentieth to the forty-first percentile in reading, and from the twenty-second to the fifty-third percentile in math. Eleventh grade scores, though slightly lower, have followed a similar trend.

The Richmond public school system has made significant gains; now the academic goals are being rasied once more: to the seventy-fifth percentile for elementary students and the sixtieth percentile for secondary students. Skeptics claim that disadvantaged urban students cannot score at the sixtieth, much less the seventy-fifth percentile. The school board disagrees. With superior resources, programs, leadership, and commitment, Richmond public school students will demonstrate unparalleled achievement.

ATTITUDES TOWARD PUBLIC EDUCATION IN VIRGINIA

One important aspect of the challenge to excellence is the input of the community. The business community is greatly affected by the products of our public education system. There is a direct relationship between the quality of education and the positive factors of economic well-being. The business community has much to contribute, other than taxes, to the more effective functioning of our public education system. Table I represents proposed ways of improving the schools of the Commonwealth of Virginia.

These data clearly indicate that both professional and lay respondents ranked improved teaching training programs as most promising for bringing about improved quality instruction in the schools. Least promising of the proposals in view of the lay respondents was additional planning time for teachers, while professionals reported lowest confidence in actions to involve the community more often in educational decisions. Both groups of respondents were of the opinion that outstanding teachers should receive special rewards and recognition for their work.

School improvement in Virginia also involves changes in the way students are prepared for further study or work after high school. In the study of Virginia education, emphasis on the teaching of reading and writing was rated most needed, and more stress on mathematics and science ranked

Table 1
Ratings of Suggested Ways of Improving Instruction

Proposal	Lay (N=347)	Average Professional (N=456)
Better teacher training program	2.54	2.62
Better in-service training	2.22	2.40
Better informed administrators and supervisors	2.04	2.18
Raising teachers' salaries	1.95	2.32
Involving community more in educational decisions	1.92	1.78
Lower pupil-teacher ratios	1.84	2.25
Employing more counselors	1.71	1.94
More equipment and materials	1.68	1.97
Employing more aides	1.68	1.98
More planning time for teachers	1.63	1.96

1 — Little improvement   2 — Some improvement   3 — Much improvement

Source: W. Thomas Rice, *A Look at Virginia Public Education* (Richmond, Virginia: Virginia State Chamber of Commerce Education Committee, 1980).

second as a needed improvement. There is public support for rebuilding a strong academic structure based on changes in the curriculum to place more stress on reading, writing, mathematics, and science.

The college board has attempted to translate the basic academic competencies essential to effective work in all fields of college study. The following was reported:

> The basic academic competencies are reading, writing, speaking and listening, mathematics, reasoning and studying. These competencies are interrelated to and independent with the basic academic subjects. Without such competencies, knowledge of history, science, language, and all other subjects is unattainable.[9]

The board's study was confined to the preparation of students who plan to attend college, but the plan has emphasized expanding opportunities for minorities. This double focus on higher-order skills and general improvement is necessary to remedy the historical failure of schools to teach the majority.

CONCLUSION

Education in urban school districts has changed significantly during the past three decades. Urban schools have become responsible for more than the teaching of the three r's. Cities composed of diverse ethnic, economic, and cultural groups have been forced to adjust rapidly to change, frequently under adverse conditions.

A preeminent consideration to reform our educational system is through effective leadership. Perhaps more than at any other time in our nation's history, the goals and policies formulated by school board members have come under sharp scrutiny. Effective schools must have explicit, clearly stated goals and objectives.

Administrators in urban school districts are responsible for the educational destiny of millions of school children, many of whom require special services. Therefore, urban school leaders have unique environments in which to operate—considerably different from those in nonurban school systems.

The struggle to improve educational conditions for urban school children will improve as the problems of urban decay and suburban indifference, of inequities and distrust of government, of organized crime and crime on the streets, of unemployment and high cost of living are solved or alleviated. All of these problems have this in common: they are all basically educational problems. How successful each of us is in this effort to improve the "quality of life" to which we have become accustomed will depend to a great extent on the knowledge and skills, values and beliefs, abilities and aspirations acquired through the process of education.

The transition to excellence in urban schools will take years before sustained gains can be observed. With increased public confidence in urban education, improved test scores, and fiscal support, the pathway to better times and places in city schools is within our grasp.

NOTES

1. Mario Fantini and Gerald Weinstein, *Making Urban Schools Work, Social Realities and the Urban School* (New York: Holt, Rinehart, and Winston, 1968): 3.

2. Raymond Hummel and John Nagle, *Urban Education in America* (New York: Oxford University Press, 1973): 9.

3. Mary Berry, commissioner on the United States Commission of Civil Rights.

4. Santee Ruffin, "Trends in Urban Education—Strong Leadership Generates Positive Image," *NAASP Bulletin,* (November 1983): 3.

5. Ronald Edmonds, "Programs of School Improvement: An Overview," *Educational Leadership* (December 1982): 4.

6. National Commission on Excellence in Education, *A Nation at Risk: The Imperatives for Educational Reform* (Washington, D.C.: U.S. Government Printing Office, 1983): 5.

7. Task Force on Education for Economic Growth, *Action for Excellence: A Comprehensive Plan to Improve Our Nation's Schools* (Denver, Colo.: Education Commission of the States, 1983).

8. Task Force on Education, *Action for Excellence,* 11.

9. The College Board, *Academic Preparation for College: What Students Need to Know and Be Able to Do* (New York: New York College Entrance Examination Board, 1983): 7.

Equality, Equity, and Excellence
A Critique

Carl A. Grant and Christine E. Sleeter

Education policy during the 1960s and 1970s was aimed primarily toward improving access to quality schooling for members of minority groups, children from low-income families, handicapped children, and females. Education policy in the 1980s has in name shifted toward improving the quality of education for children in general. Many reports and reform proposals issued during the past two years state as twin themes the pursuit of quality and the assurance of equity. In this paper we will examine how nine of the most commonly read reports have dealt with equity on the basis of race, social class, gender, and handicap.[1]

Before examining the reports, we will provide a short rationale for addressing race, class, gender, and handicap in the 1980s. Although many Americans may feel that strides made during previous decades have eliminated these as pressing social problems, a review of some current research findings shows this clearly not to be the case. After addressing race, class, gender, and handicap in society in the 1980s, we will discuss how these are reflected in and perpetuated through educational practices. We will argue that reform proposals purporting to advocate improved education for *all* children must directly address such practices. We will then examine the extent to which the reports actually do so.

RACE, CLASS, GENDER AND HANDICAP IN SOCIETY TODAY

Many Americans find it tempting to believe that racism, sexism, and handicappism are no longer major social problems; that the last three decades have witnessed such success that these factors are no longer important bases for social stratification. However, in spite of progress, there is considerable evidence that U.S. society is still very stratified on the basis of race, gender, and handicap. Furthermore, stratification based on social class is a prominent feature of U.S. society that social policy in the last three decades has made little attempt to change.

When considering racism in society, Americans often cite improvement of racial attitudes as a sign of progress. Indeed, attitudes have improved somewhat. Recent studies report that white attitudes towards blacks are much less negative than they were three-and-one-half decades ago.[2] A 1978 survey conducted by the *New York Times* and CBS, designed to replicate the study conducted by the Advisory Commission on Civil Disorder in 1968, summarizes the recent new attitude of whites very appropriately, however. It reports that whites have better attitudes about race relations and improved understanding, but not the new will to take the bitter medicine the remedies for racism require.[3] Additionally, a survey comparing 1979 with 1982 public attitudes toward the treatment of minorities concludes that treatment is not getting better, and may even be deteriorating.[4]

Improved access to public facilities is another factor often used to cite progress in race relations. While the last three decades have brought about improved white attitudes and improved access to facilities such as schools, people of color are still distinctly subordinate economically and politically. Black men earn about 80 percent of what white men with the same amount of education earn, at all levels of educational attainment.[5] In 1981, despite the average educational attainment of blacks being only slightly below that of whites (12.0 years and 12.5 years respectively), the income of black families was about 59 percent of that of white families, and had improved little in over a decade.[6] The unemployment gap between blacks and whites was the same in the late 1970s as it was in 1948. In spite of the narrowed education gap, the unemployment rate for blacks has remained about twice that of whites.[7] Mare and Winship, after studying racial inequality and joblessness among black youth, offer an illuminating observation: the growing race difference in employment results from the fact that black youth are both staying in school longer and joining the military in greater numbers, and thus no longer have a "head start" in the labor market for unskilled or semiskilled jobs. Their study suggests that "worsening labor force statistics for black youths do not denote increasing racial inequality, but rather persistent racial inequalities previously hidden by race differences in other aspects of young adulthood."[8]

People of color are also still locked out of much of the political system. Increasing numbers of big-city mayors are men of color. However, since 1971 there has been only one black U.S. senator, and the number of other senators of color has fluctuated between two and three. Between 1971 and 1981, the number of black congresspersons increased from twelve to seventeen but that still constituted only 3.9 percent of the Congress, and other representatives of color have constituted less than 1 percent of the House. Nineteen eighty-four has had the first black presidential candidate, but his white constituency was small, and his support of the Democratic nominee was considered a liability by many whites.

Women, too, are still distinctly subordinate, both economically and politically, in spite of gains made recently. Women are participating in the labor market in ever-growing numbers. However, average earnings of full-time working women are only 55 percent of those of full-time working white men. This is true of men and women who have the same level of educational attainment, at all levels. A number of studies have examined human capital factors (e.g., work experience, evidence of work commitment) that might explain this differential, but taken together, these "factors usually account for less than a quarter and never more than half of the observed earnings differences."[9] One major institutional factor perpetuating this is that "women are concentrated in low-paying occupations and, within occupations, in low-paying firms."[10]

The political position of women has improved somewhat but is still no better than the economic position. Over the last few years, increasing numbers of women have been elected to local and state offices. However, women are still a small minority of office-holders at the state level, and even smaller at the national level. Only about 12 percent of the state legislators are female, as is only 4 percent of the U.S. Congress. Only one or two states at a time have a woman governor, and only 1 percent of the mayors are women. While 1984 saw the first woman nominated by a major political party for vice-president, she needed to make herself salable to the public by emphasizing that she had fulfilled traditional roles of wife and mother in addition to pursuing a career.

The United States is a distinctly social class–stratified society. Although debates about racism and sexism have always existed, and in the last two decades have been quite plentiful, Americans have devoted much less attention to social class stratification. Yet there are tremendous inequities in the distribution of wealth. In 1978, the top 20 percent of the population earned 41.5 percent of the total income and controlled 76 percent of the total wealth, while the bottom 20 percent earned 5.2 percent of the total income and controlled 0.25 percent of the total national wealth.[11] Harrington has provided compelling evidence that the gap between rich and poor in America is widening, and that the number of poor people is growing. He has observed that,

> People who, twenty or even ten years ago, were secure in their jobs and communities now live somewhere between poverty and semi-affluence, walking the edge of an economic precipice. Their problems will be ameliorated, but far from ended, by economic recovery, if this really does come. For they, or people like them, are likely to face downward social mobility for twenty or thirty years, unless this country turns around. These are not, then, the instant "new poor" that the media discovered in that winter of American discontent, 1982–83.[12]

In spite of the popular belief that anyone who desires it can attain wealth through individual effort, Jencks et al., found occupation to be predicted largely by educational attainment, which in turn is predicted mainly by family socioeconomic background. In other words, children tend to grow up to occupy the same social class position as their parents.[13] Even when level of education is controlled for, the children of wealthy parents are much more likely to attain high-paying jobs than are children of parents who are economically less well off.[14] In addition, those controlling the greatest proportion of wealth tend to have the most political power. As Parenti has pointed out, those who are most likely to sit on state and local boards, boards for colleges and universities, and boards of corporations are from the upper socioeconomic classes.[15]

Finally, handicapped people constitute a subordinate group. Historically, public concern for their welfare has risen and fallen. The last two decades have seen a rise in concern, but if history is an accurate guide, that concern will wane. In recent years several federal and state laws have been passed to protect the rights of the handicapped, and support services have been expanded. Nevertheless, handicapped people as a group are still overrepresented in the ranks of the poor. For example, while over 80 percent of the mentally retarded adults are employed, most are in very low-paying jobs.[16] The deaf also disproportionately hold unskilled or semiskilled, low-paying jobs, and blind people are sometimes paid below minimum wage for work sighted people are paid the minimum wage or above.[17] Unemployment and poverty are particularly severe among handicapped people of color, who face double discrimination on the job market.

Handicapped people often lack the access to facilities and opportunities enjoyed by most citizens. For example, while mentally retarded people are no longer automatically institutionalized in most states, in some states in the last few years increasing numbers of them have been institutionalized.[18] Zoning laws restrict where homes for deinstitutionalized retarded people can be built. Blind, deaf, and physically impaired people have legal rights to public facilities, but in practice find it difficult or impossible to get around in many buildings, communicate with public service workers, or use some public channels of communication. The handicapped also bear stereotypes of incompetence. As Gliedman and Roth have noted, public images of the handicapped emphasize limitations, and the handicapped have no counterimage, such as "Black is Beautiful," to offset these.[19]

RACE, CLASS, GENDER, AND HANDICAP IN SCHOOLS

Schools are not insulated from racism, sexism, classism, and handicappism in society. They mirror these forms of social stratification, and in several ways contribute to their reproduction. Research in the last twenty years has contributed much information about what occurs in schools in this regard. We will briefly summarize this research, organized into the following areas: access to school resources; biases in the curriculum; attention to students' language backgrounds; testing procedures; biases in teacher-student interaction; conflicts between student learning styles and dominant teaching styles; and staffing patterns.

Access

Historically, equal access to schooling has been conceptualized mainly as the removal of structural barriers to minority students' access to instruction and material resources open to white students. Prior to the *Brown* decision in 1954, black and white students could legally be taught in different school buildings that had very unequal resources; since then federally mandated desegregation efforts have been undertaken to open minority students' access to the instructional and material resources in white schools. The past thirty years have seen progress toward effecting such racial desegregation. However, minority students still lack equal access to resources open to many affluent white students. Persell has noted that urban schools tend to have many more minority students and fewer material resources than suburban schools.[20] For example, a recent study by Orfield has found teachers in Chicago suburban high schools to be better educated than teachers in the urban high schools.[21] But in spite of such inequities in access to school resources, the federal commitment to continuing racial desegregation of schools is waning.[22]

Much less public attention has been directed toward access to quality schools based on social class. Anyon found striking differences in the quality of instruction between two working-class and two upper middle-class schools.[23] As yet, however, there has been no widespread effort to desegregate schools based on social class.

Tracking is an institutionalized feature of most schools that blocks access to instruction for many students. Goodlad, for example, recently found tracking extensively used in all twenty-five secondary schools he studied.[24] Several studies have found race and social class to be significant factors in the assignment of students to tracks in schools.[25] While lower-track students disproportionately are offered dull, unimaginative instruction that emphasizes rote learning, upper-track students tend to be offered teachers who are better prepared, imaginative instructional practices, more material resources (e.g., science equipment), and instruction that emphasizes thinking and originality. In addition, upper-track students receive more encouragement from counselors.[26]

Until 1975, there was no comprehensive protection for handicapped students' access to schooling. As a rule, handicapped students were removed from public schools, or segregated into special schools or self-contained classrooms in regular public schools, in spite of frequent findings that segregated schooling was academically no more beneficial to them than integrated schooling.[27] PL 94-142 has mandated removal of barriers to handicapped students' access to the education open to regular students. While it has led to the integration of many handicapped students into regular schools and classrooms, it has also led to the identification of many more students as handi-capped and as requiring placement in special education.[28]

Course enrollment can block access to instruction based on sex. In a nationwide survey published in 1973, Saario, Jacklin, and Tittle found en-rollment in homemaking courses to be 93 percent female and in business education, 75 percent female, while enrollment in technical courses such as metallurgy was 92 percent male. In addition, prior to 1972, female students were restricted from many school athletic opportunities open to males.[29] Title IX (of the Education Amendments of 1972) has forbidden schools from restricting access to courses based on sex, although a few studies conducted since then have noted continued disproportionate sex-stereotypic enrollment in vocational courses.[30] In addition, upper-level math and science courses tend to be disproportionately filled with male students, giving them greater access to math or science majors in college.[31]

Curriculum

Many educators have written about the power of curriculum in shaping a stratified society based upon class, race, and gender.[32] For example, they point out that curricula teach children that most important things are done by white, wealthy men; that students have little power to shape the conditions of institutions within which they live; and that injustices to some citizens of the United States are in the past tense and are no longer issues. The aspect of curriculum that has been studied most is instructional materials. Although many educators will attest to the elimination of blatant race and gender stereotypes and the inclusion of more people of color, women, and handi-capped people in materials, many of these same educators argue that instruc-tional materials still underrepresent women of color, Hispanic Americans, and poor Americans, and still highlight how handicapped people are different from, rather than similar to, other people. Also, people of color and white women are not often shown in decision-making positions.[33]

Language

School responses to the language backgrounds of students can affect their learning in school. In U.S. public schools today, almost 10 percent of the students speak a language at home other than English.[34] Haft argues that "bilingual education currently appears to provide the best means of assuring that language minority students receive an education while they learn English."[35] In this regard, experience over the last fifteen years with bilingual programs has produced evidence that children taught in programs that build upon their home language as well as teaching them English profit more than children taught in English as a second language or English-only programs. Some of the following benefits of bilingual instruction as opposed to English-only instruction have been found: better phonemic and syntactic understanding of the second language, English; better progress in mathematics; better progress in reading; competence in two languages; gain in feelings of self-worth; greater attachment to school; greater divergent thinking and creativity.[36] Positive recognition of nonstandard English dialects can also enhance children's school learning, as long as that recognition is not a substitute for teaching standard English. For example, McDermott found children of teachers who accepted their use of black English to feel more accepted and, therefore, to profit more from reading instruction than those of teachers who did not accept it.[37] Prospects for increasing numbers of children entering American schools who speak languages other than English at home suggest a need for more bilingual programs and increased sensitivity toward language differences on the part of teachers.

An often overlooked language is American Sign Language, the fourth most commonly used language among American citizens.[38] Deaf citizens tend to cluster in educational and social service institutions for the deaf because so few members of the hearing population are competent users of sign language. In spite of this, very few schools teach American Sign Language to hearing students. The teaching of American Sign Language, and its acceptance as a legitimate language, is an issue that thus far has received inadequate attention in research and policy debates about education.

Teacher-Student Interaction

Many teachers base expectations for children partly on their race, class, and gender, and interact with them in the classroom in ways that help turn their expectations into self-fulfilling prophecies. For example, several studies have found teachers to rate white children as having more academic potential than black children when presented with only pictures or tape recordings of the children.[39] Studies have also found teachers to expect more academically from middle-class children than from poor children.[40] Teachers then interact with children in the classroom in accordance with their expectations for performance. Observational studies in classrooms have found teachers to interact with, call on, ask harder questions of, and praise middle-class white male students most; lower-class and minority students are called on less and their responses are accepted, praised, and elaborated upon less. Minority male students are the targets of more negative remarks from teachers than any other group; minority female students tend to be ignored or praised more for social accomplishments, while white females tend to be praised for neatness more than males, and for academic accomplishments more than black females.[41]

Learning Styles

A growing body of literature has examined variations among cultural groups in learning styles and how cultural learning styles affect classroom learning. Ethnicity and social class are related to the strategies children learn at home for acquiring, organizing, and remembering information. Cultural groups vary, for example, in their emphasis on cooperative vs. independent learning, observational vs. participatory learning, visual vs. verbal learning, and so forth. In addition, they vary in culturally specific behaviors associated with learning, such as eye contact, body language, and patterns of verbal interaction.[42] Handicapped students also frequently have distinct learning styles. For example, learning disabled students often have definite strengths and weaknesses in auditory vs. visual vs. kinesthetic learning. Low-vision students tend to develop auditory and tactile strengths, while hearing-impaired students often develop visual strengths.

Teacher ignorance of students' learning styles can have negative effects on children. Teachers have been found to negatively describe those whose learning styles differ from their own, suggesting that teachers misperceive learning style differences as deficiencies.[43] Teachers tend to use teaching strategies that are most congruent with white middle-class learning styles, often making it more difficult for lower-class and minority children to profit from instruction.[44] These studies suggest that if teachers were more knowledgeable about and competent in using learning styles of their students, lower-class and minority students would experience more success in school. Teachers also tend to emphasize visual verbal learning, which hinders the general achievement of handicapped students with auditory or kinesthetic strengths or with sensory deficits that interfere with reading skills. Teacher flexibility in the use of varied teaching strategies would benefit handicapped students who presently are not achieving up to their intellectual capacity.

A related issue is math anxiety. Tobias has examined the failure of many girls to achieve in upper-level math courses, finding them to develop a socially conditioned fear of math and feelings of incompetence in that subject area.[45] Fox has found that when girls who fear math are taught upper-level math by teachers who use individualized learning and cooperative rather than competitive learning, and incorporate social content in problems, their achievement levels increase.[46]

Testing

Testing procedures contribute to a reproduction of social stratification in schools. In a review of studies criticizing IQ tests, Persell has provided evidence of race and class bias in their content, standardization norms, and administration.[47] Since IQ tests are an important factor in deciding who should take courses in which track or who should be assigned to special education classes, these biases have very significant consequences for children. Standardized achievement tests also have biases, although they have received less attention in the literature. Designed to assess student learning of dominant school curricula, achievement tests tend to mirror the biases in curriculum noted earlier. For example, Saario, Jacklin, and Tittle reviewed several achievement tests produced by major publishing companies, finding test items to refer disproportionately to males and the male world, and many test items to include sex stereotypes.[48] Group achievement tests are often biased against handicapped students: norm groups tend to underrepresent the handicapped; reliance on reading skills works against learning-disabled, low-vision, deaf, and retarded students; and time limits hamper the performance of most handicapped students.[49] In addition to biases in content, norming, and administration, norm-referenced standardized tests by their very nature contribute to stratification. Since they are designed to discriminate differences among students and to rank order them in terms of competence, even the most stereotype-free norm-referenced test provides a tool for sorting students into unequal categories.

Staffing

In public schools in 1980, about 27 percent of the students were minority, and 10 percent were in special education.[50] The importance of students having role models with whom they can identify and who can inspire their commitment to hard work, excellence, and future life goals is both a documented and commonsense belief among educators. The importance of white students having teachers and administrators of color, and of male students seeing women in administrative positions, is also a commonsense belief. School staff members can serve as such role models. Also, in minority communities, school staff members who share a cultural background with students can serve as linkages to the community, and can sensitize their colleagues to their culture.

In 1979, schools provided students with relatively few nontraditional role models and staff members of color. In elementary schools, 71.5 percent of the teachers were white women and 12 percent were women of color; 14.5 percent of the teachers were white men and only 2 percent were men of color. In secondary schools, 41 percent of the teachers were white women and 6 percent were women of color; 48 percent were white men and 4.5 percent were men of color. Among assistant principals, 17 percent were white women and 6 percent were women of color; 65 percent were white men and 12 percent were men of color. Finally, among principals, only 12 percent were white women and 3 percent were women of color; 77 percent were white men and 8 percent were men of color. Blacks had better representation than other minority groups. Hispanics constituted no more than 2.5 percent of any of the four positions; Asians and native Americans were each less than 1 percent of each position.[51]

The average school, then, contributes to social stratificaton in the way it allocates resources to students, in its curriculum, in its testing procedures, and in its instructional practices. These features of schooling are strengthened by tradition and taken-for-granted notions about what should occur in schools. Attempts to promote educational equity must deal with these directly. Let us examine what the nine reports we are reviewing had to say about them.

THE REPORTS

For the sake of economy in citing the reports, the following acronyms will be used:

AE	Task Force on Education for Economic Growth, *Action for Excellence*
APC	The College Board, *Academic Preparation for College*
EATC	National Science Board Commission on Precollege Education in Mathematics, Science, and Technology, *Educating Americans for the 21st Century*
HC	Theodore R. Sizer, *Horace's Compromise*
HS	Ernest L. Boyer, *High School*
MG	Twentieth Century Fund, *Making the Grade*
NR	National Commission on Excellence in Education, *A Nation at Risk*
PCS	John I. Goodlad, *A Place Called School*
PP	Mortimer J. Adler, *The Paideia Proposal*

All nine reports stated the same two overall goals of school reform: to raise the quality of teaching and learning in schools, and to do so for all students—to provide equity. The reports unanimously condemned the practice of setting expectations for achievement on the basis of students' backgrounds, and recommended that all be expected to learn. They pointed out that minority and lower-class students have often received a poor quality education, and advocated that this should stop. Three also mentioned that female students have historically been stereotyped as unscientific, unmathematical, and domestic, and recommended that this stop (AE, EATC, HC). Handicapped students were not specifically mentioned in relationship to expectations.

We examined discussions and recommendations in the reports to determine the extent to which they dealt with processes that reinforce racism, classism, sexism, and handicappism in schools. Based upon our review of the literature, we were concerned that, if recommendations were not explicitly directed toward changing these practices, they would continue, and school reform efforts would end up most benefitting those whom schools have historically benefitted most.

Access

Many recommendations centered on opening school and classroom doors to all students to give them physical access to the best instructional and material resources available. These included recommendations involving desegregation, tracking, and sex-segregated courses.

Most of the reports applauded desegregation efforts. In doing so, they tended to treat it as an accomplished fact. None advocated continuing efforts to desegregate schools racially, nor did any advocate desegregating them by social class. Instead, the reports advocated improving all schools, seeming to assume that people will willingly support efforts to bring all schools up to some equal standard. The reports' failure to recommend continued desegregation support may suggest to the readership that this is no longer an important issue blocking students' access to school resources.

Three reports specifically recommended eliminating tracking (HS, PP, PCS); a fourth pointed out that tracking usually channels lower-class and minority students into manual jobs, but did not specifically advocate its elimination (HC). The others were silent about tracking, neither explicitly supporting it nor condemning it. Three reports recommended enrolling male and female students in the same kinds of courses without regard to gender (AE, EATC, PP); the others were silent about this. In fact, in *High School,* Boyer noted that "secretarial science" courses help female graduates get jobs, without questioning why females dominate the enrollment in such courses. Again, we are concerned about the reports' silence in relationship to historic practice. As we pointed out earlier, schools have long opened and closed classroom doors to students based in part on their race, social-class background, and gender, often in the name of providing each with a suitable quality education. To recommend quality for all without recommending the elimination of differentiated education may result in a continuation of these practices.

The reports said very little about handicapped students' access to instruction. Only three stated that federal support for the handicapped should continue, and none of these elaborated on what that support should mean for programming students (AE, MG, NR). The *Paideia Proposal* qualified its recommendation that all students be educated together by noting that a small minority would not benefit from the same instruction as everyone else. *High School* recommended special programming for gifted and disadvantaged students but did not even mention handicapped students. The reports seemed to treat mainstreaming either as an accomplished fact, or as an issue not worth discussing—we are not sure which.

Curriculum

If students actually had equal access to good schools and classrooms, what curriculum do the reports recommend that they be taught? Most of them recommended eliminating inessentials in the curriculum (without necessarily defining what makes a body of knowledge inessential), and raising standards in traditional academic subject areas. Some of the reports placed most of their emphasis on increasing the quality and quantity of math and science instruction (AE, EATC, MG). Others discussed increasing requirements for mastery of reading, English, social studies, and foreign language, in addition to math and science (APC, NR, PP, HS). Most recommended more emphasis on the development of thinking skills. Only one recommended that curriculum start with the interests and experience of the student (HC).

None of the reports made any mention of racist, classist, handicappist, and sexist biases in the curriculum; none of their recommendations was directed toward redressing racist, classist, or sexist selections in what is taught, with the exception of two that recommended increasing non-Western studies (HS, PCS). The closest statement we were able to find about curricular implications of a culturally pluralistic society was a recommendation early in *A Place Called School* that schools develop appreciation of different cultural groups, but this recommendation was never elaborated on when subject area content was later discussed.

Most recommendations about curriculum were directed toward preparing the young to serve the needs of industry and technological development. There was little directed toward developing students' personal interests or affective natures, and even less toward developing their understanding of social conditions in America, outlined in the beginning of this paper, even though some acknowledged that these conditions exist. For example, the *Paideia Proposal* acknowledged that some students grow up in communities where there is much unemployment and poverty. Rather than recommending that schools help them critically examine this problem, its roots, and possible avenues for change, the report recommended only that society commit itself "to a policy of full employment,"[52] but offered no suggestions for how education might affect society's commitments to this policy.

Recommendations that all students be taught the same thing, coupled with a lack of attention to racism, classism, and sexism in the curriculum, are producing some alarming reforms. For example, California has proposed a set of standards for history and geography in grades nine through twelve that make little mention of people of color and none of women or working class groups. That would make it difficult to devote much substantive attention to these groups in history because so much else is prescribed.

Language

Related to issues of access and curriculum is the issue of language. While several reports acknowledged cultural diversity within the American population, most either explicitly or implicitly denied its language diversity. Three explicitly upheld the primacy of English as the American national language, and recommended that bilingual programs become programs for teaching English as a second language (HS, PP, MG). Several recommended that students gain competence in a second "foreign" language, but recommended that English be their first language (APC, HS, MG, NR, PP). Neither American Sign Language or Braille was mentioned as a language. Bilingualism's goals of development and maintenance of one's home language and culture *in addition to* mastery of English, and the view of America as a multilingual society, were rejected by these reports. Also rejected was bilingualism's contribution to the self-esteem, improved achievement, and interest in school of students whose home language is not English.

Testing

Four reports made little or no mention of testing (APC, HC, MG, PP). One briefly criticized the manner in which tests have been used to sort students for tracks, partly on the basis of race and class background (PCS). The other four recommended increased, rigorous achievement testing of students. Three specified that standardized achievement tests should be given regularly to determine who needs remediation and to help students decide plans for their lives after high school (EATC, HS, NR). The other did not specify the kind of achievement tests to be used, but offered the purposes for giving them (AE). Of the four reports recommending increased testing, only one mentioned human diversity, recommending that all students be held to the same standard (EATC).

We see three related problems in the uncritical way tests were advocated. The first is tied to the problems we noted earlier with curriculum. Achievement testing helps reinforce the legitimacy of the curriculum the test covers. We have no quarrel with teachers testing students over what they have taught, nor with basic-skills testing, since there is wide consensus that all students should be able to read, write, and compute. But we become very concerned when standardized testing over a common curriculum is advocated, because that constrains teachers' power to determine what is worth teaching. And we are doubly concerned when neither the recommendations for curriculum nor those for testing address issues of racism, classism, sexism, and handicappism in the material being taught and tested. It is as if efforts over the last two decades to develop multicultural curricula have been discarded. Again, the proposed curriculum standards in California, with their proposed statewide achievement testing, is an example.

The second problem in these recommendations is their complete disregard for the history of how tests have been used. Standardized tests have been used to help place lower-class and minority students in special education and white students in enrichment programs. While such testing has been proclaimed as a device to help meet individual needs, in fact it has too often served as a way to retain the advantages of middle-class white students. It is naive to assume that tests will not be used for similar purposes in the future.

The third problem concerns handicapped students. Should they be denied graduation because they cannot pass the same achievement tests as their peers? Should they be held to a different set of standards? Should increasing numbers of students be placed in special education for remediation if they cannot meet raised standards for achievement? These are no small questions, since they involve about 10 percent of the students in public schools. How to work with them in relationship to raised standards and achievement testing was not mentioned.

Instruction

Instruction was not addressed in two reports (APC, MG) and barely mentioned in the third (AE). We examined the remaining six to determine whether discussions of instruction recognized that students bring different learning styles to school. Three reports recommended giving students more time to learn, two of these specifically advocating compensatory-type programs to allow "disadvantaged" and slow-learning students to catch up before they fall too far behind (EATC, NR). Three reports addressed the narrow range of instructional strategies most teachers employ. They recommended that instruction be made more lively and exciting, and that much more use be made of instructional strategies that would improve students' skill performance and their ability to think critically and make sound judgments (HS, PCS, PP). One recommended increased funds for textbooks for "thin-market" populations such as the gifted and the learning disabled (NR). All of these recommendations about instruction assumed that students learn in the same ways, although at different rates. Only *Horace's Compromise* addressed student diversity more substantively, recommending not only that more diversified and effective instructional strategies be used for teaching all students, but also that teachers learn to recognize different learning styles, and learn to vary how they teach to match how their students learn.

As we reported earlier, there is considerable evidence that many children, particularly those from cultural backgrounds other than middle-class Anglo and those who are handicapped, often do not learn as well as they could in school because predominant strategies for teaching conflict with their preferred learning strategies. Failure to recognize and build on students' learning styles hinders their access to learning. The reports' silence on this issue implies lack of understanding or sensitivity, or tacit rejection of the importance of teachers' learning how to interpret correctly and build on students' approaches to learning.

The issue of math anxiety in many female students seems to have escaped the attention of the reports' authors altogether. While several recommended enrolling more female students in math courses, they offered no recommendations for ensuring their success there. Again, it is as if this body of research on approaches to helping students learn better had not been considered or had been dismissed as unimportant.

Teacher-Student Interaction

Earlier, we summarized research findings regarding teacher expectations of students based on race, class, and gender, documenting that teachers interact with students in the classroom differently in accordance with stereotypic expectations. We found very little in the reports dealing with this. Four made no mention of teacher-student relationships or teacher expectations of students, other than the recommendation that teachers should hold high expectations for all (APC, AE, MG, PP). Three more added the recommendation that discipline and attendance policies be enforced rigorously (EATC, HS, NR). Only two reports recognized that teachers expect and interact with students differently on the basis of home backgrounds. One of these, however, did not seem to recognize the importance of this fact. *A Place Called School* noted that teachers in white middle-class schools expressed a higher level of satisfaction than teachers in low-income and minority schools; however, the discussion of this did not explore possibilities of cultural ignorance between students and teacher, teacher stereotypes of lower-class and minority students, or teachers interacting with students on the basis of stereotypes that demean them and provoke their rebellion. *Horace's Compromise,* on the other hand, clearly stated that children of low-income parents tend to "receive limited and often careless attention from adults" in the school; however, the report lacked recommendations for changing this. Effects of gender on teacher-student interaction were not mentioned in any report.

Teachers do not automatically hold high expectations for all students and treat them in nonstereotypic manners by being exhorted to do so. Disciplinary codes, while important for establishing rules for group behavior, do not necessarily deal with this problem. In fact, telling teachers to enforce discipline strictly without helping them to recognize stereotyped expectations for students can be damaging to male, and especially minority male, students who are disproportionately the victims of punitive teacher behavior for the same rule infractions as other students. It is naive to assume that teachers will hold high expectations for all and treat all in a way that ensures equal access to instruction in the classroom without making recommendations designed to sensitize teachers to stereotypes and patterns in their behavior.

Staffing

Recommendations for staffing were made in all reports except APC. Most recommendations resolved around teacher recruitment and preparation, and improving the conditions of teaching. In statements on recruitment we looked for recommendations to recruit more people of color as teachers and administrators, females as administrators, and males as elementary teachers. We found none. HS pointed out that the average principal is white male, and AE and PCS both noted that fewer women and men of color are entering the field of education as job opportunities open elsewhere, but made no recommendations on the basis of these observations.

We studied recommendations for teacher preparation, looking for recommendations that teachers be prepared, for example, to understand culture and its effect on learning styles, reasons why females tend not to take upper-level math courses or feel confident when they do, teacher stereotypes of students based on race, class, and gender, or bias in testing. We found none. *A Place Called School* noted that special education teachers felt less well prepared than any other group, but did not develop this into a recommendation for teacher preparation.

It appears as though the reports expect teachers to offer a quality education to all students without expecting that they be taught about relationships between cultural diversity and schooling, or taught skills and attitudes that can help combat racist, classist, handicappist, and sexist practices in schools. The reports seem to assume that the handicap, sex, race, and class backgrounds of teachers and students are meaningless and that their impact on schooling can be eliminated by fiat. Such an assumption defies the findings of much research on schooling that has been conducted in the last two decades, some of which we reported earlier.

Conclusion

Have we just described minor points that we believe should be added on to basically sound reports, or are we critical of the fundamental viewpoints the reports embody? We will respond to this question after first roughly dividing the reports into two categories. Four were oriented primarily toward preparing workers for an increasingly technological economy (AE, EATC, MG, NR), while two were oriented toward developing cognitive and, to some degree, affective sensibilities of young people in order to improve the quality of individual and collective lives (HC, PP). The other three can be placed between these orientations, as they contain features of each.

The first four have a very different vision of American society from that described at the beginning of this paper. It is a vision in which most jobs will or should become highly technological, in which the nature of work people will be performing will be humanly satisfying, and in which there will be much less stratification of people in terms of reward for their work—or at least in which such stratification is not an issue. This is a naive vision, although it may serve a useful purpose. It is naive on several accounts. First, it ignores the fact that the economy is producing a much greater demand for fast-food workers than any other kind of worker. While the demand for high-tech workers is growing, it is not growing as fast as the demand for unskilled and semiskilled labor.[53] Second, routine labor, whether it consists of pushing buttons, hamburgers, or brooms, is not humanly satisfying when performed over a long period of time. This is a problem the U.S. has long recognized but has not solved. Third, the rewards for work have always been distributed in the U.S. in a manner that leaves some people scraping to get by while others have ready access to luxury.

These four reports do not stress such issues, nor do they pave the way for such issues to be addressed. But the image they project is beneficial to big business because it suggests that if everyone is prepared to fill the economic roles business requires, everyone will benefit. Business leaders, and young people who successfully secure well-paying technological jobs, will benefit. Those who push hamburgers and brooms for low wages, who history tells us will be disproportionately female, of color, and born of lower-class parents, will not necessarily benefit.

The more humanistically oriented reports have a different kind of problem. They attempt to be "colorblind" in a culturally diverse and differentiated society. As a result, they oversimplify and leave much room for their followers to reproduce racist, classist, and sexist practices. A good example is their silence about biases in the curriculum. While, for the most part, they do not make specific prescriptions about what it should contain, they discuss it as if it did not represent a selection of some groups' knowledge at the expense of others. They recommend improvements in the culturally biased curricula schools already teach, without suggesting that what counts as knowledge needs to be reexamined from a race, class, and gender perspective. Only one even entertains the notion that student experience and student interest need to be taken into account when planning curriculum. The rest discuss curriculum as if students did not bring to school personal, cultural, or gender identities with them that might affect the meaning they derive from a curriculum, and that might suggest fruitful avenues of learning for their growth. A question that haunted us as we read and analyzed these reports was why were they not more explicit in their statements about equity issues of class, gender, and race?

As these reports stand, they are inadequate at best and, in some cases, seriously flawed as blueprints for reform of schooling. They will not provide the needed guidance for ensuring that all children receive a quality education. It appears that the proposal for doing that in the 1980s has not yet appeared in print.

NOTES

1. Mortimer J. Adler, *The Paideia Proposal* (New York: Macmillan, 1982); Ernest L. Boyer, *High School* (New York: Harper and Row, 1983); The College Board, *Academic Preparation for College* (New York: The College Board, 1983); John I. Goodlad, *A Place Called School* (New York: McGraw-Hill, 1983); National Commission on Excellence in Education, *A Nation at Risk* (Washington, D.C.: Government Printing Office, 1983); National Science Board Commission on Precollege Education in Mathematics, Science, and Technology, *Educating Americans for the 21st Century* (Washington, D.C.: National Science Foundation, 1983); Theodore R. Sizer, *Horace's Compromise* (New York: Houghton Mifflin, 1984); Task Force on Education for Economic Growth, *Action for Excellence* (Denver, Colo.: Education Commission of the States, 1983); and Twentieth Century Fund, *Making the Grade* (New York: Twentieth Century Fund, 1983).

2. D. G. Taylor, P. B. Sheatsley, and A. M. Greely, "Attitudes Toward Racial Integration," *Scientific American* 238 (1978): 42–49.

3. *New York Times,* 26 February 1978.

4. E. B. Keller, "A Changing Climate for Civil Rights: Five Key Trends," *Perspectives: The Civil Rights Quarterly* 15 (1978): 10–15.

5. D. J. Treiman and H. I. Hartman, eds., *Women, Work and Wages: Equal Pay for Jobs of Equal Value* (Washington, D.C.: National Academy Press, 1981).

6. U.S. Department of Commerce, Bureau of the Census, *Statistical Abstract of the United States,* 101st ed. (Washington, D.C.: Government Printing Office, 1981).

7. U.S. Department of Commerce, Bureau of Statistics, *The Social and Economic Status of the Black Population in the United States: An Historical View, 1890–1978* (Washington, D.C.: Government Printing Office, 1979).

8. R. D. Mare and C. Winship, "The Paradox of Lessening Racial Inequality and Joblessness among Black Youth: Enrollment, Enlistment, and Employment, 1964–1981," *American Sociological Review* 49 (1984): 54.

9. Treiman and Hartman, *Women, Work and Wages,* 42.

10. Treiman and Hartman, *Women, Work and Wages,* 42.

11. Donna M. Gollnick and Philip C. Chinn, *Multicultural Education in a Pluralistic Society,* (St. Louis, Mo.: Mosby, 1983).

12. Michael Harrington, *The New American Poverty* (New York: Holt, Rinehart, and Winston, 1984): 64.

13. Christopher Jencks et al., *Inequality: A Reassessment of the Effect of Family and Schooling in America* (New York: Harper and Row, 1972).

14. R. W. Rumberger, "The Influence of Family Background on Education, Earnings, and Wealth," *Social Forces* 3 (1983): 755–73.

15. M. Parenti, *Power and the Powerless* (New York: St. Martin's Press, 1978).

16. J. W. Kidd, "The 'Adultated' Mentally Retarded," *Education and Training of the Mentally Retarded* 5 (1970): 71–72.

17. D. P. Hallahan and J. M. Kauffman, *Exceptional Children,* 2nd ed. (Englewood Cliffs, N.J.: Prentice-Hall, 1982).

18. Bill Gearhart, *Special Education for the '80's* (St. Louis, Mo.: Mosby, 1980).
19. J. Gliedman and W. Roth, *The Unexpected Minority* (New York: Harcourt Brace Jovanovich, 1980).
20. Caroline Hodges Persell, *Education and Inequality* (New York: The Free Press, 1977).
21. *Education Week,* 19 September 1984.
22. Tom Mirga, "Reynolds Asserts End of Mandatory Busing is Near," *Education Week,* 19 September 1984.
23. Jean Anyon, "Elementary Schooling and Distinctions of Social Class," *Interchange* 12 (1981): 118–32.
24. Goodlad, *A Place Called School.*
25. See, for example, J. D. Jones, E. L. Erickson, and R. Crowell, "Increasing the Gap Between Whites and Blacks," *Education and Urban Society* 4 (1972); R. B. Kariger, "The Relationship of Lane Grouping to the Socioeconomic Status of the Parents of Seventh-grade Pupils in Three Junior High Schools" (Ph.D. diss., Michigan State University, 1962); and W. E. Shafer and C. Olexa, *Tracking and Opportunity* (Scranton, Penn.: Chandler, 1971).
26. See, for example, G. Heathers, *Organizing Schools Through the Dual Progress Plan* (Danville, Ill.: Interstate, 1967); Mary Haywood Metz, *Classrooms and Corridors* (Berkeley, Calif.: University of California Press, 1978); James E. Rosenbaum, *Making Inequality* (New York: Wiley-Interscience, 1976); and J. R. Squire, "National Study of High School English Programs: A School for All Seasons," *English Journal* 55 (1966): 282–90.
27. N. A. Madden and R. E. Slavin, "Mainstreaming Students with Mild Handicaps: Academic and Social Outcomes," *Review of Educational Research* 53 (1983): 519–69; and Christine E. Sleeter, "Special Education Efficacy Studies: A Review" (University of Wisconsin-Madison, 1980, mimeographed).
28. M. C. Will, "Let us Pause and Reflect—But Not Too Long," *Exceptional Children* 51 (1984): 11–16.
29. T. Saario, Carol N. Jacklin, and Carol K. Tittle, "Sex Role Stereotyping in the Public Schools," *Harvard Educational Review* 43 (1973): 386–404.
30. See, for example, J. Gaskell, "Course Differentiation in the High School: The Perspective of Working Class Females" (Paper presented at the American Educational Research Association, Montreal, 1983); Christine E. Sleeter and Carl A. Grant, "Race, Class, and Gender in an Urban School: A Case Study," *Urban Education,* forthcoming; Linda Valli, "Becoming Clerical Workers: Business Education and the Culture of Feminity," in *Ideology and Practice in Schooling,* ed. Michael W. Apple and Lois Weis (Philadelphia: Temple University Press, 1983): 213–34.
31. A. M. Pallas and K. L. Alexander, "Sex Differences in Quantitative SAT Performance: New Evidence on the Differential Coursework Hypothesis," *American Educational Research Journal* 20 (1983): 165–82.
32. See, for example, Michael W. Apple, *Ideology and Curriculum* (London: Routledge and Kegan Paul, 1979); Geneva Gay, "On Behalf of Children: A Curriculum Design for Multicultural Education in the Elementary School," *Journal of Negro Education* 48 (1979): 324–40; Henry Giroux, *Ideology, Culture, and the Process of Schooling* (Philadelphia: Temple University Press, 1981); Jerome Karabel and A. H. Halsey, *Power and Ideology in the Curriculum* (New York: Oxford University Press, 1977); and Lenore J. Witzman, *Sex Role Socialization* (Palo Alto, Calif.: Mayfield, 1979).
33. See, for example, Robin A. Butterfield, "Multicultural Analysis of a Popular Basal Reading Series in the International Year of the Child," *Journal of Negro Education* 48 (1979); 382–89; Council on Interracial Books for Children, *Stereotypes, Distortions, and Omissions in U.S. History Textbooks* (New York: Racism and

Sexism Resource Center for Education, 1977); Carl A. Grant and Gloria W. Grant, "The Multicultural Evaluation of Some Second and Third Grade Textbook Readers—A Survey Analysis," *Journal of Negro Education* 50 (1981); W. H. Rupley, J. Garcia, and B. Longnion, "Sex Role Portrayal in Reading Materials: Implications for the 1980's," *The Reading Teacher* 34 (1981): 786–91; Katherine P. Scott, "Whatever Happened to Dick and Jane? Sexism in Texts Reexamined," *Peabody Journal of Education* 58 (1981): 135–40; and V. Wright, "Hidden Messages: Expressions of Prejudice," *Interchange* 7 (1976–77): 51–61.

34. Valena White Plisko, *The Condition of Education*, 1984 ed. (Washington, D.C.: Government Printing Office, 1984).

35. J. D. Haft, "Assuring Equal Educational Opportunity for Language-Minority Students: Bilingual Education and the Equal Education Opportunity Act of 1974," *Columbia Journal of Law and Social Problems* 18 (1983): 292.

36. T. Andersson, "Bilingual Education: The American Experience," *Modern Language Journal* 55 (1971): 427–40; A. A. Cohen, *A Sociolinguistic Approach to Bilingual Education: Experiments in the American Southwest* (Rowley, Mass.: Newbury House, 1975); M. J. Fulton-Scott and A. D. Calvin, "Bilingual Multi-cultural Education vs. Integrated and Non-integrated ESL Instruction," *NABE Journal* 7 (1983): 1–12; J. Cummins, "The Role of Primary Language Development in Promoting Educational Success for Language Minority Students," in *Schooling Second Language Minority Students: A Theoretical Framework* (Los Angeles: Education, Dissemination and Assessment Center, California State University, 1981); F. M. Goodman and C. Stern, *Bilingual Program Evaluation Support, ESEA Title VII, 1970–1971* (Compton, Calif.: Compton City Schools, 1971), ED 054-672; K. E. Hartwig, *Early Childhood Bilingual Education, Final Evaluation, ESEA Title VII 1970–1971* (Sacramento, Calif.: Sacramento School District, 1971); E. Peal and W. E. Lambert, "The Relation of Bilingualism to Intelligence," *Psychological Monographs: General and Applied* 76 (1962): R. Ruiz, *Language Teaching in American Education: Impact on Second Language Learning* (Washington, D.C.: National Institute of Education, 1984); M. E. Taylor, *An Overview of Research on Bilingualism* (Sacramento, Calif.: State Department of Education, 1970); and B. G. Trevino, "An Analysis of the Effectiveness of a Bilingual Program in the Teaching of Math in the Primary Grades" (Ph.D. diss., University of Texas, 1968).

37. Ray P. McDermott, "Social Relations as Contexts for Learning in Schools," *Harvard Educational Review* 47 (1977): 198–213.

38. T. O'Rourke et al., *National Association of the Deaf Communicative Skills Program*, Programs for the Handicapped, No. 75 (Washington, D.C.: Government Printing Office, 1975).

39. B. I. Buford, "Teacher Expectancy of the Culturally Different Student Subgroups in Texas in Relation to Student Achievement" (Ph.D. diss., Texas A&M University, 1973); Judith T. Guskin, "The Social Perception of Language Variation: Black and White Teachers' Attitudes Toward Speakers from Different Racial and Social Class Backgrounds" (Ph.D. diss., University of Michigan, 1971); L. G. Pugh, "Teacher Attitudes and Expectations Associated with Race and Social Class" (Paper delivered at the American Educational Research Association, 1974), ED 094-018; F. Williams and J. L. Whitehead, "Language in the Classroom: Studies of the Pygmalion Effect," *English Record* 21 (1971): 108–13; and D. G. Harvey and G. T. Slatin, "The Relationship between Child's SES and Teacher Expectations: A Text of the Middle-Class Bias Hypothesis," *Social Forces* 54 (1975): 140–59.

40. Tom D. Freijo and Richard M. Jaeger, "Social Class and Race as Concomitants of Composite Halo in Teachers' Evaluative Ratings of Pupils," *American Educational Research Journal* 13 (1976): 1–14; Ray C. Rist, "Student Social Class and Teacher Expectations: The Self-Fulfilling Prophecy in Ghetto Education,"

Harvard Educational Review 40 (1970): 411–51.

41. R. Byalick and D. Bershoff, "Reinforcement Practices of Black and White Teachers in Integrated Classrooms," *Journal of Education Psychology* 66 (1974): 473–80; C. S. Dweck et al., "Sex Differences in Learned Helplessness: II. The Contingencies of Evaluative Feedback in the Classroom, and III. An Experimental Analysis," *Developmental Psychology* 14 (1978): 268–76; Linda Grant, "Black Females' 'Place' in Desegregated Classrooms," *Sociology of Education,* forthcoming; G. Jackson and C. Cosca, "The Inequality of Educational Opportunity in the Southwest: An Observational Study of Ethnically Mixed Classrooms," *American Educational Research Journal* 11 (1974): 219–29; Ray C. Rist, *The Invisible Children* (Cambridge, Mass.: Harvard University Press, 1978); and Ray C. Rist, "Student Social Class."

42. Michael Cole and Jerome S. Bruner, "Cultural Differences and Inferences about Psychological Processes," *American Psychologist* 26 (1971): 867–76; Janice E. Hale, *Black Children: Their Roots, Culture, and Learning Styles* (Provo, Ut.: Brigham Young University Press, 1982); S. Kagan and M. C. Madsen, "Cooperation and Competition of Mexican, Mexican-American, and Anglo-American Children of Two Ages under Four Instructional Sets," *Developmental Psychology* 5 (1971): 32–39; Judith S. Kleinfield, "Intellectual Strengths in Culturally Different Groups: An Eskimo Illustration," *Review of Educational Research* 43 (1973): 341–59; Luis M. Laosa, "Bilingualism in Three United States Hispanic Groups: Contextual Use of Language by Children and Adults in their Families," *Journal of Educational Psychology* 67 (1975): 617–27; G. S. Lesser, G. Fifer, and C. Clark, "Mental Abilities of Children from Different Social Class and Cultural Groups," *Monographs of the Society for Research in Child Development* 3 (1965); Susan U. Philips, *The Invisible Culture* (New York: Longman, 1983); Maneul Ramirez and Alfredo Castaneda, *Cultural Democracy, Bicognitive Development, and Education* (New York: Academic Press, 1974); and Schlomo Sharan, "Cooperative Learning in Small Groups: Recent Methods and Effects on Achievement, Attitudes, and Ethnic Relations," *Review of Educational Research* 50 (1980): 241–71.

43. H. A. Witkin, "Cognitive Style in Academic Performance and in Teacher-Student Relations," in *Individuality in Learning,* ed. S. Messick (San Francisco: Jossey Bass, 1976): 38–72.

44. Philips, *Invisible Culture*; Barbara J. Shade, "Afro-American Cognitive Style: A Variable in School Success," *Review of Educational Research* 52 (1982): 219–44.

45. Sheila Tobias, *Overcoming Math Anxiety* (New York: W. W. Norton, 1978).

46. Lynn H. Fox, "Sex Differences in Mathematical Precocity: Bridging the Gap," in *Intellectual Talent: Research and Development,* ed. D. F. Keating (Baltimore: Johns Hopkins University Press, 1970).

47. Persell, *Education and Inequality.*

48. Saario, Jacklin, and Tittle, "Sex Role Stereotyping."

49. J. Salvia and J. E. Ysseldyke, *Assessment in Special and Remedial Education* (Boston: Houghton Mifflin, 1981).

50. Plisko, *Condition of Education.*

51. U.S. Equal Educational Opportunity Commission, *Minorities and Women in Public Elementary and Secondary Schools* (Washington, D.C.: Government Printing Office, 1981).

52. Adler, *Paideia Proposal,* 53.

53. R. W. Riche, D. E. Hecker, and J. U. Burgan, "High Technology Today and Tomorrow: A Small Slice of the Employment Pie," *Monthly Labor Review* 106 (1983): 50–58.

". . . for the short and long term . . ."

Rosemarie V. Rosen

The public focus on education over the last year is a phenomenon in itself. It has generated a far-reaching commentary on education, more comprehensive and more intense than in the post-Sputnik and post–Great Society eras, both of which yielded concrete changes in education. The former period gave us the National Defense Education Act, with an emphasis on science, math, and foreign languages. The latter gave us the Elementary and Secondary Education Act, with special concern for our educationally and economically disadvantaged students. To be sure, there have been and still are other influences on education. The decades of the 1960s and 1970s have brought us federal and state legislation which prescribes in great detail how handicapped and bilingual students are to be taught. The awakening of the conscience of the federal government and the courts has fostered protection of the right of access for minority populations. School boards and legislatures contend regularly with lobbying groups who seek changes in the curriculum, in textbooks, and in financing.

All of the attention on education this last year is special and is different from the other eras in a number of ways. The breadth of commentary both in source and content is great. The various task forces and commissions that have produced the reports include representatives from private foundations, colleges and universities, businesses, the education community itself, and federal and state governments. The subjects addressed include classroom activities, school climate, the curriculum, the school year, and the pay and salary structure of teachers.

Yet, within all the perspectives and comments, there is consensus that something is wrong with American public education and that we should all get down to business and fix it. Most significant, perhaps, is the fact that education has become a political priority. Education is a plank in political

Reprinted fom *Harvard Educational Review*, 1984, 54:1, 23–28. Copyright © by President and Fellows of Harvard College.

platforms all over the country and will certainly be an important issue in the 1984 presidential election.

For the practitioner who is in the eye of the storm, there are questions to be answered: What happens next? How can we take advantage of this opportunity? How can we transform the best of these recommendations into long-term improvements? What do we do in the meantime? The answers to these questions, which may offer us courses of actions, will determine whether, indeed, this phenomenon has any impact on education. Answers will need to ensure that changes occur in a commonsense way that has lasting value. Good answers must also provide guidance for the short and long term.

SHORT TERM

In my day-to-day work, I, like any public administrator facing a shortage of funds and demanding constituencies, will use this attention to say, "Yes, education has problems; yes, greater voices than mine are saying so; yes, education needs assistance; yes, we cannot carry the burden alone." In my various roles in the Boston Public Schools, I will use the most publicized aspects of the reports to futher the goals the system has already set.

As an administrator who negotiates changes in contracts with twelve separate unions, I say, "Yes, the public is not satisfied with the quality of education. It wants more time from teachers and principals, more professionalism and accountability from all for performance."

As a member of the superintendent's cabinet, working as part of a team to build higher promotion standards, a comprehensive testing program, and a standardized curriculum for Boston, I say, "Yes, the experts say the high school curriculum should place more emphasis on academics and should have higher systemwide standards which clean up the hodge-podge of undemanding courses."

As senior fiscal officer who manages a $300 million budget without a deficit and looks for maximum value for every dollar, I say, "Education is under careful scrutiny. We must spend our dollars well in order to defend the additional funds we will need to achieve better education."

For the short-term, I will take advantage of the mere existence of the reports to keep attention focused on the needs in Boston. I will use the attention to change curriculum, to seek funding, and to foster efforts already underway for institutional change; for example, to initiate a different relationship between teachers and administrators and to sharpen the focus on academics and on individual schools. I will use this phenomenon to lobby for dollars, quick changes, and leverage to maintain taxpayers' diminishing commitment to public education. I do not know how long the impact will last at levels where it will make a difference, that is, with lawmakers who not only control dollars but also can ease the regulations which force inappropriate tasks on schools.

In the meantime, I will use the reports and the political attention to gain support for activities the administration has already identified as important, We may go further in some areas, such as curriculum reform, because we have the weight of expert reports and documented opinion to help, but we will not significantly change direction. Major changes such as a reorganization of schools, a shift from grade structure to achievement as the basis for measuring student progress, a redefinition of the jobs of teachers and administrators, or a substantial revision of the school calendar require a level of organization and momentum which we do not have time to develop. Boston, like most school systems, has already chosen its battles and developed its game plan. These decisions are dictated by political expediencies and the realities of its population and its funding. These are the kinds of realities which are conspicuously missing in the national reports.

REALITIES OF URBAN EDUCATION

In the day-to-day reality of urban school systems, there is much that makes the sweeping recommendations in the national reports exasperating and irrelevant. The following examples of Boston's reality are illustrative:

1. The bulk of our teaching force is between thirty-five and forty years old. We will be working with the same group of teachers for a long time. Merit pay to people who have been alienated by the system over the last ten years is not going to make them change behavior. Further, they are already a highly credentialed work force with 75 percent at the maximum levels on the pay scale. Despite this highly trained and experienced work force, Boston's students have among the worst achievement scores in the country.

2. Nationally, the average pay for teachers is $20,500. In Boston, the average annual salary is $27,400. This is within the range of most cities where the differential is due to a higher cost of living and the need for an incentive for combat duty. Nonetheless, at these rates for a ten-month work year, the salaries are competitive with other professions, especially when one considers that salary progress in most professional environments is based on performance rather than guaranteed increments. So, for Boston and other cities, simply increasing teacher salaries will not improve education.

3. Boston has a contractual work year of 180.5 days and contractual working day of 5 and three-quarter hours. Work beyond these limits that is compensated is paid at an average overtime rate of close to $18 per hour. Through the most recent round of negotiations we may achieve 182.5 days per year and additional blocks of times for parent

meetings and remedial work with students. The salary benefits which are part of the package being negotiated will cost an additional $60 million. Longer instructional days, or a 200–220-day work year, are simply beyond the city's ability to pay.

4.   The Boston School Committee and the Boston City Council are elected every two years. The largest organized block of voters is composed of teachers and their families. In the most recent election campaign, the organization of teachers endorsed candidates primarily on the issue of guaranteed jobs and job selection by seniority.

5.   The percentage of the population with children of school age is shrinking. In Boston, only one out of ten taxpayers has a child in school, public or private. Although local polls indicate taxpayers are willing to spend more on education, they indicate higher spending priorities for increased police and fire protection. When the city righted itself fiscally after the first round of Proposition 2½ cuts, all police and fire positions were restored, but 500 teachers were not.

6.   While Boston is raising its academic standards by setting student achievement pass points and increasing middle school and high school course requirements, it must yet contend with a 50 percent dropout rate and the fact that more than half of its students entering high school are reading several years below grade level.

7.   The Boston Public Schools have a guaranteed annual appropriation of city funds of $224 million. The current operating level, without program enhancement, will require an addtional $20 million in fiscal year 1985. For that fiscal year, a deficit of $30 million is forecast for the city, at its current rate of spending—that is, at its current service levels and with no increase for the schools.

8.   Among Boston's 55,000 students, 11,000 are handicapped (20 percent) and 7,000 are bilingual (12 percent). Some 40 percent are educationally and economically disadvantaged under federal standards. Further, 70 percent belong to minority groups; their families are in the population which has the highest unemployment rate and the lowest income levels.

It is facile to say that American students should have better paid teachers who are highly trained, longer school days, and more study of math, science, and computer education. This is irrelevant to a ninth-grader who cannot read the daily newspaper and must stay home from school once or twice a week to babysit for brothers and sisters so his or her mother can keep her job. For this student the national reports will not bring help in time.

LONGER TERM—THE REPORTS CAN HELP IF WE LET THEM

In the face of all the tough realities, alongside all the measures of failure of public education, there is still cause for optimism. Practitioners in the Boston Public Schools and the school systems across the coutry are accepting the challenge of education, and within the limits of their local realities are bringing about positive changes. The most likely directions for substantial success in American education lie in three areas: governance, funding, and isolation. These are the areas of congruence between ways schools have already begun to change for the better and recommendations of the national reports.

GOVERNANCE

There are things to be learned about ways to change both the internal and external governance of school systems. Internal governing relationships include school to school, school to central administration, administration to teachers, administration and teachers to parents. The best of what is happening in education today is happening in individual schools. The most effective schools demonstrate these characteristics: clear direction from top administration as to instructional goals; decentralized authority and responsibility for administrative, as well as instructional decisions; principals who are effective managers and educational leaders; real involvement of teachers and parents; and commitment to students. The focus must remain on the individual school, which should be nurtured by its system, whose role should shift more toward policy, overall direction setting, and the maintenance of relationships with other levels of government.

Teachers and administrators should have a relationship that brings their different perspectives to bear on more than just salary and terms of employment. Through job restructuring, reorganization of time, and professional self-consciousness, teachers should have the opportunity and should take the responsibility for more curriculum and instructional decisionmaking. An increased influence over the professional work environment—that is, the classroom, school, and even the school system—will do much to enhance the holding power of teaching. Teachers who do not think of themselves as responsible for educational outcomes are on the wrong track. Unions that contend that it is more important to fight for higher mileage reimbursements or overtime rates than for higher student achievement are also on the wrong track. Neither perspective will contribute to building a better public image for teachers.

On the external side, the federal and state roles in education should continue to be that of protecting the rights of all students and funding programs to enhance those rights. What percentage of the cost of education should be paid by whom is a separate and complicated subject. It suffices to say that the cost cannot be borne by local taxpayers alone; federal and state mandates should not be issued without thorough consideration of cost burdens; and discretionary funding approaches, such as Chapter 2 of the Education Consolidation and Improvement Act are more effective incentives than categorical funds which impose substantial administrative costs and force the creation of programs which cannot be locally sustained.

ISOLATION

Schools regard themselves and are regarded by law and social policy as isolated, disconnected segments of our social and economic life. Yet, they have been given an incredible range of tasks only peripherally related to education. Schools are expected to feed children, teach them how to drive, and teach them about sex and parenting, among many other things. Whether or not schools should be doing all of these things, they certainly cannot do all of them alone. School administrations should open themselves up to collaboration with colleges and universities, business and private industry, community and cultural organizations, and other sectors of society. Such collaborations should be carefully planned so that the specific services to be provided by each member organization are consistent with its resources and missions, as well as its discrete goals and objectives.

All organizations have their own functions and financial concerns. Whatever help external organizations offer to schools will not be enough to sustain demands that do not make sense to the schools or do not seem to yield a satisfactory return in the form of better-prepared students.

On the other hand, there are many services which can be more efficiently and effectively provided through agencies in the community rather than through schools alone. For example, tackling a 50 percent student dropout rate is a task which must involve community and social agencies which provide family counseling, job referrals, daycare, and medical attention. Also, the courts and the probation system have a role in addressing the problems of older students that may have an impact on their attendance and participation in school.

The growing need for training and retraining of teachers, especially in those areas which are receiving more emphasis such as the sciences and the use of computers, can be addressed through cooperative relationships among businesses, colleges and universities, and schools. Teacher preparation programs should reflect the actual tasks that teachers face. Retraining or continuing education in state-of-the-art skills and knowledge might best be undertaken through some time-sharing arrangement with business and private industry. All of these collaborations take commitment, time, and planning on the part of all of the agencies involved.

FUNDING

Finally, an issue on which the reports are singularly silent is how to pay for all of the enhancements and changes proposed for education. They are silent because we cannot look forward to any major influx of additional dollars. Whether funds emanate from federal, state, or local sources, the taxpayers' burden and the limits which will be tolerated will continue to impose restrictions on the amount of funding that can be made available for all public services. Education must learn to compete. School administrators must become comfortable with the language and procedures of budget justifications, cost-benefit analyses, and the concept of the bottom line. If schools are not delivering a good product in a fiscally responsible way, this new interest in education will quickly turn to disillusionment. The future of public funding of education could very well include free competition, tax credits, and vouchers; if this happens, public schools will serve only those with restricted mobility and income.

In some ways, a book like *In Search of Excellence* which describes the major characteristics of effective and successful corporations has more relevance to public education today than a report like *A Nation at Risk*. This is not to say that children are to be thought of as assembly line products or that schools ought to run in ways which put cost-effectiveness before human considerations. It is to say that the basic principles of good management and fiscal responsibility have as much relevance to schools as to any other enterprise. Good management of resources, people, dollars, and time, has become and will continue to be the most reliable way in which to achieve educational outcomes because large amounts of new resources are not likely to be forthcoming.

Part 4

Reform and Educational Practice

Curriculum and the School Work Culture

Dennis Carlson

The national commissions on excellence have made a series of recommendations relating to reforms in school curriculum. I will argue in this essay that the reports, particularly *A Nation at Risk*, represent a "quick-fix" solution to perceived mediocrity in education. American schools are confronted with very deeply structured and embedded problems that the recommendations of reports like the *Nation at Risk* ignore—namely, the structure or formal organization of the curriculum, the work culture of the classroom, and the very real educational crisis in America.

My discussion begins with an analysis of the economic priorities and interests embodied in the organization and form of curriculum suggested by the reports. I will argue that such recommendations, given their economistic notions, are likely to result in "dumbing down" the curriculum rather than raising its level. I will further elaborate this point through an analysis of school work as students experience it, react to it, and give it meaning. Such an analysis will show that students actively negotiate the pace and standards of classroom work. Mediocrity is not produced by standards imposed from above; rather, it is a product of conflict between students and teachers as teachers seek to gain student compliance to the curricular production routine. The third and final part of this chapter examines teachers' work and relates excellence in educational outcomes to the organization, control, and conditions of teachers' work.

THE NEW PUBLIC PHILOSOPHY AND ECONOMIC REALITIES

The reports on the schools generally claim to speak for a broad consensus of Americans, and they present findings and recommendations as though they were self-evident to all sensible people. In *A Nation at Risk*, for example, the public is invoked again and again as "demanding" excellence from our schools, and as supporting, in one poll after another, tougher standards for teachers and students, and fewer curricular "frills." The public is said to be "responsible for nurturing the Nation's *intellectual capital*" [emphasis mine];

and patriotism is invoked to argue that Americans "know in their bones that the safety of the United States depends on the wit, skill, and spirit of a self-confident people."[1] In these and other ways, nationalism gets linked to industrial vitality and military preeminence, which gets linked to educational excellence, higher standards, and a more rigorous curriculum. The state and the corporate sphere are to work cooperatively in this "public" challenge to achieve excellence in education and in the military-industrial sphere.[2] The call, then, is for a national renewal of the schools and a public rededication to excellence, hard work, and discipline.

There is a certain appeal in this simplification of what is wrong with education, and what is wrong with society more generally. Certainly, most people support national strength and excellence and oppose a decline in standards; and everyone should support quality education that sets high expectations for learning and demands much of those in the classroom, both teachers and students, who must make learning "happen." And since the reports appear to support a more rigorous curriculum and raised standards for *all* students, the recommendations certainly sound democratic in their intent.

Henry Giroux refers to this interpretation of the crisis in education as a "new public philosophy," supposedly broadly based and consensual in its sense of what is wrong and what should be done.[3] In reality, Giroux argues, this new public philosophy represents some interests much more than others, and particularly that it legitimates corporate and state interests as the interests of all "patriotic" Americans who believe in "excellence."

Now, what specifically are some of the implications of such an economically interested "public philosophy" when we address issues of the curriculum and school work, the heart of what education is all about? The first implication is that curriculum gets apprehended as a technology for producing predetermined instructional "outputs," defined as skills, test scores, grades, class rankings, etc. The learning process is depicted as analogous to a production process in industry, and the most efficient means is sought of producing these learning outputs. This is typically done by standardizing learning tasks and procedures, by holding teachers and students accountable for what gets produced in the classroom and at what pace (a form of "quality control"), and by providing incentives of advancement within the system to those who are most meritorious, that is, "productive," in their work with the curriculum. This applies, of course, to both sets of workers with the curriculum, teachers and students, although my focus here is upon students.

A good example of such a productivity model of school work is provided by individualized instructional systems, programs, and materials. In whatever form these curricula take—objective-based workbooks, various competency-based learning "packets," or computer software programs, they all follow the same principles. They are designed to be self-guided by students, who work through a series of tasks and perform a series of specified operations on data provided to them in a logical, sequential order. By working through the sequence of tasks, which is normally linear in printed materials and branched in some computer programs, students are led to "mastery" of a "skill," the achievement of which is indicated by a passing score on an objective-based post-test that comes with the materials. The curriculum, in this case, is largely technology and format: a rationally predetermined path that guides the student, with the assistance and supervision of the teacher, to the production of test scores, with educational commodities being produced through this process. Even with more traditional textbooks, which continue to dominate especially at the secondary level, the textbook is increasingly used as a technology and a data bank to answer questions and produce grade and test scores. Students often learn to "mine" their texts to extract bits of data that are arrayed on worksheets. Once more, the process and the use of this curricular technology assumes precedence over the meaning or the value of what is being produced or commodified.

One point I want to make about this form of curriculum is that by borrowing so heavily from a dominant economic model of efficient production and work organization, it also implicitly serves the economic function of preparing young people for the types of work that increasingly characterize the adult working world. The fastest growing segment of the labor market continues to be the clerical and secretarial fields, where employees' work is typically highly standardized and involves following a prescribed sequence. This work has become more data intensive, and work tasks have become more fragmented or rationalized, as desktop computer consoles have replaced typewriters and filing cabinets. "Word processing" becomes the new operative term for this work, although it may be more accurate to call it data processing. Skills needed in data processing include: recording, tabulating, and coding or categorizing data; entering, storing, transferring, and retrieving data; and in other ways performing prescribed operations on data. Other segments of the work force may not deal as intensively with data as clerical and secretarial workers do. Nevertheless, data processing is assuming more and more workers' time in all fields of business and industry. For example, the second major growth area of the labor force is relatively low-pay, low-skill service work, from hospital orderlies, to restaurant waiters, to fast-food-chain employees, to cashiers in stores and supermarkets. Yet here too, records of accounts, transactions, and other pertinent data may now have to be punched into computers and work tasks become more routinized, One thing these new curricular forms do, then, is prepare many of our young, a growing number of them, for a working world of data processing.

These linkages between curricular forms found in schools and work forms in the broader culture provide cause to raise several issues with regard to the so-called "dumbing down" of the curriculum and the decline in students' inferential reasoning skills. First, they make one skeptical of the claim, made in *A Nation at Risk,* that a decline in educational standards comes at a time when "the demand for highly skilled workers in new fields is accelerating rapidly,"[4] since most new jobs are not dependent on rigorous training. Second, the emphasis upon organizing school work as a form of data processing routine does not appear to encourage, or perhaps even be compatible with, the development of complex thinking, reasoning, and literacy skills. Thus, while *A Nation at Risk* talks vaguely about the need for higher levels of literacy among workers, and states that all students should be able to "comprehend, interpret, and use what they read; . . . . write well-organized, effective papers; . . . . and discuss ideas intelligently,"[5] the emphases upon higher standards, more testing, accountability, and instructional efficiency are all likely to encourage a narrower and economically more functional approach to literacy in the curriculum. More empowering forms of literacy are grounded in notions of language as discourse between human subjects, in writing and reading as discursive activities, and in critical thinking as an essential prerequisite to democratic decision making and community participation.[6] One reads and writes and speaks as part of a process of growth to self-awareness, which involves an understanding of one's culture, its history, and its current dynamic tendencies, since one is always involved *in* culture, helping to shape and direct it even as one is shaped by it. The objective of literacy is to help individuals assume greater control over important decisions affecting their lives, thereby participating in the formation of the culture. When curriculum is apprehended in these ways as a framework for empowering individuals, it goes far beyond what is envisioned in economic notions of "functional literacy." Perhaps for this reason, and because it may serve to increase critical discontent with dominant work forms and relations in the economy, we hear nothing about such empowering literacy in the reports.

Another implication of the dominance of an economic functionalism in the curriculum is that most attention gets focused on curricular subject or content areas that offer a "high yield" or "high return" on investment. Currently this means math, science, and the foreign languages. In these areas in particular, the reports encourage the schools to identify the meritocratic few, the "best and the brightest" who are to receive rigorous and advanced coursework, and to pay teachers salaries competitive with industry to attract and hold the most competent in teaching. The students who are thus identified and trained will presumably go on to college and ultimately join the labor force as trained specialists, technicians, scientists, engineers, planners, and managers—the so-called "new middle class"[7]—workers who perform an important role in an increasingly knowlege-intensive reindustrialization process. The problem the schools face in providing the proper training for these types of work is that much of their time and energy is focused upon teaching data processing skills and work discipline. Especially in urban schools where few students are expected to go on to college, it is difficult to provide the highly trained and competent teachers, the small class sizes, the special curricular materials, and the other extra resources needed for a relatively small group of the "best and brightest." To circumvent this problem, we see signs of the development of a dual system of schooling, with public and private suburban schools attracting the better teachers and providing the more expensive lab equipment and extra courses needed to prepare their largely college-bound graduates. Meanwhile, urban public schools are unable to afford such programs and attract such teachers. They serve students who, largely because of their socioeconomic backgrounds and future job expectations, are not believed to benefit from a rigorous, knowledge-intensive curriculum. For these students, the curriculum is oriented primarily around data processing, direction following, and self-discipline rather than anything more rigorous. However, such a two-tiered system of education, while it may seem "rational" from a purely economically functional perspective, also generates conditions that undermine the system. Most notably, it means that there is a great "wastage" of potential talent among disadvantaged urban youth, who do not get identified or placed in a rigorous curriculum. This wastage is the result of inequalities of opportunity that lead many urban youth to delegitimate the authority of the school and the curriculum in ways that pose a threat to control.

The costs, then, of an economically efficient and functional curriculum are high. First, the emphasis upon school work as data processing and test-score production drives out or obviates the development of more complex forms of literacy and critical thinking, especially for those students who do not plan to pursue postsecondary education. Second, the curriculum content, especially for those students identified as the "best and the brightest," is heavily oriented around math and science, which have a greater utilitarian value in the economy than, for example, the arts and humanities. And third, the difficulties and incompatibilities involved in providing, or attempting to provide, distinctively different curricula to different groups of students and future workers creates ongoing problems of curricular focus and balance and exacerbates inequalities of opportunity. These problems are all structural-functional in nature: that is, they are related to the organization of the curriculum and adult work and to the "needs" of the economy for different types of workers. While such a structural-functional analysis gets us part of the way towards an understanding of the crisis in the schools, it is insufficient in itself, for it does not examine the crisis and these problems as they are "produced" in schools by human actors. To round out this analysis of school work, we must therefore turn to the everyday culture of the classroom and analyze how students respond to the curriculum as school work.

THE WORK CULTURE OF THE CLASSROOM AND EDUCATIONAL MEDIOCRITY

I have suggested that the literacy-skill requirements for many jobs in the economy are relatively low. A recent study out of Johns Hopkins University, based on survey data and interviews with business and industrial personnel officers who hire high school graduates, concludes that most employers expect their workers at this level to be able to read something as difficult as the daily newspaper and as complex as a job application form, but that literacy skills beyond this are viewed as unnecessary.[8] Nevertheless, functional illiteracy is a widespread national problem, and business is concerned that even these minimal expectations for student literacy are not being adequately met. *A Nation at Risk* views this illiteracy with alarm, noting that 13 percent of the seventeen-year-olds nationally, and up to 40 percent of minority youth, are functionally illiterate. The economic "drain" of such illiteracy is made clear in the report: "Business and military leaders complain that they are required to spend millions of dollars on costly remedial education and training programs in such basic skills as reading, writing, spelling, and computation."[9]

What accounts for the "mediocre educational performance" of American youth, and why this failure to educate at even low-skill levels? To answer these questions, we must understand something about the students' role in the educational crisis, since students tend to get blamed in these reports for "doing the minimum work necessary for the moment."[10] The first thing to be noted is that the indictment of America's youth for settling for the second rate is also an indictment that is leveled against American labor in general. The so-called "labor problem," from this managerial perspective, is that American workers are not as "productive," "efficient," "hard-working," or "committed" as they need to be to keep the economy growing and to insure that American products compete successfully on the world market. Japanese workers, then, tend to get portrayed as the ideal workers who possess these traits and also settle for lower wages.

To the degree that there is a problem in American work associated with shoddiness and inefficiency, it should not lead us to simplistically conclude that the solution is merely a toughening of standards and teaching Americans to take more pride in their work. It is not that simple. The particular character of American work culture has developed, after all, in a coextensive manner with a particular formal organization of work and a formal authority structure that separates management and workers. To use Harry Braverman's terminology, there is a clear separation in work between its "conception" (the planning, organizing, and evaluating that are management functions), and its "execution" (the actual hands-on production that is defined as a labor function).[11] As an embodiment of this separation, work is highly rationalized or fragmented into small steps to be performed in a predetermined sequence. Braverman traces this organization of work in American industry back to the early twentieth century, when Frederick Taylor and other efficiency experts began the process of revolutionizing mass-production techniques. He recognizes that it is not merely, or even primarily, an "efficient" means of organizing work tasks. It is foremost a means of better controlling workers: of dealing with the "labor problem" that existed at that time, in which supervision of workers was typically highly personal and arbitrary and therefore often conflictual, and in which workers, because they controlled and directed so much of the actual production process and possessed essential craft skills, also exercised more power over the work situation. Technical and bureaucratic control thus de-skill workers as craftspersons, reskill them as followers of a standardized format, and make supervision more impersonal and distant. Ironically, this does not alleviate the "labor problem," although some critics have argued that it has been fairly successful in containing much of the conflict, albeit at a substantial cost. [12] Part of this cost is that the clear separation of conception from execution encourages a "them versus us" mentality among workers. They come to view their work as an imposed routine through which their labor is appropriated; and because they do not find much room for self-expression or a sense of accomplishment through their work, they differentiate their interests from work and cease to view it as a "central life interest." As work gets redefined as drudgery, efforts are made by workers to lessen the demands of the work routine and slow down the pace at which they must labor.

Now let me relate this discussion to the work culture we find in classrooms. Especially in those working-class neighborhoods where young people find these attitudes prevalent among adult role models, and where the curriculum is most likely to be presented to students as an imposed routine, we find that students are the most differentiated from the curriculum and seek to minimalize their involvement with it. David Hogan remarks in this regard that "the school becomes a workplace whose ostensible purpose is to make young people work—to extract labor from labor power—but without the protection of unions or the rights to engage in collective bargaining."[13] This means that the school, more often than the adult workplace, is a site of overt work conflict, and that students unburden much of their general discontent upon teachers as the human representatives of the curriculum and the school routine (although students also unburden their hostility upon one another, especially along racial, ethnic, and gender lines). This is also why classroom control, or classroom "management," as it is more often called these days, is such a central concern among teachers and administrators; why the classroom encounter with the subject matter of the curriculum so often seems secondary; and why the engagement between teacher and student sometimes resembles a pitched battle and, at other times, a long, protracted guerilla war on the part of students, without, however, any winners.

Of course, overt conflict of this sort is still the exception rather than the rule, at least in many schools. More commonly, another form of adaptation by teachers and students prevails: a negotiated trade-off. Here, I think we can see in a very direct way how mediocrity gets produced as an everyday accomplishment in our schools. To gain student compliance with and acquiescence to the curricular production routine, teachers may give up much in the way of expectations about the quality of students' work and the pace at which it gets done. Students use their individual and collective power to slow down the flow of work; they subvert the official production goals; and they carve out their own sphere of personal interaction with classmates. If students with this orientation towards the curriculum are not pushed too hard, overt conflict can largely be avoided, and the classroom work gets done, albeit a bit behind schedule and of dubious quality. The so-called "dumbing down" of the curriculum I referred to earlier is not just a response to the minimal literacy needs of many jobs. It is also part of this negotiated trade-off, a way of expecting less of students in terms of wrestling with complex issues and dealing with new and challenging concepts and language. The corollary of this is that the educational production process is prone to periodic breakdowns and work stoppages when students are pushed to produce more at a faster pace, or when critically minded teachers ask their students to dig deeper in their textbooks, or to draft thoughtful and complete essays, rather than hastily scrawled and half-legible responses.

One of the most important recent studies of classroom life that documents this trade-off mentality among teachers and students is that by Paul Willis.[14] He studied a group of delinquent working-class youth, "the lads," in an English secondary school, and concluded that little was expected of them in the classroom as far as serious work was concerned. Teachers allowed them to get away with much nonwork behavior so long as they kept classroom disruptions "within limits." Willis recognizes that students, such as "the lads," exercise real power in the system and act to resist the authority of the curriculum and the institution in significant ways. He also recognizes that their rejection of school work as an oppressive routine, and their refusal to compete for advancement are in many ways insightful and penetrate the ideology of credentials. They recognize, for example, that advancement is always for a few, and that most of them cannot succeed within the school hierarchy. Finally, however, Willis recognizes that the types of resistances and accommodations that "the lads" make to their school work are also part of a self-induction into working-class jobs and lifestyles after schooling. In an ironic way, he concludes, working-class youth often collude in their own subjugation as the price they pay for a refusal to compete. Of course, the refusal to take school work seriously and the refusal to compete for rewards of credentials and advancement also leave the system in a state of crisis. It can hold out few incentives to these students, and to gain their compliance through the use of more authoritarian methods only exacerbates conflict. Settling for less, aiming for mediocrity becomes the most expeditious course of action.

But what about those upwardly mobile youth, primarily from middle-class but also from socioeconomically disadvantaged backgrounds, who do not merely "get by" in schools but seek to use the schools as an avenue for advancement, and who therefore choose to compete and to conform to class-room work norms? Even here there are problems that could reach crisis proportions. For among these competitive students, work gets apprehended in a highly instrumental manner. One produces top test scores in order to get good grades, in order to get accepted in the right college, in order to build a career. Discontent often lies close to the surface. Some, as the shallowness of this instrumentalism as a grounding for their learning and their growth in life becomes apparent, may too become apathetic, withdrawn, defiant, or feel trapped by school and by life in general. Others, who see their possibilities and perceptions of achieving social mobility through schooling continue to decline, recognize that the grading and credentialing system no longer serve as an adequate instrumental "pay-off," and the system loses its credibility and legitimacy.[15] In one form or another, then, the failure of the schools to reach students and to convince them that school work serves their interests is both broad and deep.

TEACHERS AND THE CRISIS IN EDUCATION

The crisis in education is as much about teachers' work—its organizaton, its control, and its conditions—as it is about students' work; and, as I have sought to convey throughout this essay, the work of both groups in the classroom is inextricably linked. Both groups also tend to get apprehended in the reports as too lax in their standards, too mediocre in their achievement, and too willing to settle for the second rate. That is, they are understood in terms of the dominant "labor problem" ideology. To hold teachers more accountable (to school management), *A Nation at Risk* recommends that they be evaluated on their performance (which also means their students' performance, as indicated by test scores). To make them more "professionally competitive," they are to be rewarded with merit pay and master teacher status.[16] The commission decries the fact that "individual teachers have little influence in such critical professional decisions as, for example, textbook selection."[17] But it says nothing about enlarging teachers' influence in more important spheres, such as curriculum design, planning, and evaluation; and it does not envision significantly altering the conditions under which teachers labor. Giving teachers more power to choose predesigned curricular programs from competing corporations, where the differences are often minimal, is associated with "professional" decision making. Meanwhile, teachers' real power over the curriculum and how it is presented continues to erode, and they are de-skilled in the "craft" of teaching.[18] I do not, however, mean to totally dismiss new curricular technologies and forms—such as individualized curricular packets and computer programs—as merely part of an oppressive apparatus of control that de-skills and alienates teachers as well as their students. Such technologies may well serve a useful supplemental role in the curriculum, when they are not overused; and the possibilities for creating one's own programs opens up some creative possibilities for an otherwise highly predetermined technology. But my fear is that such uses will not be effectively realized so long as their development and adoption in schools are pegged to increased instructional accountability and efficiency within a dominant production metaphor for education.

Because of these conditions, teachers appear to have interests in promoting change in education that are more fundamental and more politically progressive than those promoted by the reports. These interests have to do with overcoming some of the artificial barriers between conception and execution in the curriculum that divide teachers and students, as well as teachers and administrators, and that lock both teachers and students out of more control over the form, content, and "output" of the learning process. Teachers also have interests in promoting a more socially productive and personally meaningful work experience for students: without proper motivation, teaching becomes mainly control, and conflict is intensified.

Of course, not all teachers understand their interests and their discontents in this way; and among those who do, many become demoralized and leave the profession after one or two years of mounting frustration. Others become cynical and resigned. Still others take out much of their discontent on students and their parents, just as I have suggested that students unburden their hostility on teachers. But some teachers also continue to work, against great odds in many schools, to realize some of their ideals in practice. They also work collectively through their organizations to do what they can to redirect some of the priorities of the schools. Teachers' discontent, unlike students' discontent, is thus at least potentially more political and empowering. Countervailing efforts among teachers and other groups of educators in the schools, including school administrators in some cases, need to be supported as they challenge and question dominant interests in the schools and dominant forces that shape the curriculum. Through such efforts teachers may lead in the articulation of an alternative "public voice" in the debate on the schools, one that articulates a starkly differing picture of what is wrong in the schools, what needs fixing, and how we must proceed, both within education and more broadly on a political and cultural front, to rise to the challenge of the crisis that confronts us.

NOTES

1. The National Commission on Excellence in Education, *A Nation at Risk: The Imperative for Educational Reform* (Washington, D.C.: U.S. Department of Education, 1983): 17.

2. Joel Spring provides a fascinating account of this type of cooperation between big business and big government in the design of a new "national curriculum" in math, science, and the foreign languages, which was spawned by the National Defense Education Act (NDEA). That piece of legislation, enacted in 1957, appropri-

ated government monies to design the curricula, which were then turned over to industry to produce and market to local schools, which in turn used government grant monies to purchase materials and to retrain teachers in the "new" math and science (Joel Spring, *The Sorting Machine: National Educational Policy Since 1945* [New York: David McKay, 1976]).

3. Henry Giroux, "Public Philosophy and the Crisis in Education," *Harvard Educational Review* 54 (May 1984): 186–94.

4. National Commission on Excellence in Education, *A Nation at Risk*, 10.

5. National Commission on Excellence in Education, *A Nation at Risk*, 25.

6. The work of Paulo Freire is important in this regard, for treating literacy in a nonreductionistic, self- and community-empowering manner (Paulo Freire, *Pedagogy of the Oppressed* [New York: Seabury Press, 1970]).

7. See P. Walker, ed., *Between Labor and Capital* (Boston: South End Press, 1979) for a discussion of theoretical issues involving the so-called "new middle class."

8. See Robert Crain, "The Quality of American High School Graduates: What Personnel Officers Say and Do About It," a paper of the Center for Social Organization Schools (Johns Hopkins University, 1984).

9. National Commission on Excellence in Education, *A Nation at Risk*, 9.

10. National Commission on Excellence, *A Nation at Risk*, 14.

11. Harry Braverman, *Labor and Monopoly Capital* (London: Monthly Review Press, 1974).

12. See Stanley Aronowitz, *False Promises* (New York: McGraw-Hill, 1973); and Richard Edwards, *Contested Terrain: The Transformation of the Workplace in the Twentieth Century* (New York: Basic Books, 1979).

13. David Hogan, "Education and Class Formation: The Peculiarities of the Americans," in *Cultural and Economic Reproduction in Education: Essays on Class, Ideology and the State*, ed. Michael Apple (London: Routledge and Kegan Paul, 1982): 32–78.

14. Paul Willis, *Learning to Labour: How Working Class Kids Get Working Class Jobs* (Westmead, England: Saxon House, 1977).

15. See Martin Carnoy, "Education, Economy and the State," in *Cultural and Economic Reproduction in Education*, ed. Michael Apple (London: Routledge and Kegan Paul, 1982): 79–126. Carnoy argues that as the extrinsic value of education falls in the marketplace, the grades given for a given level of effort must rise to ensure a given level of performance.

16. National Commission on Excellence in Education, *A Nation at Risk*, 30.

17. National Commission on Excellence in Education, *A Nation at Risk*, 23.

18. For a discussion on de-skilling of teachers' work through new curricular forms, and of resistances by teachers, see Michael Apple, "Curricular Form and the Logic of Technical Control," in *Ideology and Practice in Schooling*, ed. Michael Apple and Lois Weis (Philadelphia: Temple University Press, 1983): 143–66; Dennis Carlson, "'Updating' Individualism and the Work Ethic: Corporate Logic in the Classroom," *Curriculum Inquiry* 12 (no. 2, 1982): 125–60; and Andrew Gitlin, "School Structure and Teachers' Work," in *Ideology and Practice in Schooling*, 193–212.

Teacher Culture and the Irony of School Reform

Linda M. McNeil

The current reform reports, or "excellence" reports, on secondary schooling are replete with complex descriptions of public school practice. Their suggestions for improvement vary widely, including philosophical rationales for classical core-curricula, shifts in school funding policy, new career patterns for teachers, alternative conceptualizations of education that include components for public-service and esthetic and ethical education, intense concentration in special areas such as math and science, and general upgrading of currently common educational practice. This diversity of description and prescription has been lost in the public press for immediate reforms. The sense of immediacy aroused by the overwhelming evidence that America's secondary schools are less than excellent has led to a reform movement that differs dramatically from the educational reforms of the past two decades, which have primarily focused on specialized school functions and which have originated at or been largely supported by federal initiatives. Unlike Headstart, Title I, and other specifically targeted areas of school policy, the current reforms aim at raising overall quality in public schools. And unlike the many programs in such areas as special education, the current reform effort is occurring principally at the state level.

There is a clear reason for this locus of initiative: the Reagan administration's attempt to preempt Democratic candidates' call for increased aid to education. To balance this preemptive policy issue, the Reagan administration had to seize on education as an issue without alienating its usual constituency for decreased federal support of social and educational welfare. The solution was to endorse the commission report on public schools while tossing the responsibility back to the states. This satisfied those constitutional conservatives who note that education, by its absence as a stipulated federal issue, is one of the responsibilities reserved to the state in the Constitution, and who have never been happy with the use of other constitutional provisions (especially the civil rights amendments) as federal leverage over local schools. It also served well the current economic reality of needing to cut rather than increase federal spending. Thus, education reform was a convenient state policy issue.

The definitive history of how state legislatures came to accept this pressure and act on it has yet to be written. Many states were already actively increasing school requirements and raising teacher pay before the reform reports of the past two years were issued. What is interesting is that indeed many states have appropriated this issue as a legislative one, not because of federal default on the issue but in response to perceived local default on school quality.

Once the issue of school reform becomes the domain of state legislatures, several forces take over. One is the need for speed: the swiftness of many states' enacting of new regulations for their schools challenges old models of innovation and implementaion that assume that after scholars and practitioners come up with new ideas, those ideas will perk through various school districts or classrooms, encountering local variation or inertia that renders the original intent problematic. The current reforms, by contrast, are addressed to all the states' schools at once, leaving little time for filtering, processing, and experimenting with ways to implement the intended changes.

A second force at work is the need for comparable changes across wide diversities of geography, population, and school structure. A legislature accepting responsibility for setting school policy seeks changes that can be implemented in all schools. These include visible, concrete aspects of school practice, such as credits needed for graduation, and ignore individualistic aspects of schooling, such as teacher personality or collective school culture. The dominant impact of this need for comparability is that improvements are being expressed in terms of outcomes, especially measurable outcomes. Most commonly, these outcomes are the students' scores on standardized tests (nationally normed achievement tests, SAT tests, and statewide assessment tests), though they also include such measurables as length of school day, attendance figures, and teachers' standardized test scores. When standardized or comparable models of improvement are desired, the results cannot be left to the local or building personnel of the schools to design their schools' improvement policies or measure of effectiveness.

This leads to the third force at work in these reform efforts: the shift of school improvement from a classroom or subject-field issue to an administrative one. And in this case, that administrative initiative is not relegated to district administrators but to state agencies, as mandated by their legislatures. The legislatures are assuming the role of local school board, principal, and even teacher in deciding what should be taught and how students should be graded.

These forces of speed, standardization, and centralization merge in a top-down model of school reform, a model in which directives issue from those in highest authority (legislatures and state agencies) for implementation by those in the bureaucracy having least authority (classroom teachers). The purpose of this chapter is to discuss why this model of school improvement is inappropriate for addressing what is wrong with schools. Although the fallacies of this model extend to students, to the communities, and to the subject fields, the central purpose here is to examine the reasons this model of school reform is the wrong one to raise educational quality because of its negative impact on the quality of teaching. As examples of classroom teachers already working under typical new guidelines will show, state-mandated reforms measured by standardized scores on tests of standardized curricula deprofessionalize our best teachers. In doing so, they cause both teachers and students to further disengage from the teaching and learning process.

Ignoring teachers and the personal nature of teaching has historical precedent in school reform. Top-down school improvement did not begin with *A Nation at Risk:*

> The citizens disputed the purposes of public schools. They could not agree on who should be educated, on what kinds of education should be available to different classes of students, nor on how teachers should conduct class. A new superintendent was hired, bringing in a new wave of school reforms. Principals would supervise teachers more closely, and teachers would report in more detail with specified measures of student performance. Business leaders were asked to offer advice on curriculum content and on the management of schools. Constant drill in fundamentals was followed by testing thousands of students to determine how many achieved 100% mastery of reading, arithmetic and writing. When teachers requested more resources to help with mandated school improvements, the superintendent declined to provide them, placing the responsibility for "improvement" on the teachers.

This top-down view of school improvement is not a current case study. The year was 1924; the city, Chicago. Into a decade-long dispute among organized labor, organized teachers, and business leaders over the purpose of public schools in Chicago, William McAndrew was hired to make schools more efficient and productive. His plan reduced teachers to the level of powerless workers, in need of "constant and specific direction from superiors."[1]

The model for McAndrew's plan for reforming schools was the industrial factory. Following the lead of other social-efficiency school men, McAndrew saw the constituents of public schooling to be business leaders, whom he described as the "customers" of the factorylike processing of students into labor-force categories wanted by industry. He thought of students as "human output." He even invited business elites to inspect and quiz elementary students at a "Citizens' Sampling Day."[2] These "customers" could interrogate the students, mainly on facts, to determine the schools' level of success in making them into acceptable products of schooling. Adults came and inspected to see if the children had clean hair and clean teeth; they asked children to spell hard words, recite facts, and answer questions about who paid for their schools.

Labor force leader John Fitzpatrick was invited to join other "stockholders in the public schools" in this exhibition of the efficiency of public school expenditures. He declined, with this written response:

> I cannot understand what you and your assistants are thinking about when you talk about "output, customers, stockholders and sampling day" unless you imagine that you are running some kind of a mill or factory while you are grinding out a certain kind of product or material and you are going to get the "stockholders and customers" together and bring forth your "samples" as an exhibit of your output." . . . This "samping day," as you present it, is nothing more or less than an exhibition of the effort and result of eight years' schooling to make the youngsters think and act alike . . . . And the customers will be shown that the products of our public schools jump when the string is pulled and they will be splendid material to draw upon for employees in stores, offices, shops, factories or elsewhere.[3]

Children's advocates today may be less eloquent, less blunt, but they are repeating Fitzpatrick's theme that standardized reforms arising from the imperatives of the workplace do not necessarily serve the educational needs of children. The current wave of educational reform, with its call for standard tests and top-down policies, is hailed as the solution for schooling in a highly technological society; but its high-tech rhetoric is rooted in the tradition of industrial social efficiency that dominated school reforms in the early part of this century.

The goals of social efficiency, besides elevating school administrators to executive positions comparable to industrial management, were to make school processes and school curricula standard for large aggregates of students. Highly reductive course content enabled teachers to function as replaceable parts in the processing of students for their future destinies in the workplace; most of these students expected to end up as replaceable parts in the human capital of manufacturing. The social-efficiency movement attempted to apply rational planning to public education. In reaction to large and diverse groups of immigrants, increasing numbers of secondary school students, and the technical demands of a changing economic structure, social-efficiency experts deduced curricula from adult activity, established standard measures for assessing student capabilities ("raw material") and learnings ("outputs"). Justifying public expenditures in reaction to years of corruption and mediocrity, industrial-efficiency experts arranged the components of the school as parallel as possible to those of assembly-line manufacturing to make schools more accountable. With a pessimistic and distrusting view of teachers and an assumption that schooling was something done *to* children, the reforms by McAndrew and others defined "school reform" as applying broadside solutions to aggregate problems.

These reforms challenged growing urban political corruption, brought secondary schools onto the agenda of public education, and made public schooling a public issue. But they had the ironic effect of threatening school quality by alienating teachers, the very group essential to any school reform. Their rationale sounds disturbingly familiar. For those acquainted with the secondary school reforms of the 1920s, the current reform movement presents an unsettling case of déjà vu. Both involve quickly implemented, easily monitored standardized solutions for large aggregates of students in mediocre schools. Both address symptoms rather than causes and confuse accountability (counting costs against the value of "outputs") with legitimacy (having value based on a social purpose). In doing so, they set in motion policies that inadvertently exacerbate, rather than solve, the problems at the heart of what is wrong with schools. Those central problems have to do with teaching and learning. Visitors, both casual and professional, to our nation's high schools have a clear sense that teachers and students are meeting in a ritual of instruction that often holds little interest or commitment for either. This disengagement from school processes is the basis for students' and teachers' feelings that something is very wrong with our schools. This disengagement is not only widespread, but also deeply embedded in what our secondary schools have become. It cannot be engineered away with top-down policy mandates. Its symptoms may be the declining test scores, but it often persists even when test scores are high; its symptoms may be drop-out rates for teachers or students, but it can be found even in schools where attendance and retention rates are high.

There is a commonsense feeling that the new reforms coming out of state legislatures are misguided; critics have attacked particular elements of the new laws and agency directives. But there has yet been no systematic attempt to explore the shakiness of the assumptions upon which these reforms are constructed and to analyze the complex factors at work in schools that mitigate against their success.

This analysis attempts to begin that process by examining one "problem" of secondary schools, the quality of teaching. *A Nation at Risk*[4] and other reform reports lay much of the inadequacy of America's public schools at the feet of the teachers. This report is typical in suggesting that bad teaching is caused by recruiting and retaining bad teachers. Standardized credentialing policies and increased economic rewards are two solutions proposed in almost every state involved in reform. Their logic is that the requisite characteristics of teachers are known, are generalizable across the population of teachers, and are measurable. If individuals with those characteristics can be hired and paid higher salaries, school teaching will improve. The logic also calls for testing in-service, as well as pre-service, teachers at intervals to maintain their quality.

Two sets of case studies of classroom teaching document that the logic of these reforms is not grounded in the realities of classroom practice. The causes for poor teaching range beyond finding people who qualify on standardized tests and beyond the powers of management to monitor teacher quality through standardized measures. The case studies indicate in fact that the reforms currently being adopted in many states will only lower educational quality in many schools. As presently constituted, the legislated minimum standards will feed rather than reverse cycles of lowering expectations in schools.

It is important to trace the logic of these reforms into classrooms for several reasons. First, when tested against what we already know about teaching, the current reform movement is seen to omit our understandings of the professionalism of good teaching, of the nature of teaching as craft. Schools recently portrayed by Lightfoot and Lipsitz[5] as "good" or "successful" schools earned these labels by utilizing teachers' unique capabilities and commitments to meet the needs of particular groups of students. At best, such teachers worked in schools having a shared vision of purpose and a structure and community supportive of the exercise of teachers' professional judgments and expertise in building programs. At the least, where administrative structures were not actively contributing to such professionalism, they receded into the background of the total school program and did not overshadow instructional efforts.

Second, despite the slogans of the current reform movement, we know that schools do not exist merely to "raise achievements." Public schools have many purposes, many of those mutually contradictory. Although many of the currently popular policies set standardized content for curriculum and standard measures for assessing "learning" of that content, the resulting achievement measures will tell us little about the quality of instruction, the nature of students' learning, or the "effectiveness" of the school, including its contribution to those test scores relative to other factors in the students' biographies. As the examples below will suggest, the current reforms' emphasis on outcomes such as achievement measures misses the dynamics by which teachers play out the multiple purposes of schooling. These include meeting institutional demands for course credits and teaching loads, maintaining order and sorting students for future labor categories, teaching and learning, and merely getting through the day. As teachers and students construct their meanings of what goes on in schools, those meanings are shaped by these competing purposes. Reforms that address only those that can be measured omit the critical fact that teaching and learning take place in an institutional setting, about which much is already known. In his classic treatment of school changes, Sarason warned that innovations always come up against the behavioral and programmatic regularities of the institution.[6] In schools, many of those regularities are contradictory, at cross-purposes, as the culture of the school embodies the meanings of the participants with different purposes for being there and differing means of warranting judgments about what should be changed. Some of these purposes do include increasing "learning," with all that the term implies; others arise more from goals of institutional maintenance, controlling student behavior, or producing externally mandated products, such as attendance figures and course credits.

Finally, we know that formal labels and categories in any organization do not capture the realities of the organization as lived by its participants. With schools this is especially true because of the intangible quality of education. Just as we know that course titles are not always accurate indicators of course content, we know that achievement measures based on multiple choice tests tell us how students do on that multiple choice test but do not tell us how students assimilate or synthesize those disparate bits of information. Attendance and homework figures tell us about "being there" but give no hint as to the nature or quality of involvement. So much is known in organizational literature and in schooling literature about the obliqueness of formal organizational titles and indicators that reforms based on these should be immediately suspect. And yet the currently legislated reforms rely on such formal educationist labels to describe what should happen in schools. So long as the rich culture behind these labels is ignored, aggregate reforms may "succeed" in reaching their own goals (raising achievements) but will fail to improve education.

This becomes especially clear as we look at the impact of the reforms on high school faculty. In the first case studies, we will see how the reasons for declining educational quality fall outside the capacity of the management paradigm to take account of them, much less solve them. In the second case study examples, the beginnings of implementation of the top-down reforms will be shown to contribute to reducing instructional quality where it had been outstanding by standard aggregate measures and by traditional wholistic standards of "good teaching."

BEFORE

The assumption of the current reform movement regarding quality of teaching is that low pay has encouraged only the least competent college students to prepare for teaching and has encouraged the best teachers to leave to higher-status, more lucrative professions. The reforms also suggest that administrators need to monitor teachers more and set more standard rules about test scores teachers must have and maintain to stay in teaching. Like the Chicago superintendent, many state legislatures are implying by their new policies that teachers when left to their own devices will be mediocre at best; they must be told what to teach and how to measure student progress. Room for random teacher initiatives is shrinking.[7]

An intensive study of midwestern high schools reveals a very different picture.[8] In those schools, teachers were well educated; compared to national averages, they were fairly well paid. One was a Phi Beta Kappa history major from a fine university; all kept up reading in their fields. They were the kinds of teachers the current reform reports say we should recruit and retain for our schools.

When observed over a semester, these "good" teachers in a "good" high school were seen to water-down content, to restrict or eliminate student reading and discussion, to call for little or no student writing. Their U.S. history courses treated most information in the form of lists, brief descriptions, or slogans. Rare were significant student questions, in-depth explanations, attention to varied student abilities within the classes.

If the subsequent interviews had not revealed more complex teacher knowledge, the observations would have indicated that these teachers were weak in their subject fields, were ill-prepared in instructional methods, were in need of administrative monitoring or supervision. The teachers would have seemed to be prime targets for the kinds of reforms currently being aimed at teachers.

These top-down measures could not have solved the "problem" of teacher quality in this school. The teachers had deliberately adopted their teaching styles in accommodation to top-down administrative strategies. They had developed a teacher culture around the need for authority and efficiency in an institution that they felt did not provide either. They felt their authority over content, in this school with broad latitudes for teachers in curriculum development and instruction, to be threatened by the elimination of ability grouping, an administrative decision made against teachers' recommendations. With heterogeneous classes, teachers who for years had based instructional strategies on student diversity (when that diversity was represented across their teaching day rather than within each class) felt unable to "really teach" with so many abilities in one room. They taught to the lower-middle (perceived lower-middle) level, lecturing, tightly controlling all information, eliminating outside resources previously used with "brighter" levels of students. They rightly noted that their pedagogical wisdom had been ignored in the detracking decision. They also correctly pointed out that while charges of discrimination and elitism had brought about the administrative decision to detrack basic subject classes, no administrative efforts were exerted to give teachers resources or planning time to reassess their instructional patterns and adopt them for heterogeneous classes. Similarly, no administrative oversight followed up on the detracking to see if, indeed, it eliminated discrimination or fostered better education for students perceived as being left out in the previous policy of ability tracking. Like the teachers in McAndrew's schools, these teachers were not to question administrative policy nor ask for resources implicit in policy changes; they were merely to carry out the polices. Having their authority over schoolwide decisions ignored in this and several other issues, they reacted by tightening their authority over content with their students.

In addition, the teachers believed that the administrative concern with order keeping and the processing of students through required course credits ignored teachers' priorities for instruction. Having their day interrupted with patrolling duties (in hall, cafeteria, restrooms) and their communications with the administration limited to memos and meetings on paperwork and outcome measures (teacher-based, not standardized in this system), the teachers responded by creating their own efficiencies in the ways they conducted their classes. Having what they saw as too little time to work together on lessons (one teacher was not interested but the other two had planned together before they lost their common planning time), little schoolwide attention to program quality, much schoolwide attention to minimum standards, they reduced their paperwork and nonclass time by limiting student writing, by pacing lectures to minimize student discussion, and generally bringing their treatment of history down to the level of ritual preparation for tests.

For these teachers there was a clear conflict between their ideal of teaching and, in two cases, their memories of how they "used to teach," and the minimal teaching rewarded within their school. They felt the educational purpose compatible with their professional ideal to be in conflict with the administrative emphasis on controlling. These teachers rejected top-down management; they successfully fought against having the superintendent's model of management-by-objectives imposed on classroom teachers. They felt it would demean their professional identity as subject matter experts. Yet in response to administrative policies of control, they participated in their own de-skilling or de-professionalizing by putting barriers between their students and their personal store of knowledge about their subject, about student diversity, and about the importance of varied instructional techniques.[9]

Within this school, the social-control purposes, as exemplified in administrative priorities in staff time, resources, attention (or inattention) to effects of administrative changes—these overwhelmed the instructional purposes of the school as defined by the teachers' personal conceptions. Metz has described faculty culture as the shared assumptions and understanding of institutional processes that are so much a part of the common sense of the group as to go unarticulated.[10] In this school, the part of the faculty culture that was articulated was that each was doing the best he or she could "under the circumstances." The circumstances of a cavalier administration prevented "real teaching." In the absence of administrative supports for professional judgments from teachers, teachers had to find their own means of maintaining professional authority, even at the expense of low student participation. One reason these teachers wanted to retain authority over content was that they were afraid students would become cynical if they discovered too many social problems. Ironically, by tightly controlling information and presenting a sanitized, factual history, devoid of discussion, the teachers (according to many students interviewed) engendered not only cynicism about social problems and social institutions, but about the credibility of school knowledge.

Students, apparently passive in the pace of the lectures, were found to be negotiating just how much teacher-supplied information to believe. They did not understand the reactions of teachers to the administrative context, but did see minimal efforts on the part of teachers and minimal requirements for their own participation.[11] Students were not unaware of the low expectations the assignments (or lack of them) implied.

Students responded quite logically: they disengaged from the classroom interaction, content to take notes, answer short-answer tests (or essay answers that must match preconceived right answers), and basically be present in exchange for the required course credit. They remained unaware that the administration, whom they perceived as distant except in direct matters of attendance or discipline, had even the slightest impact on what their teachers were teaching. But they were aware that content was often trivialized (reduced to outlines on a transparency in one class; more interesting, but not always more detailed in the other classes) and "schoolish."

In these classes, the social relations of the classroom were interwoven with the instructional processes. In these classes, teachers controlled content in order to control students, to control classroom pacing and efficiency. I have described their style as "defensive teaching,"[12] because in many cases their rich store of knowledge of history did not prevent them from apologizing for assignments or backing-off assignments in order to gain minimal student compliance.

The link between social relations and classroom knowledge was not anticipated when that study of economics curricula was undertaken. It emerged as patterns of instruction were traced first to the teachers' knowledge and level of academic preparation, to their experience as teachers, and to their biographies (as middle-aged teachers in an established urban high school). Next these patterns of instruction were linked to the administrative policies from which teachers felt so excluded. This linkage was made because teachers made it; their perceptions of having no effect over the overall school program led them to increase their control over their students so that class time and student outcomes would become fairly predictable and nonintrusive on teacher time. The linkage of teacher practice to student responses was important because it connected the cycle of lowering expectations. As little was required of students, they disengaged from classroom interactions, not in active or collective resistance but in privatized remoteness and minimal participation. Administrators, and some teachers, saw this as a motivation problem and increased their attention to controlling student behavior.

None of these social relations is addressed by the current reforms aimed at improving school quality through standardized assessments. The student disengagement and cynicism observed cut across all levels of student achievement on standardized tests and all levels of student performance within the observed classes. One could not have deduced from testing how the teacher taught nor how well the students learned. Beyond the facts of the lesson, the teachers were teaching content they did not always believe, and students were in many cases "learning" that content for tests but planning to "forget" it as soon as the test was past.

A second study carried the analysis of these linkages into schools chosen for specific variation in administrative structure and policies from the first school.[13] Within those other three high schools, it was observed that where school resources and personnel were concentrated on the social control goals of the school, rather than the educational purposes, teachers exhibited this same pattern of controlling content, limiting student participation in learning, exerting minimal effort in reaction to what they perceived to be insensitive administrative policies. Where students saw this kind of teaching, they responded with minimal effort.[14] Students were very aware when their administrators spent much of the staff time on controlling halls, interrupting class to talk on the intercom about litter and cafeteria manners, making up rules to lock students into the library over lunch so that those entering would not later make noise in the halls if they left before the bell rang to end lunch hour. The students under such conditions maintained distance between the school and their personal involvement; they did not recognize that these same policies were having an impact on their teachers' levels of effort.

In the one school where the credentialing and behavior-control functions were subordinated to the teaching functions, teachers acted as professionals, creating and teaching rich lessons, bringing their own personal knowledge into the teaching of the subject, risking inefficiencies of time, and risking conflict by permitting, even encouraging, students to discuss. In these classes, teachers exhibited the organic link between persona and craft that had been missing in the schools where the tension between educational purposes and social-control purposes had been resolved at the administrative level in favor of the social-control purposes of the school.

These schools were observed before the current wave of reforms. These secondary school teachers shared a professional culture as subject matter experts. As I have discussed elsewhere,[15] they had rejected management objectives and prepackaged curricula that they had seen imposed on elementary teachers. In resisting these forms of imposed de-skilling, they had asserted a professional ideal of teaching. But they had unwittingly begun to participate in their own de-skilling in their reactions to administrative controls. Because their de-skilling was participatory rather than institutionalized, there existed the potential for individual teachers to break out of the patterns of defensive teaching, of minimal standards, of reductive content contrary to their personal expertise in their subject. *This potential would not have been released by standardized mandates to reform their least professional teaching.* In fact, its subjugation by the reward system in the institution pointed to a need to decentralize administrative policies rather than tighten them, to involve teachers in resource allocations, including those of staff time as well as finances. These teachers, according to their own memory and those of several former students interviewed, remembered a time when they had "really taught." That was a time when the shared vision of the school included instructional excellence, rather than overemphasis on controls and course credits. The teachers had been actively involved in developing programs for their schools in those days; when that was taken away and their advice ignored in later policies (tracking being only one of these), they reduced efforts and, as a result, lowered instructional quality.

DURING

The first set of case studies, briefly sketched here but treated at length in related publications, raises serious questions about the locus of control over instruction and its effect on instructional quality. In a second set of case studies, the teachers in a large urban district have found themselves under increasingly strict district and state directives on course content and assessment measures. The schools observed are magnet high schools, established with distinctive programs to encourage voluntary desegregation.[16] Two of the schools are based on career-related topics (engineering and medical professions) and have no distinctive pedagogy beyond a philosophy of serving all races of students in ways that will give them the knowledge and skills needed to pursue their career or higher education goals in these fields. The third school, for gifted students, has a distinctive pedagogy centered on involving the students in creative and in-depth treatment of traditional core subjects. Teachers are recruited to these schools on the basis of their sensitivity to students' individual ability differences, cultural heritages, and varied social circumstances; their subject matter expertise; and their commitment to high academic standards.

While not all magnet teachers attain these ideals, there is a definite shared culture that magnet teaching is unique, is important, is "real teaching." Because they are to go into greater depth and offer diverse learning experiences, these teachers have to have an optimistic view of student development. They have had to take the inefficient risks the previously described teachers avoided: risks of opening their authority to challenge from student questions; risks of inefficiencies of student participation and open-ended projects. While many of the teachers do have a special interest in gifted children or in the area of career emphasis, many others say that they teach in magnet schools because these are the only schools in this area where they are allowed the autonomy to do what they consider to be real teaching. Here the faculty culture is not tacit but frequently articulated. Recent policy changes have made teachers especially verbal about their shared culture of values and expectations.

The policy changes bring us back to the model of McAndrew and Chicago: top-down dictates about content, based on businessmen's advice about priorities of schooling and based on business accounting applications to student assessment. These policies have originated with the state but are elaborated and implemented by the district, which has a strong commitment to the standardized model of reform typical of new state mandates. These teachers are interesting to study because they represent what these standardized reforms can do to teaching by people who are considered to be good teachers, a kind of teachers *A Nation at Risk* says we should hire and offer better pay.

Two years prior to the magnet school observations, the state legislature responded to the state's long history of mediocre and inequitable schooling by legislating a uniform curriculum K-12 for all public schools. The state education agency was empowered to draft the "esssential elements" of all basic subjects.[17] Each district could adapt these for its students but had to account for "covering" them, since eventually students would be tested on them. A statewide test given at three levels was already in place and additional tests were being devised; in addition, the plan was to tie local school-district accreditation and possibly some resources to adherence to and implementation of these essential elements.

As implemented in the district where the magnet schools are located, the essential elements took the form of a numbered set of "proficiencies" for each subject in each grade. These proficiencies, first introduced in high schools, set the specific content for each course. For instance, learning the simple formula for photosynthesis is an essential element or proficiency of ninth-grade biology. The plan was to give proficiency tests that would become the course grade, thus equalizing not only content but also grading across the district, eliminating the idiosyncrasies and unpredictability of teacher lessons and grades. Because the scores on the piloted test were so low, the central administration revised the policy to make the proficiency test count only 20 percent of any course grade.

In addition to testing student performance, these multiple-choice tests were designed to "catch" bad teachers, teachers who let students play cards in class or talk football, teachers who take fifteen minutes to call roll, teachers who do not know their subjects or only go through the motions of teaching. Given the widely ranging quality of teachers in this state and in this district, and the history of low pay, such an assessment policy does have some basis in real need for reform. The difficulty is that its first impact is to reduce the quality of instruction in the "good" teachers' classes.

The proficiencies, combined with new attendance policies that make curricular trips into unexcused absences if they take time from more than one subject, have had the effect of shifting the locus of curriculum control away from teachers. Magnet teachers, hired specifically to develop specialized curricula with attention to student diversity, are seeing even magnet school courses subjected to the regimentation of the proficiencies. The district supplied teachers with "pre-tests," lists of proficiencies to "cover," and, finally, the post-test. They are expected to teach to the proficiencies all semester; teaching to the test in the form of cramming brings swift, negative repercussions.

These magnet teachers have a store of varied instructional pedagogies and a commitment to teaching students how to learn, how to synthesize and analyze, how to intepret information. To do these tasks, they must treat some topics in depth, make professional decisions about proportionate time for in-depth and survey treatment of course topics, and must make lessons open-ended enough to encompass student contributions. Procedurally, they must allow class time for group work and individual research, since most magnet students ride buses and cannot meet together or with the teacher after school. In addition, the sparseness of school labs and libraries prompts most of these teachers to schedule guest speakers (including those provided by an extensive and widely praised cooperative effort between the schools and the corporate sector), field trips to local public and university libraries, and other off-campus activities to supplement less than adequate school resources. The new attendance rules, designed primarily at the state level to keep small-town athletes in class more, have had the effect of reducing field trips to these resources. Reminiscent of McAndrew's answer to the Chicago teachers, the district has no plans to supplement school resources to compensate for reduced out-of-building excursions.

Rather than raise quality, these broadside policies, which standardize overt behaviors of schooling, induce semantic games for symbolic compliance, cause teachers to eliminate complex lessons in favor of simple coverage of testable proficiencies, or increase teacher alienation among even those dedicated and competent teachers. These *actual* effects are missed when the outcomes that are assessed are those that can be expressed in numerical measures. The result is that *counting up* is resulting in *dumbing down* in many classes. Several examples will demonstrate the range of teacher responses to these imposed standardizations. One English teacher has many years of experience in curriculum development, and both a file cabinet and a head full of enriching activities to promote writing, literary analysis skills, and reading. Each day on the back chalkboard she lists the district proficiency related to the day's lesson. Since in English these are rather general, she is able to write something like "the student will gain an appreciation for the language of poetry and know the role of imagery," then go on with the lessons she developed in previous years for teaching poetry through the poetry of music. Her course has not been drastically changed by the proficiencies, but the justification is written for all the class to see.

In history and the sciences, the proficiencies are based more on factual content than on skills related to reading and writing. The purpose, again, is to make sure all teachers assigned to "cover" U.S. history include the major events, names, dates, and places. One teacher at the gifted school continues to teach history as issues, as important public policy concepts, as historiography. In her class the names and dates serve a larger purpose in helping students understand historical events and processes. Teaching them how to learn about history, how to evaluate historical sources, and how to understand the contemporary world as the product of past occurrences are all interwoven in her lessons. While this sounds like competent history teaching, it is in conflict with the district-supplied proficiencies because of their lack of attention to conceptualization and their lack of emphasis on students' roles in analyzing, rather than mere memorizing of, historical sources. An example is the period of U.S. history following the Civil War. According to the district-supplied proficiencies, there are four points to "know about" this period: industrialization, urbanization, immigration, and labor-management conflict. The teacher's interest is in having the students understand the period rather than memorize these four major trends. She wants them to learn to investigate how social processes imply certain values, and how different social groups interpret history according to their own perspective. Her lectures for this period, and the assigned common readings, are merely the basis for the primary activity: the trial of the robber-baron industrialists for their industrial growth policies, based on charges brought by those who were out of power during this period. Each student role-plays a figure representing the interests of industrial giants, political and labor leaders, sharecroppers, recent immigrants, injured packing-plant employees. The student must not only represent the attitudes of this person during the trial but also must, through his or her testimony, convey to the class key information regarding this segment of society. Despite scanty library resources, the students gathered impressive amounts of information (written and submitted for a grade), developed their characters, and challenged each other's characters in a two-day trial. By the end of the activity, they were very confident in their understanding of the conflicts and values of the period, as well as the names of key leaders and events. Designers of the proficiencies would point to this class as evidence that proficiencies serve only as minimum standards, and not as upper limits on what teachers can do. However, this teacher's accommodation to the proficiencies extended further than her numbering those unit objectives related to the district's proficiencies. In order to have this lesson that demanded student selection, comparison, and analysis of information resources, the teacher had to compress a subsequent lesson into worksheet format in order to "cover" the fall proficiencies before the December tests.

A science teacher articulated this conflict best when she said that she feels she is under two conflicting rules: as a teacher of the gifted, she is required to give students depth and learning skills; as a teacher in the district, she is required to cover fragments and high spots over great breadth. These teachers want their students to do well on the proficiencies so that the gifted programs will not be singled out as weakening students' achievements. In reality, their concerns are not great because in order to test into the program, students had to perform substantially above district averages. However, as specific content, rather than aptitudes or general math-verbal skills, is tested, that content will consist of reductive pieces of course content from presumed survey courses. And as having student aggregate scores above the district average is tied to teacher pay and career ladder promotions (as intended over the upcoming phase-in of that portion of the proficiencies policy), teachers will feel more and more pressed to cover the material, even superifically, rather than stop running through facts in order to teach learning skills and give students opportunities for involvement.

My own informal interviews with magnet teachers at middle and elementary schools indicate that the problem of teacher professionalism over content and instructional method is dominating teachers' concerns. They feel stripped of the very expertise they were hired to have. Many know that there are numbers of weak teachers and welcome methods to bring who those teachers are to light, possibly even to give them disincentives for remaining in schools. But they also know that these standardized reforms will not produce excellence but short-term results, "products," in the language of social efficiency. As my university students do their observing in nonmagnet schools, they are discovering the same phenomena. Teachers, only recently the lobbyists for school reform, have seen reforms enacted by a legislature that wants instant accountability rather than long-term learning development in children. Surely their purpose was not to impose so many grammar proficiencies that a teacher who has street kids enthusiastically reading in a listening-to-learn program has to cut back on student reading in order to cover noun proficiencies for students who are not ready for them and who are failing all their classes but her reading class. Surely, in focusing on extracurricular absence policies rather than substantive issues of reforming science education, the designers of essential elements and proficiencies did not intend for a creative biology teacher to drop a three-day biology trip, whose length is necessary to conduct longitudinal studies of sample specimens. Their purpose was surely not to lower quality of instruction; yet in these and many other cases, where teachers do comply with legislated rules, that lowering results.

AFTER

We have seen two patterns of deprofessionalizing teachers. In the schools observed before widespread standardized reforms were instituted, educational purposes were seen to be in tension with the control functions of schools. Where those tensions were resolved at the administrative level in favor of the control purposes of schools, teachers participated in their own de-skilling by creating their own authority and efficiencies in the classroom; reducing their efforts at curriculum development and instruction; limiting student assignments and participation; and trivializing content in order to accommodate their time and energies to institutional policies over which they felt they had no control.

These teachers' autonomy, even in those schools, greatly exceeded the autonomy and range of discretion left to teachers whose requirements to teach to specific district- and state-mandated tests caused them to have to compromise their own view of what real teaching is all about. Only the teachers in the school where the administrative policies of control were subordinated to educational policies treated school knowledge as extensions of the personal knowledge they and their students brought into the classrooms. Only under conditions where the educational functions superseded the control functions did teachers feel great latitude in teaching students to learn as well as teaching them a subject.

The magnet teachers observed have been working under such a model, having schools established by the courts and the district to serve unique educational needs. Now they see that uniqueness in tension with pressures to conform. It is not yet known what effect the minimum standards will have on our worst teachers. Because the proficiencies of this particular district have been in place even as other states and districts are beginning to enact policies of standardized assessments, we have these magnet school teachers as an example of the possible negative effects these reforms can have on good teachers. Several talk of leaving teaching; if teaching becomes acting as a replaceable part in a credentialing factory, many of these teachers will seek more satisfying employment.[18] Others feel great conflict with the pressure to keep student scores above district or state averages because this will penalize teachers committed to working with children with learning problems. Others feel that fragmented tests ignore aspects of the content that they consider to be basic, to be central: these include values and issues as well as learning skills, and are not easily reducible to multiple-choice testing. At any rate, they are not shared as "basic" goals of instruction by those who have devised the proficiencies and essential elements.

McAndrew of Chicago and numerous state legislatures around the country have made the assumption that there is a positive correlation between management and educational quality. They have equated time with quality and have recommended extending school days or school years. They have confused testing with assessment and built a model of testing on assumptions that content is reducible and that instruction is deducible from those reductive test answers. Most important, they have confused management with leadership. The vague calls for "leadership" in many of the reform reports have translated, for lack of a common language of what leadership means, into top-down management strategies that presume labor to be inept and resistant, products to be predictable, and short-term accounting to be indicative of significant results. Such assumptions ignore the evidence that many of the inadequacies of teaching are caused by inadequate administrative support, misplaced administrative priorities, and misapplied administrative controls. It is ironic that so many of the reform reports call for improved teaching but leave school administration, except for some new standardized tests for administrators, as a given in public schools.

It might be said that in schools, as in many industries, centralized controls and short-term accounting are evidence of the failure of management. Decentralized management strategies imply taking risks, risks that the individuals involved may go off in unpredictable directions, with unpredictable results. But education itself is such a risk; in its true definition of drawing out the potential of the individual, education is a venture of risk, of inefficiencies and false starts and uncertain growth. The external pressures for immediate accountability have convinced many school administrators that they cannot take such risks with their school program, even at the expense of some of the programs of unique quality. Interestingly, in many states, the legislatures perceive public pressure to improve schools to be so immediate that they are likewise reducing their risks by centralizing content and assessment at the state level, deprofessionalizing local school boards and administrators as well as teachers.

This rush to reduce uncertainties and standardize outcomes has its history in an era that shared similar problems of student diversity, immigration, shifting financial bases, and calls from the press and public, especially business leaders, for prompt reforms. In the days of Superintendent McAndrew, school management policies had to confront organized teachers' resistance and the insistence of parents in organized labor that schools not neglect their children. In the absence of such organized, articulate dissent today, the language of testing remains the language of accountability. If there is a lesson to be learned from these examples of the ways top-down administrative controls become counterproductive in schools, it may be that there is a need for a language of accountability that will not reduce teachers to the level of drone workers or students to identification by their measured proficiency tests.

That such a language is needed is already well known. With so much research documentation that supports the need for school staffs to be empowered, with so much commonsense perception that teachers must have something to say and something to give, rather than mere content to cover, it is uncanny that the standardized aspects of the current reform movement have come to dominate school policy. One can only speculate that, ten years hence, the public outcry will again be directed against the failures of our high schools. Journalists and politicians will wonder aloud why our schools have resorted to teaching to tests and leaving teachers with so little autonomy. They will berate schools whose students have fewer skills at synthesizing and discovering information than filling-in bubbles on computer-graded score sheets. The realization that the current standardizations of curriculum and assessment trivialized education and reduced it to a parody of itself will assuredly come. The problem of reform in that instance will be what to do with the teachers who know only proficiency-based teaching, and how to find and reclaim those teachers who left when their ability to teach was compromised by these external impositions. Observers will note the irony that it was the mediocre teachers who stayed and most easily adapted to the de-skilled roles that teachers played in implementing the reforms of the 1980s.

NOTES

The author is indebted to the National Institute of Education, U.S. Department of Education, for support for the research cited herein. The data on the de-skilling of teachers in an administrative context in which social control goals supersede educational goals were drawn from case studies in "The Institutional Context Controlling Classroom Knowledge," Grant #NIE-G-78-0015, Organized Processes divison; final report entitled *Contradictions of Control.* Examples of teacher responses to district-supplied proficiencies and state mandates for standardization are taken from case studies in "Structuring Excellence: The Potential for Constructive District-Level Intervention," in progress, Grant #NIE-G-83-0042. The analysis is that of the author and does not represent NIE policy or endorsement.

1. Julia Wrigley, *Class Politics and Public School: Chicago, 1900-1950* (New Brunswick, N.J.: Rutgers University Press, 1982): 176.

2. Wrigley, *Class Politics,* 178-80.

3. Wrigley, *Class Politics,* 180.

4. The National Commission on Excellence in Education, *A Nation at Risk* (Washington, D.C.: U.S. Government Printing Office, 1983).

5. Sara L. Lightfoot, *The Good High School* (New York: Basic Books, Inc., 1983); and Joan Lipsitz, *Successful Schools for Young Adolescents* (New Brunswick, N.J.: Transaction Books, 1984).

6. Seymour Sarason, *The Culture of the School and the Problem of Change* (Boston: Allyn and Bacon, 1971).

7. For an overview of the state reform movements being enacted by legislature and state educational agencies within the past two years (including several in progress before the publication of *A Nation at Risk*), see *The Nation Responds* (Washington, D.C.: U.S. Department of Education, May, 1984). This state-by-state review of recent educational policy changes reveals that almost all states are responding to issues of teacher quality by enacting standardized tests of people applying to enter the profession, of students entering colleges of education, and/or of practicing teachers. Career ladders, master teacher plans, teacher assessments are almost all standardized or warranted against standard norms, including students' test scores on standardized achievement or proficiency tests. Only a handful of states include entrepreneurial or professionally innovative incentives such as mini-grants or other resource offerings that would decentralize curricular or instructional decisions, and these are almost all as footnotes to standardized models. The preponderance of "reforms" assume that there is "one best way" to educate children, to assess teachers, to raise school quality.

8. Linda M. McNeil, *Contradictions of Control* (Boston: Routledge and Kegan Paul, 1985). See also *Contradictions of Control,* report to the National Institute of Education (1982).

9. For a fuller discussion of the tendency of productivity models typical of capitalist production to divorce labor actions from purposive and conscious content, to split craft into rationally sequenced components of behavior disembodied from the personal and intelligent functions of the worker, see Harry Braverman, *Labor and Monopoly Capital* (New York: Monthly Review Press, 1974). The current reforms in education call for systematic new analysis on the effects of controls on teacher labor,

on the nature of de-skilling and reskilling of teachers in the context of these shifts in control levels and techniques. This chapter is an attempt to begin that analysis.

10. Mary H. Metz, "Faculty Culture: A Case Study," paper presented at the annual meeting of the American Sociological Association (San Antonio, Texas, August 1983).

11. Linda M. McNeil, "Negotiating Classroom Knowledge: Beyond Achievement and Socialization," *Journal of Curriculum Studies* (Winter 1981).

12. See Linda M. McNeil, "Defensive Teaching and Classroom Control," in *Ideology and School Practice,* ed. Michael W. Apple and Lois Weis (Philadelphia: Temple University Press, 1983), for a documentation of the processes by which teachers simplify course content, or otherwise make it less accessible to students, in order to gain from students at least minimal compliance with academic and behavioral requirements.

13. See McNeil, *Contradictions of Control.*

14. Students' explanations for their resistance to school-supplied knowledge and their silent negotiating of its credibility and utility for them are analyzed in McNeil, "Negotiating Classroom Knowledge."

15. McNeil, *Contradictions of Control,* especially chapters 3–6.

16. This research is funded by the National Institute of Education, Grant NIE-G-83-0042, and is conducted under the auspices of the Department of Education of Rice University. This ethnographic study includes extensive classroom observations over a semester per school in selected magnet high schools; teachers, administrators, and students are interviewed; and historical investigation into district policy is supplemented with analysis of current legislative and district policy changes. Identities of school personnel and students remain confidential.

17. For a brief overview of these state-level legislated reforms, see Michael G. Killian, "Local Control—the Vanishing Myth in Texas," *Phi Delta Kappan* (November 1984): 192–95. Although the article accepts at face value the assumption that these legislated curricula and assessments in Mr. Killian's state will improve education, he is more analytical in examining the shift of control from local ("independent") school boards to the state legislature and education agency.

18. Interesting demographics are at work in teacher hiring and retention in this and, presumably, other districts. Whereas at one time, young women working before having children constituted a significant portion of the teaching profession and were presumed to be short-term employees, this group of often bright, young women are now attracted to professions that once were closed to women, but are now more accessible and more remunerative, more likely to provide avenues of professional advancement and autonomy. These include law, medicine, engineering, and numerous science, business, and commercial roles. Schools now have, or seem to have, more women who are returning to teaching or remaining in teaching because they need an income as divorced parents with custody of their children. They are attracted to teaching not only because of their earlier training and perhaps teaching experience (and perhaps the lack of other professional training), but also because the hours remain flexible for caring for their own children after school and in summers; such flexibility is rarely available in private sector employment. A number of these women have expressed declining satisfaction with teaching as the profession becomes less professional, more controlled. Several have indicated that when the trade-off between flexibility for child rearing and the decline of professional satisfaction comes to the point of strictly controlled curriculum and test-based pay scales, they will seek other employment. These are, by and large, committed, talented teachers who would like to stay in teaching if the structure of schooling would permit their functioning as "real teachers" (their words).

Teachers and Reform

Albert Shanker

To most teachers, the many reports that are the basis of the excellence movement seemed like more of the same criticism they had grown accustomed to. Along with most of the general public, teachers did not read the full reports. They relied on newspaper and television coverage, and much of that highlighted the failure of schools to teach and of students to achieve in recent decades. In the past teachers have not found reports such as these particularly helpful. First, a picture of failing schools rarely results in increased resources. On the contrary, people tend to believe that if the schools are so bad, it would be a waste to spend additional money on them. Second, the critics usually are good at telling educators what needs to be changed, but it is the professionals in the schools who are left to pay the price of making the changes while the critics move on to some other topic that interests them. And, third, most teachers are struggling to succeed against great odds; they resent the frequency with which they are blamed for the failures.

It is precisely because school people think that this set of reports is like all those that have come before that full deliberation is needed. This time things really are different in a number of very crucial respects. First, previous reports were issued at times when public education generally was held in high esteem and its continued existence was not in question. This time it was different. Public education was in great trouble. Because of the decline in the birth rate and the greater longevity of our population, the percentage of voters who have a direct interest in public schools because their children attend them is very low—at the 20 percent mark. Public confidence in our schools, as measured by the annual Gallup Poll (and others), was at an all-time low when the excellence movement started. The economic problems faced by our country pointed to bleak prospects for public education. With the real purchasing power of many citizens declining or standing still, few were inclined to generosity in financing public schools. And, there were other major needs that demanded huge amounts of money: reindustrialization; the modernization of our industries so that we could compete successfully; rebuilding our infrastructure, our roads, bridges, harbors, water conduits, sewer systems; and maintaining an adequate defense system.

In addition to less support by direct users, a very poor public image, and increasing competition for limited financial resources, there has also been the growing threat of tuition tax credits and vouchers. Public support for tuition tax credits actually reached above the 50 percent mark in the 1983 Gallup Poll, and those who thought they need not worry about tax credits because the Supreme Court would declare them unconstitutional had that hope shattered when the Court refused to overturn tuition tax deductions in Minnesota.

So bad were the prospects for public education that it would not be too far off to compare public schools with our auto and steel industries. Only a few years ago the idea that the United States might not have auto and steel industries was unthinkable, about as unthinkable as the idea that we might not have a public education system. There were all kinds of warnings that auto and steel were in trouble. Many Americans visited Japan, Germany, Korea, Taiwan, and other places that were putting in place more efficient systems than we had, but to change American industry so that it could really compete was too painful, both to management and to labor. Major changes, painful ones, would have to be made. They were not. Perhaps both sides hoped that things would work out well because Americans would not switch from the domestic cars they had always bought, or because Congress would act to prevent major American job losses by preventing foreign products from coming in in large numbers. But these hopes turned out to be wrong.

The beginning of the excellence movement was much like the earlier period in auto and steel. All could see the declining power of the schools, that there were fewer resources and greater demands for public financing of private education. The school excellence movement, at least for the time being, has turned things around. Whether or not they stay that way will depend upon what happens next. But there are, to start, at least three good reasons for optimism. One, the reports at the heart of the excellence movement repudiate tax credit and voucher proposals. There is no doubt that all these committees and commissions had advocates of tax credits on them and that abandoning public education—or, as tax credit advocates would have it, strengthening public education through competition—was considered or debated. But the idea was not accepted or recommended by a single report. Two, every one of the reports exudes confidence that American public schools can be greatly improved, and that they need much more in the way of resources. And, three, there is the new and productive involvement of the business community in support of public education. Leaders of major American corporations served on the commissions, and many more have themselves become active, involving their businesses, in improving public schools. Their clear emphasis has been on the need to improve education as a key to successful economic development, on the folly of trying to compete successfully in world markets with a strategy that invests in industrial capital and in the infrastructure but that fails to invest in and build our human infrastructure. (Unlike some earlier interest in public education by the business community, the current support is not a demand for narrow vocationalism. On the contrary, business seems to be pressing for something that closely resembles traditional academic education.)

Also, in spite of great economic difficulties, in a number of states the business community has supported huge increases in financial support for public schools at the state level, even where this has meant an increase in taxes. In all cases this support had strings attached. It was not money to do the same old things. Rather, the money was accompanied by proposals for major change.

What were these changes? What do teachers think of them? One set of changes centered around which courses students would be required to take. Many schools permitted students to take soft electives instead of hard subjects. It came as no surprise that if students were not required to take difficult subjects like math, science, and foreign languages, most of them did not. Under pressure from the excellence movement, most states now spell out the courses to be taken in high school. For the most part, teachers applauded the moves. Most of those who teach in our schools were themselves good students, enjoyed and excelled in a given subject, and became teachers so that they could do for their students what some other teacher had once done for them. The new requirements allow them to do what they became teachers to do: teach the subject of their specialization. Also, teachers as a group never accepted the 1960s fashion that became dominant in so many of our schools—that students should take only courses that they find "relevant," that students should be permitted to select the courses and read the books they enjoy, and that teachers and other adults had no right to impose their (irrelevant and old-fashioned) values on their students. Teachers know that many things need to be learned that are not fun, and that students are not the best judges of what they must learn. Few students take to Shakespearean plays at first sight, but many people enjoy Shakespeare throughout life because they were once forced to read and study a play against their will.

Another set of reforms is also popular with teachers: the end of "social promotion" and "social graduation." For many years it has been a practice in most school districts to move students from grade to grade, whether or not they had mastered what they were supposed to. In many schools they were promoted even if they did not attend school, and the same philosophy prevailed when the time came to hand out diplomas. Teachers are not sure that holding a student back twice (and just what do you do with the six-foot sixteen-year-old who is still at second-grade level in reading and math?) will do that student much good; but they do believe that many students who might work and study harder and achieve more don't do their work or master their subjects because they see that those who don't do their work—and even those who don't attend classes—get the same rewards. The policy that rejects automatic promotion or graduation may not help the hard-core nonachieving child to learn, but it will spur the learning and achieving student on to greater efforts.

Almost all the reports deplore the disappearance of homework, or at least its decline. Most teachers agree. Students cannot learn it all in school. Homework increases time on task, and it tests a student's ability to work independently. Homework can be part of a process of inculcating good work habits and responsibility. But it is easier for legislators and administrators to mandate homework than it is for teachers to deal with some of the problems homework creates. One is the time it takes the teacher to correct homework assignments. Suppose a high school teacher has five classes a day with 30 students in each. Marking 150 papers would take almost eight hours, assuming that each paper takes only three minutes to mark. Many papers take longer to mark, and many teachers teach 175 or even 200 or more students each day. Of course, smaller class size and the use of outstanding college students as helpers could reduce the load, but new burdens have been placed on teachers while the help is still to come. Another problem with homework centers around students who don't know how to do it when they get home and who have no one to help them, or students who repeatedly refuse to do it. What does a teacher do when half the students have done the assignment and half have not? Proceed as if all had done it, leaving half the class in the dark? Go over the work so that those who did not do it can catch up, leaving those who did it to question why they did? Clearly, the existence of such problems is no argument against homework, but teachers should not be left holding the bag. School policies and resources are needed to back up the teachers.

Another reform idea has been less controversial among teachers than among their unions, the requirement that teachers be tested before entering teaching. Most teachers accept the idea in spite of the campaign against it by the National Education Association. The NEA has argued that passing an exam in math or English does not prove that a person is going to be a good teacher. Of course that's true. Knowing your subject is a necessary but not sufficient condition. Passing the test is not enough to make one a teacher; other qualities need to be looked for. But if the test is failed, that should be enough to decide that the person will not be a teacher, no matter what other qualities he or she has. It is also argued that requiring an examination is an insult to the prospective teacher and the college or university he/she went to, but that argument doesn't hold up very well. What about graduates of law schools who take bar exams, and the exams taken by doctors, accountants, actuaries. Teaching, up to now, has been the only profession or skilled occupation in which an examination has not been required, and recent evidence shows the results. Very large numbers of teacher applicants in states that require an examination fail to pass, and the examinations that they fail rarely test more than knowledge the students are expected to have at the same elementary or secondary level the teacher will be teaching.

Finally, teacher exams are criticized because they have an adverse impact on the hiring of minority teachers. Some have gone so far as to call either the examinations or those who advocate their requirement racist. Fortunately there are few buyers for this line. Teachers must know their subjects. If black and Hispanic applicants do not pass the test in sufficient numbers, the solution is not to throw out the tests or standards but to do a better job of educating minority students, so that when they take the test, they will pass it. An unqualified teacher can do as much damage as an unqualified doctor or airline pilot. There is no more justification for abandoning standards in this field than in the others.

There are other recommendations for excellence and reform that have received a much cooler reception from teachers. There has been a push for a longer school day, but if students are now to be required to take many tough subjects and to do homework, how much time is left? Should we not wait to see the effect of these changes before requiring a longer day? Should we not do the same about a longer year? There are a few issues involved here. Are there other changes that would give us the same improvements for less money or greater achievement for the same money? In addition to these issues, however, is the fact that most teachers feel that the time they now spend in school teaching is already too much. The general public may not understand, but any mother who has spent two or three rainy days in the house with two or three children ought to appreciate the plight of the teacher locked in a room with twenty-five, thirty, or thirty-five. It's a job full of tension. Most teachers are exhausted with their current workload. Any required additions to the day or year for teachers must take into account the impact of such changes on retaining our present workforce and attracting able new recruits. If more work is required without a higher salary, the effect would be devastating. It may be almost as devastating even if more money is given.

Most opposition from teachers and their organizations has been directed at merit pay proposals and those career ladder schemes that really are traditional merit pay plans. Teachers have asked: Who does the evaluation? How can personal bias be eliminated from the process? What is evaluated? If some teachers are designated "merit teachers," "master teachers," or "superior," will all the others who are doing an acceptable job be viewed as inferior, inadequate, incompetent? What happens to teacher morale? Will student ability or socioeconomic status, rather than teacher superiority, play the more important role? If the criteria include student performance, will teachers refuse to accept students who are more difficult to teach? Will parents complain and feel cheated if their children do not get the merit teachers? Would the teacher who is politically supportive of the administration be rewarded with merit? Would the teacher who creates good public relations for the system be rewarded? If the numbers who can be granted merit raises are limited by budget, will there be resentment among deserving teachers who are bypassed? Will time spent on evaluating teachers to determine merit take away from the time that should be spent with students? Will teachers give guidance and help to each other, will they cooperate, if they are competing for merit raises? Is the process of evaluation needed to find the merit teachers too costly and time consuming? Would teachers avoid less showy projects for more showy ones? Has any merit plan in operation now, or used in the past, been credited with educational improvement? If not, should any merit pay plans be put into widespread use until several are found to be successful in limited experiments?

In spite of serious reservations and outright opposition to merit pay, many teachers have shown a willingness to entertain such proposals since the excellence movement began. The reasons are clear. In a number of states, merit pay was an inseparable part of a package, and teachers, though still opposed to merit pay, were not about to kill a package that contained many improvements because they did not like one part of it. But there has also been the realization that much of the hope for future improvements in public education rests with a continuing relationship with the business community. Outright rejection of merit pay or of any other reform proposal could very well lead our newfound allies in the business community to the conclusion that public schools cannot be changed, that the bureaucracy is too rigid, teacher unions, too powerful. They might well say, "Nothing's more important for the future of the country than good education. We've been giving much of our valuable time, and we're willing to give support for more taxes. But what do we get for it all? A wall of opposition. Abuse. Unwillingness to change. We tried, but now we're convinced—public schools can't be improved." Such an experience on the part of the business community might lead not only to a loss of its vital support, but to its outright opposition; to abandonment of public schools in favor of other alternatives such as private schools, through tax credits and vouchers. How teachers respond to the business community, governors, legislators, and the general public will determine the future of public education. There is no reason for teachers to merely swallow what they do not like or believe in. They should share their beliefs, their fears, and their experiences. They have every right to argue for their points of view. Most of the time, since they are the experts, their views will be accepted. But, even when they are not, the stakes for public education are so great that compromise is better than confrontation.

What is most wholesome about the current reform movement is the realization that none of the reforms will work unless there are competent teachers in sufficient numbers. Here there are real danger signs. The reports, rather than being critical of our teaching staff, actually indicated that the teachers we now have are the best we are likely to see for a long time. Schools benefited in the past from problems elsewhere in our society. Many good teachers came to us because there were no other jobs during the Great Depression. Others came because they preferred to fight in the classrooms rather than in Korea or Vietnam, at times when teaching in a difficult school meant a draft exemption. The largest pool of talent was provided by women, who found the doors to most professions closed. But we no longer enjoy these advantages. People no longer seek refuge in teaching. There is no depression-level unemployment. Indeed, we are about to experience a nation-wide labor shortage as members of the "baby bust" period enter the work-force. There is no military draft, and women are now free to enter many other occupations, and they're doing so. For the first time in modern school history, schools will have to do what most businesses have always done: compete on the open market for the talent they need. A million or more new teachers will be needed during the next decade. There are not enough enrolled to become teachers to meet the demand, and, if we give tests to keep out those who do not know their subjects, many who are training to be teachers will not be accepted. What must be done? How can we attract and keep good teachers?

It's likely that nothing short of a revolution in our schools will make teaching a profession and attract high-caliber people into our ranks. The revolution has to be dramatic, it has to be soon, and it has to be thorough. It has to involve compensation, conditions, and a level of management skill that is far better than what is typical today. Let us look at some ingredients of this revolution.

COMPENSATION

We have to make it possible for teachers to live decently, like other pro-fessionals. That means far more money than they now earn. The baby boomers of the sixties who are now coming into the workforce were weaned on the good life they saw on television. They are searching for careers that will enable them to provide it for themselves and their children, and, at the moment, teaching is not such a career. Starting salaries are a particular sore point, with teachers averaging about $14,500 to start while similarly educated people get anywhere from $5,000 to $12,000 more: accountants, $20,176; statisticians, $22,416; social workers, $23,907; computer analysts, $24,864; engineers, $26,844. Even those with virtually no educational qualifications start higher. Sanitation workers begin at over $20,000, and in New York City, those who repair the window shades in the schools with the $14,500-starting teachers begin at more than $19,000. With the exception of the most dedicated, those who see teaching as a calling in the same way some see the ministry as a calling, bright young people today are simply not going to make that kind of sacrifice for the first years of their careers. Yet these are the people we need to staff our schools.

But it is not just starting salaries. Teachers take inordinately long, far longer than any other college-educated people, to reach a maximum that is below that of most other professional careers. It takes fifteen to thirty years for a teacher to reach the $35,000-$40,000 salary range, often with a Ph.D. requirement, in the few places where $40,000 is even a possibility. "Beyond the Commission Reports/The Coming Crisis in Teaching," the July 1984 Rand Corporation study by Linda Darling-Hammond, recommends a salary range of $20,000-$50,000 to address what it projects as a severe general shortage of teachers over the next few years. Unfortunately, by the time such salaries are widely instituted, the salaries will probably have to be higher to remain reasonably competitive with other fields.

DISCIPLINE

It is pretty much a problem everywhere, but it hits hardest in the big cities: where classes are larger; where a huge percentage of the student population learns its social behavior—often its antisocial behavior—not in stable middle-class homes but in poverty-ridden ghetto streets; where children have more economic deprivation and more emotional and physical problems that they bring to school with them; where inadequacy in the English language is often a barrier to the most rudimentary communication. There are no easy answers to the discipline question, and most of those that have been proffered—such as educating children who chronically misbehave in separate facilities until they are ready to return to the mainstream—require additional funding. But unless we deal with discipline, we are sacrificing not only the education of the other children, those who are shortchanged when a teacher's time is taken up with one or two disruptive or even violent students, but also the capacity to attract the best teachers to the urban schools that need them most. Teachers want to teach the subjects they love, not to be a policeman or a jail warden. Morever, teachers tend to have come from working-class homes, and teaching was seen as a way up and out. Many simply do not want to return to the climate of urban disruption and violence they had hoped to leave behind. Until we make all the schools in our big cities safe and calm places where teachers can teach and students can learn, we will be confronted with a serious disincentive for the best and brightest to join or remain in teaching ranks.

WORKLOAD

I discussed the issue of class size earlier, and it is a burning one for most teachers. It has to come down. But while we are reducing the number of students teachers see and providing some help with paperwork genuinely related to their teaching, we had better do something to reduce the nonteaching chores that eat up a teacher's day and turn off the most talented veterans and recruits. Here's how Darling-Hammond described this aspect of a teacher's life in the Rand study:

You spend roughly 12 hours each week correcting papers, because you believe your students should write a theme each week. You feel guilty that this allows you to spend only 5 minutes per paper. You spend another 6 hours each week preparing for your five different sections, mostly writing up the behavioral objectives required by the system's curriculum guide, which you find meaningless and even counterproductive to your goals for your students. you do all of this after school hours, because your one preparation period is devoted to preparing attendance forms, doing other administrative paperwork, and meeting with students who need extra help. Between classes, you monitor hallways and rest-rooms, supervise the lunch room and track down truants.

Are there many young would-be teachers who graduated with honors in English who want to spend a large part of their time in school keeping attendance, prowling corridors and bathrooms, dodging flying objects in the school cafeteria? I suspect not. There are other people to whom such tasks can and should be assigned—guards, clericals, paraprofessionals, and others. Teachers ought to teach—and be provided with time to think.

MATCHING

If we want to retain and woo good teachers, it is time for school systems to do a better job of looking at teachers as individuals and matching them with the students *they* are interested in and capable of teaching. Some teachers prefer to have a broad range of students every year. Others would like to be paired with one age or intellectual level in a given year and a different group the next. Some teachers would be terrified to confront classes of very bright students every day, while others who are expert in their fields would thrive on that challenge. In any school system of substantial size there are different kinds of schools that may be appropriate for some teachers, inappropriate for others. The business of assigning teachers almost at random and certainly without regard to their individual talents and desires is wrong for both teachers and students and counterproductive to attracting the kind of people we need in teaching.

Some years ago the principal of New York City's High School of Music and Art, a specialized school that selects students competitively, based upon their talent in these fields, telephoned me in desperation. Could I possibly speak to someone high up at the board of education to make sure that the talents of the teachers being assigned to the school were equal to the challenge of educating these precocious youngsters? He was losing teachers who did not feel up to it—and doubtless there were extremely fine teachers in less selective schools who were leaving out of boredom, because they and their students were mismatched. I made the call, but, frankly, I don't know how much was done about it. I have a feeling that teachers are still being assigned more or less randomly not only to what is now the Fiorello H. LaGuardia High School of Music and the Arts at Lincoln Center, but also to such equally selective academic high schools as Stuyvesant and Bronx Science, where budding young geniuses are perfectly capable of wearing out their teachers in no time at all. Of course, school systems have other things on their minds, including civil rights mandates (the worthwhile business of integrating school faculties, for example). But here's an issue whose resolution would seem to be in the interest not only of teachers but of the students as well.

"Matching" should also go beyond pairing up certain teachers with specific schools or groups of students. Intelligent school administration should be able to assess the professional needs and desires of individual faculty members and endeavor to meet them. Some teachers are perfectly happy to be doing in their thirty-fifth year exactly what they were doing in their first. Others need to be challenged by doing something different each year or every couple of years. There are many jobs within a school that some teachers will enjoy and others will not—working with the student newspaper or magazine, for example. There ought to be much more effort to match the right teacher to the right activity, based upon individual talent and preference. Of course, this means that the principal really has to know and understand his or her teachers and not regard them as interchangeable parts on a factory assembly line. Which brings me to the most important issue of all.

PROFESSIONALISM

The word *professional* has had a checkered history in our schools. For the most part it's been used in an Orwellian way, to mean exactly the opposite of what it means to most people. "Act like a professional" is something management thunders when it wants teachers not to rock the boat, not to be critical, not to be disobedient. But when most of us talk about a person who is a professional, we mean someone who is expert in his or her field, and by virtue of that expertise is relatively unsupervised and has a high degree of independent decision-making power. That's what distinguishes a professional from another kind of worker, one who has the whole job laid out by someone else or by an assembly-line process that requires close supervision. Professionals exercise their own judgment and take action based upon that judgment most of the time.

Are today's teachers in today's schools professionals? Far from it. For the most part, school management continues to adhere to old, ritualistic practices that date from a time when supervisors were the only adults in schools who had college degrees and, therefore, were in a position to tell teachers what to do and how to do it. That teachers are just as highly educated as supervisors now—with many teachers far more qualified in their fields than those supervising them—seems to have made no difference at all. Teachers are treated like children. Principals admit that when they were teachers, the procedure by which their principals "observed" them—that is, sat in the back of the room, watched a lesson, wrote an evaluation, and discussed it with them—helped them not at all to become better teachers. Yet they continue to follow the same practice with those they supervise today, although none can give a satisfactory response as to why they adhere to this useless ritual. Some principals require teachers to prepare lockstep lesson plans. A couple of years ago New York City high school teachers were in a state of great demoralization because most principals were demanding that they prepare detailed plans, written according to a particular management-by-objectives approach. Since most of these teachers were specialists in their fields, many with Ph.D.'s, and had taught for years without this rigid requirement, they bitterly resented what they saw as just another time-consuming power play by the principals. Of course, teachers do plan, especially high school teachers, but there doesn't seem to be any reason why all the plans have to follow the identical format, why they all have to be inspected on the same morning—or why an outstanding teacher may be given an "unsatisfactory" rating for failing to meet the planbook mandate, while a marginal teacher (or perhaps one who is truly unsatisfactory) who submits to all the rituals is given high marks.

If anyone thinks that schools can continue to treat teachers so unprofessionally, indeed like children, and attract bright, young self-directed college graduates into teaching, he or she is sadly mistaken. Even after we have solved the problems of providing adequate compensation, dealing with discipline, reducing the workload, achieving a better match of teachers with students and with the teachers' professional interests, we are not going to get good teachers or keep them so long as school management rewards blind obedience to authority above creativity and excellence—so long as teachers are regarded as incapable of making their own professional judgments.

Incidentally, the problem is not only with principals and other supervisors, nor even with superintendents and school boards. In the wake of the excellence reports, legislatures in nearly all the states—and sometimes governors—are busy telling teachers what to do and how to do it, including which textbooks to use. The decision-making power is not devolving upon teachers as it should. Instead, we seem back in the era of about twenty years ago, of designing "teacher-proof" curricula and materials, once again refusing to permit teachers to make professional judgments and act on them. It won't work. It will spur the best to bail out sooner and the best prospects to look to other careers.

Isn't it time to take the professional education decisions away from bureaucrats—near or distant—and put them into the hands of teachers? What kinds of decisions? On textbooks—teachers are the ones who use textbooks with children, know what works and what doesn't, should evaluate and select them. Curriculum design—why not have teachers shape the courses they will teach and build in the flexibility most teachers know they need? The very way a school is organized—teachers should be able to help determine, let's say, whether a high school has a large number of students who engage in independent study, some large-group instruction, and some seminar-type smaller groups. Teacher evaluation—until teachers are given and accept the same type of peer evaluation as exists in other professions, teaching will continue to be something less; teachers should be engaged in training, helping, and evaluating the newcomers, and in making the decisions as to who gets tenure and who doesn't. In Toledo, Ohio, the union and school management negotiate such a peer review system that deals not only with newcomers but with veterans who, by the consensus of their peers, may be in need of collegial "intervention."

Will all teachers want to serve on the committees charged with doing these things? No, but most will welcome the opportunity to do so. Will some be better at it than others? Of course, and the selection cannot and should not be on the basis of popularity, activity in the union, or any other irrelevant consideration but, rather, on the basis of recognized expertise and excellence. I believe existing teachers are eager to be trusted to engage in this kind of decision making—and that we will only get the talented newcomers we need if they see this kind of professional challenge as a vital part of their future career.

There is another plus. Some teachers do not mind being locked up in classrooms with children for their entire careers. But many, perhaps most, would welcome the opportunity to deal with other adults, colleagues, in the course of their work lives. (Recently in New York City, a teacher encountered an officer of the union on a city bus. In the course of conversation on professional issues, the teacher noted, sadly, that in the course of seventeen years of teaching in the same Lower East Side school, she had never had the opportunity to see another teacher teach!) Interacting with other teachers in these professional areas would enable teachers to fill that void—and it would do much more. It would give them a sense of ownership of the enterprise—a stake in the outcome—that is a much more powerful motivator than being treated as a hired hand.

But even if we do most of these things, it will be hard to get the staff we need, especially in those areas for which there is great competition in the private sector, the military, and other government work. I'm thinking particularly of those trained in mathematics and the physical sciences. A number of new and promising strategies are emerging: (1) Provide college scholarships for the best and brightest high school students who promise to teach one year for each year of scholarship support given. Many do not want to spend their entire lives in teaching, but would agree to give four or five years. The presence of a large number of academically outstanding teachers would be a big plus for the schools, and when they leave for important positions in the outside world they can provide a continuing base of support and understanding. (2) Give graduate fellowships for an M.A. to the best and brightest college seniors who are willing to commit to teaching for a period of time. (3) Offer to pay for a one-year graduate program, an M.A. in teaching, for retirees between the ages of fifty and sixty who have degrees in math, science, and other fields, have retired from successful careers in business or government, and are willing to teach for five or more years.

The excellence reports were a good way to bring about some fast and mostly needed changes. But they neglected some of the critical teacher-related issues I have discussed above. And there are one or two additional issues that received scant mention and need more emphasis. The first is the so-called equity issue, which ought to be better defined. There are many students in school who are learning students. They can and do learn. The new requirements imposed by the excellence movement will mean they will learn more. But there are also many nonlearning students. The excellence movement, so far, does nothing for them. To use an analogy: If you take a pretty good swimmer who has been swimming only a few yards a day and set a standard that he must swim x yards each day, he will do it. But if, at the same time, you make the same demand from an absolute nonswimmer or one who has tried to swim many times but has completely given up, throwing him into the water and demanding that he meet this new and higher standard will not lead, as in the case of the first swimmer, to higher levels of performance and achievement but, rather, to drowning. There are at least two approaches that ought to be tried to address this kind of inequity.

Most of the reports dealt with the high schools, because that is where the students are who are about to go to work or to college. But problems seen in the high schools represent, in many, perhaps most, cases the accumulation of neglect in earlier years. The best evidence we have in terms of cost-effective investment is the latest longitudinal report on the disadvantaged youngsters enrolled in the Perry Pre-School Project in Ypsilanti, Michigan, at age three and followed until they were age nineteen along with a closely matched control group not exposed to the advantage of a high-quality preschool program. The research (reported in *Changed Lives*, The High Scope Press, Ypsilanti, Michigan, 1984) showed that the preschool group had nearly double the rates of employment and participation in college or vocational training after high school of the control group. The preschool girls as teenagers had just over half the pregnancies that the control group females had. The preschoolers were involved in 20 percent fewer arrests and detentions, and nearly 20 percent less had dropped out of school. The economic benefits to the Perry graduates and to society were estimated at more than seven times the cost of one year's operation of the program. Clearly, high-quality preschool education ought to be at the top of the excellence agenda. Yet it is not even discussed in most of the reports.

Also absent from all of these reports—and the current discussion—is the near-universal experience that children who do not learn to read, write, and count fairly well by the time they are in the fourth and fifth grades do not learn in school later, no matter what kind of remediation we provide. A child who has been in a classroom with a teacher, chalkboard, books, and fellow students from kindergarten through third grade or fourth—four or five years —and hasn't made it feels himself a failure, believes he is stupid, will not continue to believe that he can learn, and will not try. The evidence is clear. Some stop coming to school. Others come and act out disruptively or even violently, preventing others from learning too. Some sit in the back of the room, sleep, or read comic books or scan rock magazines, as if to say, "Teacher, you leave me alone, I'll leave you alone." Will these students ever learn to read and write? Some do, but not in school. Some learn later at work. Some in organizations such as the Boy Scouts. Why shouldn't schools provide out-of-school alternatives for those who have lost faith in themselves by the fourth or fifth grades? Experimentation is called for here since, for the school and for these students, nothing could be worse than doing more of the same.

"Excellence" and Student Class, Race, and Gender Cultures

Lois Weis

Just then Jack turned around. "Hey, you guys, my brother says he and some guys from the high school are going to put on a kegger [of beer] next week over in Forest Grove. I'll bet we could get a ride over."

"OK," Steve said emphatically. "Can you get a bag [of marijuana]?" Jack said, looking at Don. "I'll manage." Don smiled on his way into the science room. As we sat down, the four of them—Jack, Don, Steve, and Morris—began a chorus of their favorite song.

"'And I said no-no-no-no, I don't smoke it no more, I'm tired of waking up on the floor; No thank you, please, it only makes me sneeze, And then it makes it hard to find the door.'"

The bell rang. Mr. Franks barked out, "Class, turn to page 328 in your science books. And stop the singing back there. Don, yesterday you remember . . . , I told you about igneous rocks . . ."

(from Robert Everhart, *Reading, Writing and Resistance*)

Many of the recent reports on "Excellence in Education" tend to assume that student cultures can be manipulated easily. The production of "excellence," for example, has been linked in the various reports to a longer school day, pay increases for teachers, more rigorous teacher training, a "core" curriculum, less federal and/or state control, increased attention to the traditional academic subjects, and increased attention to science and technology. The attempt is to alter certain school-related factors, with the assumption that altering such factors will produce higher achievement scores among students.[1]

The reports which fall under the rubric of "Excellence" do not say the same thing.[2] As Kelly points out in this volume, there are striking differences within the current set of proposed reforms, and it is a mistake to view the reports as monolithic. They differ internally in terms of the criteria by which they assess schooling in the first place, the kinds of prescriptive statements made with respect to the curriculum, the extent to which they support teacher autonomy, and the level at which they lay responsibility for implementing proposed reforms.[3]

There is agreement, however, that our educational system needs improvement. There also seems to be tacit agreement that a key level in the system is the secondary school. The American high school is in deep trouble, whether because of low achievement scores, student boredom, or lack of attention paid to the creation of students capable of consuming and especially producing high-level scientific and technological knowledge presumably linked to the maintenance of America's position as a world power. While the criteria through which the schools are assessed and the proposals for reforms themselves are different, there is general consensus that *something* is wrong with the nation's schools.

Although the reports differ in some rather profound ways, they all assume student cultures can be *made* to change. This assumption—that student outcomes are a simple function of certain within-school factors and can be altered if only these factors are manipulated—is incorrect. Student outcomes are tied rather directly to the cultures students themselves produce within the institutions in which they reside. These cultures do not arise in relation to within-school factors alone. While elements of student cultures may represent a response to certain school practices, the practices that might elicit such response are not pinpointed in the reports.

John Goodlad and Theodore Sizer both acknowledge the importance of student cultures in relation to school outcomes. Goodlad, for example, talks about the intensity of nonacademic interests among students and indicates that "research findings regarding the youth culture lead one to wonder why we have taken so little practical account of them in schools."[4] Sizer is even more straightforward when he discusses the effects of student culture. Whether students go along with the structures of the school or not, he argues, they possess "the autonomous power not to." The fact that most students go along with the system masks the actual power students hold—they can always collectively, whether quietly or not, decide to say no.[5]

Despite the fact that Goodlad and Sizer acknowledge the importance of student culture in relation to school outcomes, neither take serious account of these cultures in their proposals for reform; and neither address the reasons why student cultures take the shape and form that they do. The remainder of the proposals do not, for the most part, take student cultures into account at all. This lack of attention to these cultures, and the reasons why such cultures arise will, as I argue here, contribute to the almost certain failure of this newest round of reforms.[6]

This chapter challenges the assumption that student outcomes can be altered easily through a change in factors, such as those outlined in the reports. It will be argued that student cultures play a key mediating role in the production of school outcomes, and that such cultures are not a simple response to practices either within or outside the schools. Student cultures are, rather, semi-autonomous and, as such, cannot be controlled easily or directly. They arise in relation to structural conditions in the larger society and the way in which these conditions are mediated by both the experience of schooling and the lived experiences of youth in their own communities. None of the proposals for reform address these issues. Since student cultures are closely linked to school outcomes, such outcomes cannot be altered in any substantial way by manipulating within-school factors, such as those noted in the reports.

This chapter addresses the following questions: what do student cultures look like; what gives rise to them; and to what extent might they respond to school-based alterations such as those proposed in the excellence reports? I will explore these issues through an examination of recent work on class, race, and gender cultures by Paul Willis, Linda Valli, Robert Everhart, Angela McRobbie, John Ogbu, and myself.[7] The overriding question is, to what extent can we alter student outcomes, given the cultures students themselves produce within educational institutions and the reasons why such cultures take the shape and form that they do? I use the organizing categories class, race, and gender since these constitute areas of key structural tension. Such structural tensions are worked on and through at the level of student-lived culture, producing distinct cultural forms. The school provides an arena in which such tensions are lived out, worked upon, and partially created anew.

SOCIAL CLASS

Paul Willis's study of working-class boys in England provides an excellent example of the way in which student outcomes are at least partially created at the cultural level by the students themselves, irrespective of input at the official or pragmatic operating level.

Learning to Labour is an ethnographic account of a group of working-class boys at an all-male comprehensive school in an industrial area of England. Rather than internalize messages distributed through the school, the "lads" self-consciously reject school-based meanings and spend their time "working the system," in order to gain some control over obligatorily spent time: they use school time to "have a laff." The "ear 'oles," in contrast (so named by the lads because they simply sit and listen), comply with educational authority and the notions of qualifications and credentials. The lads actively differentiate themselves from the "ear 'oles" and school culture generally, categorizing them as effeminate and unrelated to the masculine world of work.

The most obvious dimension of the lads' culture is generalized opposition toward authority and school meanings. The lads engage in behavior designed to show resentment while stopping just short of outright confrontation. They also exhibit extensive absenteeism, signaling their generally oppositional stance; their "struggle to win symbolic and physical space from the institution and its rules and to defeat its main perceived purpose: to make you 'work'."[8] The core skill here is being able to get out of any given class, thus preserving personal mobility within the school. Personal mobility encourages the preservation of the collective--cutting class means meeting friends elsewhere. This can be seen as a limited defeat of "individualism."

Willis's ethnography is important in that it demonstrates that we cannot assume that meanings distributed through schools are internalized by students. Just because schools legitimate certain norms and forms of knowledge does not mean that students necessarily accept these valuations. In the lads' case, though the school encouraged independence and achievement (as it relates to specific knowledge forms), the lads inverted these valuations and embraced the opposite. Opposing school-based meanings was valued at the lived cultural level. It became as important to the lads *not* to succeed as it was to school authorities that they *do* succeed.[9] Thus school "failure" is not necessarily defined as such on the cultural level.

Willis's analysis goes further, however, in important ways. By rejecting the world of the school and the compliance of the "ear 'oles," the lads rejected mental labor, cross-valorising, patriarchy, and the distinction between mental and manual labor. Thus, manual labor became associated with the social superiority of masculinity, and mental labor with the social inferiority of femininity. Since, as Harry Braverman, Michael Buroway, and others have argued, hierarchical capitalist social relations demand the progressive divorce of mental from manual labor, and certainly profit from (if not demand) gender-based distinctions, the lads' rejection of the world of the school, and the way in which this rejection is linked to masculinity, reproduces at an even deeper level the social relations of production necessary for the maintenance of a capitalist economy.[10] Although the lads live their rejection of the school as a form of cultural autonomy and freedom, they help, at the level of their own culture, to reproduce existing social structures.

It must be clear, however, that cultural production (and the shape and form that lived cultures take) is not a conscious response nor does it lie in any individual act. Its logic lies only at the *group* level; the behavior represents a creative response to a set of lived conditions. It arises out of definite circumstances in a specific historical relation. While not predetermined and certainly not conscious, it is also not accidental.[11] I will return to this point later in the chapter.

In highlighting Willis's study, I do not mean to imply that the English and American cases are identical, nor that working-class students in Britain are the same as working-class students in the United States. Britain has had a more overt set of class antagonisms than the United States and a sense of "working classness" will differ to some extent simply on that basis. My point here is not to suggest that American students are like Willis's lads; they may or may not be. What is important is the way in which student culture acts to shape school outcomes. It is not the case that the lads are less "intelligent" (as measured by standardized tests) than "successful" students. In fact, a number of the lads had been among the most intelligent students, relinquishing this position only when they decided to become a lad.

A second example of working-class cultural forms comes from Robert Everhart's ethnography of a junior high school in the United States. Unlike Willis, Everhart does not focus on those students who create overtly oppositional forms in school. He focuses, instead, on those who compromise with school culture, giving the bare minimum, taking care to complete necessary assignments without causing undue trouble.

That Everhart's students complete assignments and do not overtly reject school content or form does not mean that they are involved with the process of schooling, nor that their valuation of achievement qua achievement is any different from that of the lads. All it means is that they don't value the specific and overt negation of school meanings in the same way that the lads do. Students view school as a place to meet friends, "goof off," smoke a joint, and pursue other activities that are not related to the official learning process. To students at Harold Spencer Junior High School, it was important "that one should conform to the requirements of the school in sufficient detail so as to 'get by,' all the while creating a separate culture that permitted the maximum elements of self-determination."[12]

Students create their own cultures within schools and these cultures have a great deal to do with the production of academic outcomes—with what students "choose," so to speak, to value. It is not simply within-school factors (teachers, curriculum, etc.) that "create" student "success" as the current reports on the schools suggest. Outcomes are mediated by the culture students produce themselves.

Such cultures are materially grounded. They are, in many ways, sensible responses to existing social structures—structures that are strikingly unequal by class, race, and gender. While Willis and Everhart offer different explanations for the culture students produce, both are, at their root, structural, while at the same time allowing for some creative response to existing conditions. It is not simply that working-class students come from homes where education is not valued (which is not necessarily the case in any event) and that they, in turn, act on this valuation in school. Such students are not necessarily less intelligent than middle-class students either. It is also not true that working-class students become working class simply because schools prepare them specifically to do so by offering them only course work in vocational areas.[13]

Willis suggests that the basic determinants of cultural form can only be found below the surface of ethnography in a more interpretive mode. He argues that the lads' rejection of so much of the form and content of schooling stems from an unconscious (and correct) realization that while working-class youth can succeed as individuals, schooling will not work for the working class as a whole. Only the destruction of the entire class structure could do the latter.[14] This insight is only partial, however. Paradoxically, insights about schooling that the lads exhibit on the cultural level are "bound back finally into the structure they are uncovering in complex ways by internal and external limitations. There is ultimately a guilty and unrecognized—precisely a partial—relationship of these [insights] to that which they seem to be independent from and see into."[15]

Everhart also stresses the relative autonomy of student cultural form. He draws attention to what he calls reified knowledge—knowledge that while abstract, tenuous, and problematical is treated as if it is concrete and "real."[16]

> Such knowledge is treated unequivocally as a fact and as information to be used in the formation of real (empirical) relationships said to exist between these facts . . . . The world of education is that which supplies objective facts, concrete and agreed upon, that are to be learned, manipulated, and applied in an empirical fashion towards predefined ends.[17]

In contrast, regenerative knowledge is that which students themselves produce. It is based on mutuality of communication and "created, maintained, and re-created through the continuing interaction of people in a community setting and because what is known is, in part, dependent upon the historical forces emerging from within the community setting."[18] Regenerative knowledge is *experienced* by students as socially constructed—they feel that they have a hand in its creation. This is not the case with reified knowledge. Student regenerative knowledge is oppositional to school knowledge. While students exert no control over reified knowledge (either its production or the process through which they are supposed to consume it), they exert substantial control over regenerative knowledge. Furthermore,

> regenerative knowledge and its creation and recreation among students reveals that the deterministic forces of the school, as exemplified by reified knowledge, do not always take root and in fact may scarcely be paid any attention to at all. The student culture and the regenerative knowledge that grows from it may serve to resist that alienative aspect of learning by creating oppositional forms that contradict the mechanistic process of school learning.[19]

Everhart conceptualizes students qua students as a class. In school they learn that they have little control over either the process or product of their own labor. They, in turn, create their *own* knowledge—their own set of valuations and styles[20] that includes humor, jokes, and "goofing off" rather than, in Robert Dreeben's terms, the norms of independence, achievement (as it relates to school knowledge), universalism, and specificity.[21] Students create a "separate reality"—one that is under their control and not the institution's. (It does, of course, emerge dialectically in relation to the institution.) Within their own culture, students accord little value to official school knowledge and maximum value to humor, "goofing off," and control of their own space and time within the school.

Willis and Everhart make it clear that shcool outcomes are not under the control of school authorities alone. Outcomes are, in some rather serious ways, under the control of the student culture--a culture that is produced within educational settings and differs by class, race, and gender.

RACE

The issue of race is particularly important.The American population as a whole is aging, but the youth population among blacks and Hispanics remains large and is proportionately increasing. In 1980, less than one-third of white Americans were nineteen years old and under. Forty-three percent of Hispanics and 40 percent of blacks were of comparable age. In 1981, 52 percent of white families had children of school age whereas 71 percent and 75 percent of black and Hispanic families, respectively, had children under eighteen years old.[22] This has profound significance for schools of the future: the population of minority students is growing and this is precisely the group with which schools have been least "successful."

Both John Ogbu and I explore minority student culture in schools. While Ogbu focuses on the common school and I focus on the community college, our conclusions regarding the elements of minority student culture are rather similar.

Ogbu's study begins with the question, why do some children do so badly in school, especially minority children? The main thesis of his study, which was conducted in Stockton, California, is that the "high proportion of school failures among subordinate minorities is both a reaction to and adaptation to the limited opportunity available to them to benefit from their education."[23]

While it is often argued that minority parents do not care about their childrens' schooling, thus accounting for the high failure rate among these groups, Ogbu suggests that this is not the case. There is strong indication that the educational goals of "Burgherside" parents and their children are, in general, higher than those of white working-class families and higher than they were some years ago.

It is nevertheless true that the failure rate of minority students is exceptionally high. Ogbu documents this for Burgherside and suggests that this phenomena must be rooted historically. Blacks and Mexican Americans did not have equal access to the occupational structure. Minorities do not achieve well in school because of adaptations they made in the past, when members of subordinate minority groups were not allowed to receive social and economic benefits from education. Burghersiders fail to meet their *own* educational goals, not because they try and cannot do the work but because they do not even try to do the work.[24] Thus a major component of minority "lived culture" in school is the minimization of effort. This minimization must be seen historically; blacks and other subordinate minorities have not had equal access to valued goods in the society. Ogbu argues as follows:

It would appear from their tradition of collective struggle in the field of education that caste-like minorities have looked to formal education as a means of improving their social and occupational status, if not for achieving full status with the dominant group. But their expectations have not been met because their education is not designed to help them do so and because of institutional barriers against them in adult life. They have responded to this situation, it appears, in a number of ways that have actually tended to reinforce their educational preparation for marginal economic participation. Some of these responses include conflict with the schools, disillusionment, lowered efforts, and survival strategies.[25]

In my recent ethnography of black students in the community college, I draw similar conclusions. Like Ogbu, I find that student cultural form is, in itself, contradictory: students embrace and reject schooling at one and the same time. They affirm the process that is education but drop in and out of school, arrive late to class, exert little effort, and engage in extensive drug use that serves to distance them from the process of schooling. As I argue in *Between Two Worlds,* the effects of the culture are twofold: (1) an exceedingly low graduation rate per entering class, and (2) the reproduction of deeply rooted race/class antagonisms in the broader society.

Unlike the case for working-class whites, the form and content of education is, on one level at least, affirmed by blacks. At the same time, this affirmation is contradicted at the same lived cultural level.

Given that race has its own dynamic in the United States and that the economic position of white workers and black workers is different, it is not surprising that the elements of student culture differ by race. Along these same lines, cultural form is also affected by the nature of historic struggle for particular groups. The black struggle in the United States has, by necessity, taken a different form than the struggle for a better life among working-class whites. Blacks have, until recently, engaged in what Gramsci calls a "war of maneuver"—a situation in which subordinated groups seek to defend their territory from assault and develop their own society as an alternative to the existing system—a system in which they are relegated to the lowest possible status. Based on the strength gained through a "war of maneuver," black Americans were able to mount a subsequent "war of position"—a strategy that has sought to transform the dominant racial ideology in the United States, to rearticulate its elements in a more egalitarian and democratic discourse.[26] Both the fact that blacks constitute a castelike minority in the United States and the particular form that struggle had to take in the black community exert an impact on the shape and form of student culture.

While working-class white students overtly reject much of the form and content of schooling and act on this rejection within educational institutions, black student opposition will be coded differently, given my points above. Like working-class whites, however, blacks have understood the unequal reality they face. While they do not reject the form and content of schooling (this must be seen as historically oppositional in and of itself), their own lived culture reveals these impulses. Students realize to some extent the "true" value of education for blacks. Thus the pattern of exerting little effort that Ogbu uncovers, and the cultural elements that I describe at the community-college level must be seen as impulses within the culture toward a true understanding of the group within the social whole, despite the current ideology of "equality of opportunity" that suggests otherwise. Part of this is consciously understood by blacks.[27] This can be contrasted to working-class whites where this process is largely unconscious.

Black student culture arises in relation to social structure. Black students are, as a group, responding to very real conditions in the society, both historic and current. As Michael Olneck argues, the rates of return to schooling for blacks and whites are not the same. "The cost of being black" in the United States is that whites get greater rewards for any given amount of schooling than nonwhites. This is particularly true for elementary and secondary education; it is only upon completion of the bachelor's degree that the expected status advantage is larger for nonwhites than whites.[28]

While the cultures students produce in schools differ by class and race and represent a creative response to lived conditions, cultures are, in the final moment, bound to the social structure. Students do not respond *simply* to factors within schools. While such factors cannot be ignored (especially since certain school factors tend to parallel race/class lines in the United States), student culture cannot be seen in relation to institutional factors alone. Student cultures are dynamic, produced on-site, and linked in important ways to economic and social structures.

GENDER

Gender has its own dynamic in classrooms and schools. The very "stuff" of schooling normalizes the separation of prime responsibility in public and private domains for males and females. Sexist meanings and practices are embedded within authority and staffing patterns, subject-matter staff segregation, the formal curriculum, differential treatment within the classroom and school, and counseling.[29] There is no question but that the school "acts upon" students to reinforce gender-based meanings.[30]

My purpose here, however, is to focus on the culture females themselves produce. As in the case of class and race cultures, the reproduction of patriarchical relations on the cultural level cannot be seen simply as a response to educational policies and practices *or* broader economic and political arrangements.

Angela McRobbie's research on working-class girls in England is helpful here. While McRobbie's "girls," for the most part, endorse traditional "femininity," they do so as a creative response to their own lived conditions rather than as a passive acceptance of meanings imposed by either school or family. In spite of the fact that they know, for example, that marriage and housework are far from glamorous, they construct a fantasy future in which both realms are glamorous by elaborating what might be called an "ideology of romance." Like Willis's lads, these working-class girls create an anti-school culture, but one that is specifically *female* in that it consists of interjecting sexuality into the classroom, talking loudly about boyfriends, and wearing makeup. As McRobbie argues,

> Marriage, family life, fashion and beauty all contribute massively to this feminine anti-school culture and, in so doing, nicely illustrate the contradictions in so-called oppositional activities. Are the girls in the end not doing exactly what is required of them—and if this *is* the case, then could it not be convincingly argued that it is their own culture which itself is the most effective agent of social control for the girls, pushing them into compliance with that role which a whole range of institutions in capitalist society also, but less effectively, directs them towards? At the same time, they are experiencing a class relation, albeit in traditionally female terms.[31]

The extent to which working-class girls "achieve" in school is linked to the culture they produce within the institution. This culture, rather than express a valuation of achievement, expresses instead a valuation of the ability to work the school system to their own, specifically female, ends. These ends, like those of working-class males, are largely unconnected to the official culture of the school. The girls' culture is rooted in but not totally determined by the material position that they occupy—their social class, future role in production, and present and future role in domestic production.

Linda Valli's study of working-class girls in an American high school extends our understanding of the way in which gender culture and school outcomes are linked and the reasons why gender cultures take the form that they do. Valli studied a group of girls in a cooperative education program, a vocational program in which senior high students go to school part time and work part time in an office. She explored the way in which students construct work and family identities and, more specifically, the way in which ideologies regarding the family and the social and sexual division of labor impact upon the production of cultural forms.

Valli clearly documents the way in which gender culture shapes school-related behavior and choices. Taking the office preparation curriculum is "not the result of either 'office career aspirations' or an oppositional school culture. Instead, it represented a sensible accommodation to their future possibilities and probabilities as the students and their parents saw it. This view of future probabilities resulted not only from a realistic perception of the job market, but also from a notion of what was a good job 'for a woman'."[32]

Taking the office curriculum was perceived as the best of available options. Openings exist in the clerical area and the work was not seen as derogatory to the students' sense of femininity. Once in the program, the training the students received further marginalized their identities as wage laborers. The identity as workers outside the home was presented as secondary to a home/family identity. "While in some minimal ways the women may have rejected the ideology of male supremacy," Valli argues, "at a more fundamental level, they affirmed it, granting superiority and legitimacy to the dominance of men in a way that appeared spontaneous and natural."[33]

The girls' culture must be situated within ongoing social structural arrangements. In many ways, choosing the office work curriculum represents a "sensible" accommodation to sexist structures, in giving them *some* control over their own labor.[34] Unfortunately of course, such "choices" reproduce the very structures that give rise to them to begin with. As Valli states,

> Given the scarcity of professional level or interesting career-type jobs and the difficulty of handling such a job along with home/family responsibilities, the emphasis the co-op students placed on a traditional feminine code exhibited a certain amount of good sense. Reproducing a traditional culture of femininity can be interpreted as a way of escaping the tedious demands of wage labor and of denying it power over the self. It can even be seen as an unconscious resistance to capitalist domination. The irony, of course, is that this culture both reproduces patriarchical domination and fails to alter capitalist exploitation which is quite amenable to a segment of the skilled labor force having a tangential relation to it.[35]

In the final analysis, the girls, at the level of their own culture, opted out of academic areas and placed a low valuation on school knowledge and achievement. Once again then, culture mediates outcomes.

CULTURE AND "EXCELLENCE"

I have argued here that student cultures are tied to the production of academic outcomes. The current reports on the schools suggest that factors such as teacher training, curricular offerings, degree of federal and/or state control of schools, and so forth, "create" student "success." While this may be true to some extent, outcomes are linked to a far greater extent to cultures students themselves produce within schools.

These cultures arise in relation to existing social structures—structures that are strikingly unequal by class, race, and gender. Any proposal for reform that seeks to alter achievement levels but does not take into account these structures is doomed to almost certain failure. Given that cultures do not arise simply in relation to teachers, for example, how can we expect raising teacher salaries to impact on the form that student cultures take? How will changing curricular requirements impact upon student outcomes, given that valued practices and styles among students do not arise solely in relation to curriculum? Can we really affect student cultures through a set of within-school reforms that do not directly address the structures that give rise to them to begin with? I think not.

As I have argued throughout, student cultures must be seen as sensible responses to existing conditions. What students "choose" to value represents a creative response to the material conditions of their lives—to their position, as they experience it, as classed, raced, and gendered persons in a society such as our own. This does not mean that the form of such cultures is totally unrelated to what schools do. The cultures students produce in schools are at least partially a response to school practices themselves. In the case of the lads, for example, their working-class culture would not necessarily have produced in them the kinds of within-school actions that it did had the school not been so ignoring of their culture to begin with. By attempting to impose uncritically a middle-class cultural and reward system on students, the school elicited a stronger collective working-class response than might have been the case if the school had been more sensitive to working-class culture. My point here is that schools *may* be related to student culture in significant ways, but these relationships are tied to the lived experiences of students *outside* schools—to the material conditions of their lives, and the extent to which these material conditions are affirmed, denied, or simply ignored within educational institutions. At present, we possess relatively little knowledge about the ways in which school practices are actually linked to the production of student cultural form. This needs to be a central focus for future research on schools.[36]

It is possible, of course, to argue that the proposed reforms will produce higher test scores among those students whose lived culture reflects a valuation of academic achievement to begin with—in other words, middle-class students. While this is possible, I am uncomfortable with this notion for a number of reasons. To begin with, it is not at all clear to me that middle-class students haven't made similar compromises regarding school knowledge and culture. Linda McNeil's excellent study suggests that they have; that middle-class students also give the minimum, what they perceive as necessary to attend college, thus maintaining their positon in the class structure.[37] Secondly, the reports themselves tend to emphasize that "excellence" must be accompanied by equity, in which case the points raised here about class, race, and gender cultures are critically important. America is still not interested (at least on the ideological level) in totally abandoning equality of opportunity. This is reflected in the reports.

It is difficult for me to oppose the concept of "excellence." I support a number of the proposed reforms in that I would like to see more academic content in the schools, and I have never been a supporter of tracking.[38] All students should, I believe, be exposed to a solid academic curriculum. Teachers should be paid more, and they should exert more control over their own labor in the classroom. There is too much time wasted in school and there are too many classroom interruptions, often from the office by means of the public address system. Philip Cusick has pointed out that over three hours of a seven-hour school day is spent in procedural and maintenance details. A large part of the students' day is spent in a state of spectatorship during which time he or she simply watches and waits.[39] Others have made this same comment, most recently Everhart and Goodlad. Surely we have need for improvement simply on that score alone.

Stating that I support some of the proposed reforms does not mean that I believe that any of them will, *in and of themselves,* have the desired effect of raising achievement levels. In order for student cultures to change, there must be change in other sectors of the society. Class, race, and gender conflicts are historic in this country, and cultural creation in schools reflects historically rooted oppression, struggle, and adaptations on the part of different groups. These struggles have been waged and continue to be waged in a system that is highly unequal by class, race, and gender. Unless we address these inequalities and tensions directly in the economic, political, *and* cultural sphere where schools lie, we will not substantially affect school outcomes. Within schools, we need to acknowledge and legitimate the lived experiences of all students. At the same time, we must work toward altering society itself so that opportunity structures are more equal.

Even if such structures change, however, we will not see quick shifts on the cultural level. Culture embeds a peoples' historic trajectory—as such, it does not change overnight. I support some of the reforms because they are what I value. I also believe that extending a more serious academic curriculum in an across-the-board fashion may enable more individuals to attain the social mobility this country promises. Over time, this may lead to some alteration in the social structure, in that inequality may be more randomly distributed across class, race, and gender lines than it is currently. To think that we can alter school outcomes easily, however, is a mistake. We have much more to learn about *why* students behave in schools as they do before we assume we can control outcomes.

NOTES

I would like to thank Philip Altbach, Gail Kelly, and Linda McNeil for their comments on an earlier version of this chapter.

1. Although couched in different language, this is reminiscent of studies within the Coleman Report genre, where the attempt is to locate within-school factors that predict academic achievement. See, for example, Central Advisory Council for Education, *Children and Their Primary Schools,* Vols. 1 and 2. The Plowden Report (London: Her Majesty's Stationary Office, 1967); and James Coleman et. al., *Equality of Educational Opportunity* (Washington, D.C.: U.S. Government Printing Office, 1966).

2. Numerous reports fall under this rubric. The ones I am dealing with specifically include: National Commission on Excellence in Education, *A Nation at Risk: The Imperative for Educational Reform* (Washington D.C.: Government Printing Office, 1983); Ernest Boyer, *High School: A Report on Secondary Education in America* (New York: Harper and Row, 1983); John Goodlad, *A Place Called School: Prospects for the Future* (New York: McGraw-Hill, 1983); Theodore Sizer, *Horace's*

Compromise: The Dilemma of the American High School (Boston: Houghton Mifflin, 1984); Mortimer Adler, *The Paideia Proposal: An Educational Manifesto* (New York: Macmillan, 1982); and The National Science Board Commission on Precollege Education in Mathematics, Science, and Technology, *Educating Americans for the 21st Century*, 2 vols. (Washington, D.C.: National Science Foundation, 1983).

3. Gail Kelly, "The Reports on Excellence: Setting the Boundaries of Debate about Education," in this volume, 29–40.

4. John Goodlad, *A Place Called School*, 75–76.

5. Theodore Sizer, *Horace's Compromise*, 138–40.

6. The reform effort may fail for other reasons as well, of course. To begin with, reforms on paper are often not implemented. As Kelly points out in this volume, the proposed "excellence" reforms are themselves contradictory as well.

7. Paul Willis, *Learning to Labour: How Working Class Kids Get Working Class Jobs* (Westmead, England: Saxon House Press, 1977); Linda Valli, *Becoming Clerical Workers* (Boston: Routledge and Kegan Paul, 1986); Lois Weis, *Between Two Worlds: Black Students in an Urban Community College* (Boston: Routledge and Kegan Paul, 1985); Robert Everhart, *Reading, Writing and Resistance: Adolescence and Labor in a Junior High School* (Boston: Routledge and Kegan Paul, 1983); Angela McRobbie, "Working Class Girls and the Culture of Femininity," in *Women Take Issue*, ed. Women's Studies Group (London: Hutchinson, 1978): 96–108; and John Ogbu, *The Next Generation: An Ethnography of Education in an Urban Neighborhood* (New York: Academic Press, 1974).

8. Paul Willis, *Learning to Labour*, 26.

9. My point here is that the structure of the school promotes the consumption of a specific body of knowledge and set of norms. "Success" is measured by the extent to which students master this knowledge and act in terms of the norms. While "failure" may be functional in terms of the broader social structure, it cannot be argued that school authorities *want* to promote failure. Tracking may, of course, promote the "success" of one group over another.

10. See Harry Braverman, *Labor and Monopoly Capital* (New York: Monthly Review Press, 1974); and Michael Buroway, "Toward a Marxist Theory of the Labor Process: Braverman and Beyond," *Politics and Society* 8 (no. 3-4, 1978): 247-312.

11. See Paul Willis, *Learning to Labour*, 120-21, for a discussion of this important point.

12. Robert Everhart, *Reading, Writing and Resistance*, 121.

13. The latter point must be seen as a debate with the structuralists such as Althusser and Poulantzas. For a discussion of the culturalist/structuralist controversy, see Michael Apple, ed., *Cultural and Economic Reproduction in Education: Essays on Class, Ideology and the State* (London: Routledge and Kegan Paul, 1982), chapter 1; and Richard Johnson, "Histories of Culture, Theories of Ideology," in *Ideology and Cultural Production*, ed. Michele Barrett et al. (New York: St. Martin's Press, 1979): 49-77. For a structuralist perspective see Nicos Poulantzas, *Classes in Contemporary Capitalism* (London: New Left Books, 1975); Louis Althusser, "Ideology and Ideological State Apparatuses, in *Lenin and Philosophy, and Other Essays* (London: New Left Books, 1971); and Samuel Bowles and Herbert Gintis, *Schooling in Capitalist America* (New York: Basic Books, 1976).

14. Here I am simplifying a rather complex argument. For elaboration see Paul Willis, *Learning to Labour*, especially chapters 5 and 6.

15. Paul Willis, *Learning to Labour*, 119.

16. Robert Everhart, *Reading, Writing and Resistance*, 86.

17. Robert Everhart, *Reading, Writing and Resistance*, 86.

18. Robert Everhart, *Reading, Writing and Resistance*, 125.

19. Robert Everhart, *Reading, Writing and Resistance*, 129.

20. Such valuations on the cultural level are linked to the wider system of commercial youth culture that supplies a lexicography of style, with already connoted meanings that are adapted by various groups to express their own located meanings. These located cultural forms, in turn, affect the shape and form of commercial youth culture. This theme is pursued more extensively by Mike Brake, *The Sociology of Youth Culture and Youth Sub-Cultures* (London: Routledge and Kegan Paul, 1980).

21. Robert Dreeben, *On What is Learned in School* (Reading, Mass.: Addison Wesley, 1968).

22. Ernest Boyer, *High School*, 5.

23. John Ogbu, *The Next Generation*, 12.

24. John Ogbu, *The Next Generation*, 197.

25. John Ogbu, "Equalization of Educational Opportunity and Racial/Ethnic Inequality," in *Comparative Education*, ed. Philip Altbach, Gail Kelly, and Robert Arnove (New York: Macmillan, 1982): 269-89.

26. This is Omi and Winant's point. See Michael Omi and Howard Winant, "By the Rivers of Babylon: Race in the United States," *Socialist Review* 71 (September/ October 1983): 56.

27. Ogbu and I draw different conclusions here. Ogbu stresses the way in which castelike minorities consciously understand their subordination and therefore "blame the system" for their failure. I argue that, at least on the community college level, black students also blame themselves for failure. My point is that a tendency to blame the system exists side-by-side with the tendency to blame oneself.

28. Michael Olneck, "The Effects of Educaton", in *Who Gets Ahead?* Christopher Jencks et al. (New York: Basic Books, 1979): 150-70. For a careful analysis of the historical position of blacks in the American economy, see Michael Reich, *Racial Inequality* (Princeton, N.J.: Princeton University Press, 1981).

29. See Gail Kelly and Ann Nihlen, "Schooling and the Reproduction of Patriarchy: Unequal Workloads, Unequal Rewards," in *Cultural and Economic Reproduction in Education*, ed. Michael Apple (London: Routledge and Kegan Paul, 1982): 162-80.

30. This is true for class and race meanings as well.

31. Angela McRobbie, "Working Class Girls and the Culture of Femininity," 104.

32. Linda Valli, *Becoming Clerical Workers*, 102.

33. Linda Valli, *Becoming Clerical Workers*, 252.

34. Jane Gaskell points to the way in which sexual harassment also influences "job choice" for women. While there is certainly harassment in an office setting, it is less intense than that which is experienced in a traditionally male working-class area. See Jane Gaskell, "Course Differentiation in the High School: The Perspective of Working Class Females," (Paper presented in Symposium on Race, Class and Gender Analysis in Education—Implications for Curriculum Theory, Meetings of the American Educational Research Association, Montreal, April 1983).

35. Linda Valli, *Becoming Clerical Workers*, p. 263.

36. I must point out here that student cultures can serve to inform school practice in positive ways. Resistance in schools based on class, race, and gender cultures can, if understood, be taken into account in some kind of productive manner. One example might be the way in which the assertion of minority culture has impacted upon literature choice.

37. Linda McNeil, "Economic Dimensions of Social Studies Curricula: Curriculum as Institutionalized Knowledge," unpublished Ph.D. diss., University of Wisconsin—Madison, 1977.

38. Sizer's *Horace's Compromise*, for example, recommends the elimination of tracking.

39. Philip Cusick, *Inside High School: The Students' World* (New York: Holt, Rinehart and Winston, 1973).

Educational Reform and Teacher Education

Hugh G. Petrie

Somewhat surprisingly, the recent national reports on educational reform, with few exceptions, have had little to say about teacher education.[1] The major exception has been the Carnegie Foundation Report, *High School: A Report on Secondary Education in America.*[2] In this report Ernest Boyer calls for a revision of teacher education programs that would lead to establishing a five-year course of study. Students would, typically, spend the first four years of their college careers pursuing a standard liberal arts degree. They would follow this experience with a special fifth year devoted to pedagogy, albeit a revised pedagogy from that currently in existence in most colleges of education. In the Carnegie program teachers would study four subjects—schooling in America, learning theory and research, teaching of writing, and technology and its uses—in addition to participating in a variety of clinical experiences.

Another report, *Education for Economic Growth,*[3] calls for improved standards of teacher certification. Changes in certification, such as those called for in this report, would eventually have an effect on schools and colleges of education. John Goodlad, in *A Place Called School,*[4] gives passing and almost resigned acknowledgment to the necessity for improving teacher education. His major thrust is to call for two years of professional education, along with closer ties with school districts and more focused use of the research on effective teaching. Outside of these examples, most of the national reports simply do not address teacher education directly.

However, as many of us in colleges of education wryly remarked to each other when the national reports first began to appear, "Enjoy the lack of attention to teacher education while you can. We're next." And indeed we were. Once the broad-gauge issues of the national reports were translated into specific policy recommendations at the state level, teacher education began to receive its share of criticism and suggestions for reform. The cover story of the September 24, 1984, issue of *Newsweek,* "Why Teachers Fail: How to Make Them Better,"[5] was largely an attack on teacher education.

What happened was that the various national reports concentrated on teaching and teachers, correctly identifying the teacher as the key to educational reform. The issue of the quality of the nation's teaching force became a central issue in the reform debate. As that debate progressed, the states began to take stock of the policy options available to them to improve the quality of teaching.

The most obvious policy change, to attempt to attract higher quality candidates into teaching by raising teacher salaries, is being pursued to some degree. However, with the continuing financial difficulties of the country, this option cannot be relied upon as the sole means of improving quality. Indeed, most policy makers have said that more money will be available only if there is some hope that more money will bring improvements. There has been no desire to simply pay for more of the same. Consequently, states have turned to a consideration of nonmonetary policy options, and a number of these options emphasize the links between teacher quality and teacher preparation programs.

The various state-level initiatives and recommendations for educational reform, along with the indirect implications of the national reports, affect teacher education in a variety of ways. The problem is that many of the critics have taken only a superficial look at teacher preparation, and the recommendations they make often do not reflect the critical analysis of the situation for which one might hope. Although the issues affecting teacher education identified by the critics are indeed important, the typical suggestions made for dealing with these issues are often indefensible. In some cases the common wisdom, if pursued, would actually make the situation worse, rather than improving it. In other cases, it is time for colleges of education to realize that teacher education is not a monolithic whole and that some radical reforms are in order. In what follows I will consider the issues of pedagogy, certification, tests, institutional variability, and continuing professional development as these affect teacher education.

PEDAGOGY

Nothing seems so clear to many critics of education as the proposition that teaching teachers how to teach is a waste of time. According to this line of argument, pedagogy takes time away from the subject matter that teachers must master. In addition, courses in "methods of teaching" are thought to be universally dull, boring, and without intellectual merit. Furthermore, it is claimed that a good internship with a practicing teacher is really all that is required for pedagogical training. Thus, it is implied, we can get better teachers by eliminating the nonsensical hurdle of teacher education. It is assumed that bright students will flock to teaching if only we eliminate education courses.

Perhaps the most direct attck on teacher education has occured in the state of New Jersey, where traditional college-based teacher education has been bypassed entirely. As an alternative to the longstanding requirements for at least some courses in pedagogy in the preparation of teachers, New Jersey has established a system whereby any person with a bachelor's degree can become a teacher without any education courses at all. The only requirement is that the district in which the graduate is hired must provide a year-long apprenticeship program. Florida is considering a similar system.

Typically, the pedagogical component of teacher education programs is composed of courses in methods, the behavioral and humanistic foundations of education, and student teaching. If courses in methods of teaching were to be eliminated and student teaching given over to practicing teachers, then only foundations courses would be left. They could probably be taught by liberal arts departments almost as well as they are presently being taught in schools and colleges of education. In short, if there is no good argument for pedagogy, there is no good argument for teachers' colleges.

There is, however, a logical fallacy in the line of argument that suggests that education courses are unnecessary. The question is not *whether* anyone will learn how to teach. The question is rather *where* and *how* people will learn how to teach. Will they pick up hints in the teachers' lounge? Will they simply model teachers they have had? Will they be able to reflect upon and improve their teaching? Will they have the knowledge of instructional theory, classroom management, and curriculum design to adapt to new and changing circumstances? There is a significant difference between those professions or crafts in which one can simply pick up the tricks of the trade on the job, and those professions where a knowledge of the processes involved allows for critical reflection upon and improvement of one's performance. Perhaps plumbing can be taught solely by apprenticeship, but unless we wish education to stagnate, teaching cannot. If methods courses are inadequate, let us improve the methods courses. Let us not make the logical blunder of assuming that the question of how to teach will disappear if *courses* on how to teach disappear.

There is another point to be made in this connection. The last twenty years have seen a remarkable increase in our knowledge of how to prepare good teachers.[6] The effective-schools research, the work on classroom management, direct instruction, and time on task have all begun to place the practice of teaching on a firm knowledge base. As this work continues, it will improve our knowledge of how to train better teachers. This knowledge is not of recipes, but of principles. A knowledge of principles not only allows the practitioner to deal with routine and repetitive situations, but also to adapt to novelty and creativity. Teachers cannot simply be technicians. They must make too many individual decisions about effective instruction every moment of the day to simply follow instructions, no matter how detailed. The total failure of some twenty years ago to try to devise "teacher-proof" curricula demonstrates this point rather dramatically.

In any event, there is a widespread misconception of how much of a teacher's education really occurs in a teachers' college anyway. According to a recent study conducted by the dean of education at Texas Tech,[7] at the major universities in the United States, the average elementary-education student takes approximately 25 percent of his or her coursework in education courses, including student teaching. The average secondary student takes slightly less. Thus, if Johnny's teacher cannot write a coherent note to Johnny's parents, the problem is probably that of the English department rather than of the college of education. It is important to note that this study looked at practices at the major institutions in the country. It did not include regional universities or small private colleges. Thus, at least at many of the major institutions in the country, there is no substance to the claim that teacher education is under the control of "educationists" with no standards.

These data show that the liberal arts already predominate in the education of a teacher. The best teacher preparation programs combine the skills of faculty in education with those of faculty in the liberal arts. However, the contribution of the liberal arts is by no means limited to the content of what the prospective teacher will teach. As a member of a Task Force of Deans of Education in the Association of Schools and Colleges of Education in State Universities and Land Grant Colleges and Affiliated Private Universities, I have suggested four areas in which the liberal arts make, or can make, a critical contribution to the training of teachers.[8] These are in basic, or general, education; the teaching of higher-order skills of analysis and problem solving; the content area being taught; and in improved methods courses.

Basic education is clearly essential for good teaching. Teachers must be able to read, write, calculate, and have some general knowledge of the natural and social world in which they live. Higher-order cognitive skills are essential for a teacher. Given the myriad problems of strategy, implementation, classroom management, and individualization in a modern classroom, it is essential that teachers be able to analyze their situations, pose appropriate questions, and devise adaptive solutions to their problems. Such skills have traditionally been the province of training in the liberal arts, but have seldom been emphasized in a teacher education program. Knowledge of what a teacher is to teach, the content, is, of course, essential. The problem is that many people seem to believe that this is all that is required from the college or university experience.

The most interesting suggestion, however, is the idea that the liberal arts can also help improve methods courses. The assumption is that the goal of learning how to teach is to be able to relate the structure of that which is being taught to the student's cognitive map by means of effective instructional strategies. To carry out this kind of integrative task requires that the prospective teacher not only know the details of the discipline being taught, but also its structure. It is only in that way that instructional strategies can be developed that ensure that the student is neither bored by material that is too easy nor frustrated by work that is too difficult. The liberal arts could, if they would, teach the structure of the disciplines, and contribute to the integration of that structure with learning and curricular strategy in truly challenging new methods courses.

What this discussion indicates is that pedagogy cannot be ignored. At the same time, it may well be too important to leave solely to teacher educators. The role of the liberal arts in teacher preparation is critical, not only in the content areas, but also in a revised conception of methods of teaching.

It is important to note that the conception of the contribution of the liberal arts to teacher education sketched above is an integrated one. Although I believe that adequate teacher preparation will require more than the typical four-year baccalaureate program that is currently the norm, I differ from those, such as Boyer,[9] who call for a fifth, and a separate, professional year. A proper understanding of the role of the liberal arts in teacher preparation makes it evident that the liberal arts must be integrated throughout the program, rather than being separate from it.

CERTIFICATION

All fifty states have some form or other of initial certification for teachers. Since education is a state responsibility, the state monitors the quality of teaching in a variety of ways, with certification being one of them. Typically, certification requires competence in a variety of areas, including professional education as well as subject matter content. The concern over "unqualified" teachers, therefore, can take a variety of forms. It might mean a teacher who has not received the appropriate professional education training, or it might mean a teacher who has not had the appropriate subject-matter courses.

One of the major difficulties for colleges of education with regard to certification has to do with the distinction between program approval and transcript evaluation. "Program approval" refers to that process whereby a state agency approves the program of a given college of education, usually as the result of an independent evaluation, including a site visit. After approval, all graduates of the approved program are automatically certified by the state. One difficulty has to do with the fact that once approved, programs are almost never disapproved, even though there is usually a nominal periodic review. Furthermore, program approval requirements vary significantly from state to state in terms of the quality and rigor of the standards employed for approval. Over the past ten years there has been an *increase* of over 10 percent in the number of teacher education programs approved nationwide, while at the same time there has been over a 40 percent decrease in the numbers of graduating teachers.[10] The criteria for receiving program approval do not appear to be very rigorous.

Program approval is, however, a paradigm of rationality when compared to transcript evaluation. This system of certification, in use in some form or other in all states, involves an educational bureaucrat looking at the transcript of a student, counting up courses, and issuing certifications on the basis of the courses taken. The problem here for colleges of education is that students who might flunk out of an approved program at one school can, nevertheless, shop around at other schools until they have completed all of the requirements for transcript approval, and then be certified by the state. The extent of certification by transcript review is large and growing. In New York, nearly 50 percent of initial certificates are issued by the transcript review process.[11]

The only handle colleges of education have on the quality of such students is that the colleges largely control the student teaching experience. Even here, however, there are moves afoot as, for example, in New Jersey, to allow for alternative modes of practice teaching, thereby posing a serious threat to colleges of education in their attempts to provide integrated, professional education experiences. A simple collection of courses does not necessarily constitute a real program.

One might point out, however, that there is no research on the differences that graduation from an approved program makes on the quality of the teacher. However, the research cannot stop simply with comparing the difference in effects between approved programs and certification via transcript review. The variability in quality of approved programs could end up obscuring any real differences that might be found between high-quality teacher education programs and teachers who are certified through transcrpt review processes. Colleges of education must face these certification issues squarely. If graduation from a high-quality teacher education program really does make a difference, then research should show it. Colleges of education should undertake that research. If graduation from an approved program does not make a difference, colleges should either improve their programs, or, perhaps, some of them should get out of the business of teacher education.

In addition to the certification issues surrounding the professional education component, there are also concerns with the content portion of certification. This concern has surfaced in the national reports and in state-level policy forums in the guise of worries about the lack of mathematics, science, and foreign-language teachers. Many teachers in these areas, both experienced and newly graduated, are forsaking teaching in favor of more lucrative positions with industry and government. Thus, one hears of "unqualified" teachers teaching math and science.

Many believe that a solution to this problem lies in tapping the reservoir of technically trained and qualified people who would become teachers if only required courses in pedagogy were removed. Emergency certification has not worked in the past, but perhaps this time it would be different. As a remedy such a move would need to be tracked with caution. Colleges of education would need to monitor several things very closely: the number of teachers actually attracted in this way, how well such teachers perform, and whether they stay in the profession. As noted earlier, waiving the pedagogical component of certification requirements does not eliminate the necessity for these teachers to learn how to teach. The question remains of how they will learn to teach well.

There is another, more serious problem with the content portion of certification requirements. This problem can be illustrated by the situation in New York. Similar situations occur in other states. In New York, because of union contracts, education law, and tenure policies, a district with a lack of qualified teachers in a given area, say, mathematics, cannot simply go out and hire new mathematics teachers—at least not if that would mean laying off any existing teachers. Rather the district must first ask existing teachers who might be overrepresented in another field, say, English, to teach one of their five classes out of certification, in mathematics. This policy must be followed virtually throughout the system before the district can even begin to require the English teacher to start taking courses to become certified in mathematics. In areas of the country where there is still a declining school population, this situation often occurs. In such a case we do indeed have teacher shortages in certain areas, but cannot hire people competent in those areas, whether certified or not.

The implication of this for colleges of education is a sort of catch-22. In an effort to do something for these teachers teaching out of certification, most of the colleges of education will offer some kind of "quick-fix" course in the new field so that the teacher does not approach the job totally cold. Districts may even aid and abet the colleges by providing incentives for such teachers to take these courses. However, no college of education can require the teacher to take the amount of work really needed. Then when parents complain that their children are being taught by unqualified teachers, the college of education will receive at least a part of the blame. It will be a rare college of education that will be able to resist the temptation to gain additional enrollments by offering these quick fixes, especially since the colleges' budgets are largely determined by enrollments. Even if colleges were not swayed by the self-interest argument, they might well believe that such courses would be better than nothing for the students who must learn from the unqualified teacher. Thus, certification pressures can push colleges of education into practices that will dilute or obscure the contributions that can be made through strong professional training programs.

What colleges of education must do in the certification area will require courage and leadership. They are often perceived as benefiting from the hodgepodge of state certification policies and as working hand-in-glove with state departments to prevent any real reforms. They must fight for more rigorous standards of certification. They must take up the challenge of demonstrating that completing a teacher education program really is superior to amassing a collection of courses. Perhaps most importantly, colleges of education must insist on stiffer entrance and exit requirements—both in the extent of subject area knowledge and in the skills and capacities of teaching—so that their students truly are well qualified. If states then continue to insist upon less demanding requirements, the colleges can point this out. Otherwise, the strong teacher education programs will once again be lumped together with the weakest links in the teacher preparation system.

TESTS

The national reports have focused on the issue of the quality of the classroom teacher. One of the policy options open to states for trying to improve the quality of teachers in the classroom is to try to impose stiffer requirements for becoming and remaining a teacher. In today's context the call for stiffer requirements for teachers most often translates into tests of teachers. Over and above completing an approved program or amassing a set of courses, more and more states are requiring a variety of tests for certification. Most such tests are still aimed at beginning teachers, but several states, most notably Arkansas, are also requiring such tests of practicing teachers as well. Although teachers' unions on the whole reluctantly accept tests for beginning teachers, they vehemently oppose them for experienced teachers. They argue, with some degree of logic, that other professionals are not required to continually demonstrate their competence, so why should teachers? The fact remains, however, that the use of such tests is here to stay and will doubtless increase.

These tests, the National Teachers Exam is a good example, tend to be paper-and-pencil tests purporting to evaluate a variety of areas. Typically these include communications' skills, general knowledge, professional education knowledge, and subject matter knowledge. Very few tests attempt to determine how well teachers actually teach. The reason for this, from a policy standpoint, is very simple. Tests that could hope to measure the actual performance of a teacher by observation, peer evaluation, administrator visits, student response, and so on, would be enormously expensive, far more expensive than very many states seem able to afford.

Because of the expense of evaluating actual teacher performance, the alternative of assessing teachers by pupil achievement has been suggested. This procedure has at least two fatal flaws at the present state of the art. First, teachers are by no means responsible for everything that affects a child's learning. They have no control over television watching, latchkey children, poverty-stricken children, parental indifference, and so on. All of these things strongly affect learning, as we well know. Since teachers cannot control such things, it seems wholly inappropriate to judge teacher performance solely on student achievement.

Second, the state of the testing art simply does not allow us to measure very accurately the "value added" by any given teacher to a child's education. By this I mean that a teacher who brings a marginal child's performance up to average may have added much more value to that child's education than a teacher who brings a "B" student up to an "A." Yet in most schemes of measuring teacher performance by student achievement, the latter teacher would be judged superior. Perhaps the worst problem is that a single, objective test score does not even come close to reflecting the results of education. Professional test constructors understand this point, but policy makers often do not.[12]

Because of the difficulties of measuring actual teacher performance, most states have resorted to paper-and-pencil tests of an abstract knowledge that they piously hope will translate into improved performance. But there are significant problems with this approach as well. First, almost all paper-and-pencil tests correlate very highly with general verbal and mathematical ability. Good students will test well on these exams whether or not they can teach or relate to children at all. The other side of the coin is that minority students proportionately perform much less well on such tests than do other students. This is a particularly distressing policy result when we are faced with rapidly rising proportions of minority children to be taught. Indirectly, this implies that schools of education have particular challenges facing them in preparing minority students or other students who have low-aptitude scores to pass these tests.

The most direct implication of the testing movement for schools of education, however, lies in the potential use of test scores of an institution's teacher graduates to judge the quality of the institution itself. Florida, for example, intends to close down teacher education institutions that do not have an acceptably high proportion of their students' passing the state tests. If these tests arguably measured actual teaching performance, this would not be too bad, but in the present context, such a policy will largely affect institutions with large minority enrollments.

Nevertheless, there are certainly areas in which such tests do seem appropriate, the areas of communication skills, general knowledge, and subject matter competence. If would-be teachers do not know how to spell or write a grammatical sentence or are deficient in elementary and secondary subject areas, then they ought not be allowed to teach, no matter how well they relate to children. Colleges of education should welcome tests in such areas. In addition to improving the general quality of teachers, such tests will help focus attention on the liberal arts components of teacher education. If an institution's teacher candidates fail general knowledge tests, then questions can and should be asked of the quality of the liberal arts training those students are receiving in that institution. Colleges of education contribute only a small part of the total education of a teacher. It would be extremely salutary for the rest of the institution to come to recognize its role in teacher preparation.

INSTITUTIONAL VARIABILITY

Recent studies indicate that the number of institutions offering teacher education programs has actually risen over the past ten years; at the same time the number of teacher graduates has fallen by about half.[13] Now, nearly 1300 teacher education programs in the country produce approximately 150,000 graduates per year.

The most plausible explanation for this fact is that many small colleges, faced with declining enrollment figures, have added teacher education programs because they are cheap and, even in a glutted market, there are still fairly large numbers of students desiring teacher training. Concomitantly, large, prestigious institutions have tended to cut back on basic teacher education, sometimes transforming their programs into graduate schools of education. Such graduate schools tend to be closer in spirit to the academic values of the rest of the institution, stressing research and scholarship at the expense of teacher preparation. It has been estimated by the one hundred or so colleges of education comprising the prestigious Association of Schools and Colleges of Education in State Universities and Land Grant Colleges and Affiliated Private Universities that they produce less than 15 percent of the teacher education graduates in any given year.

In addition to the variability of kinds and types of teacher training programs cited above, there is also the much-noted fact that on a national level students indicating an interest in teacher education on SAT applications tend to have the lowest scores of almost any students. This fact is a major piece of evidence cited for the declining quality of teachers. At the same time several institutional studies indicate that, at least in some colleges and universities, teacher quality, as measured by test scores and grade point averages, is very similar to the average quality of all students at the given institution. This seems to hold true for the California State University system and for the units at the State University of New York. However, when one puts together the variability of teacher training institutions with the possibility that would-be teachers are close to the overall quality of the institution from which they graduate, an interesting possibility emerges. It may be that the low average-quality of teachers nationwide is due primarily to the fact that a disproportionate number of them graduate from third- and fourth-rate institutions.

This possibility, if largely true, could have enormous implications for colleges of teacher education. One approach would be to devise policies to shift more of teacher training to the higher-quality institutions that, because of their higher selectivity, would likely result in an increase in the average quality indicators for teachers. Of course, it must be assumed that these higher-quality institutions would retain their selectivity, even for teacher education students. However, even if the within-institution quality of teacher education students were slightly lower than the institutional average, the overall effect on quality would still be in an upward direction if more students were educated at the better institutions.

There are, of course, a host of difficulties that emerge in pursuing the distinction between higher- and lower-quality educational institutions. For present purposes, standard considerations of institutional prestige, measures of the quality of the student body, and programs of solid research and demonstrated effectiveness may be acknowledged as defining higher-quality institutions. However, there is one caveat. Almost all of these measures focus on the quality of the institution to begin with. They do not consider the "value added" of any program. Standard measures are particularly inappropriate in measuring the quality of programs devoted to serving predominantly disadvantaged or minority students, who typically do not score well on entrance exams such as the SAT.

However, granted the difficulty of precise definition, it still appears reasonable to pursue the goal of educating more teachers at higher-quality institutions. One way would be simply to close many of the lower-quality institutions' teacher education programs. Indeed, this has been suggested, but the political problems would be enormous. Since the programs at these institutions are approved by state education departments, local political pressures would be brought to bear upon such departments were they to try to impose rigorous standards on such programs. Because of the general distrust of colleges of education in their role of providing pedagogical training, the better colleges of education are tarred with the same brush as the weaker ones, and policies are adopted that do not allow conditions under which more effective pedagogical training would be demonstrated.

A second way of attempting to shift more of teacher education to the high-quality institutions would be for those institutions to expand their programs, maintain high standards for admission, and adopt measures to try to attract more students into teacher education. This tactic makes a good deal of sense because it can be combined with the improvements in teacher education that could flow from increased interaction with the liberal arts noted above. The higher-quality institutions also usually have higher quality liberal arts faculties that are currently suffering from some enrollment problems of their own. Such faculties may be enticed into cooperation with colleges of education, both by the curricular challenges posed by redesigning truly effective teacher education programs as well as by the possibilities of increasing their own enrollments. Although liberal arts faculties traditionally look down upon teacher education, perhaps the time is ripe for a marriage of convenience and challenge for the purpose of actually producing qualitatively improved teacher education programs.

In any event, forces seem to be at work to break down the heretofore nearly monolithic structure of teacher education that has seldom discriminated the better programs from the weaker programs. The time has come for the higher-quality colleges of education to unite and collectively begin to define what a paradigm teacher education program should look like. If this entails that some of the weaker institutions in the education community no longer measure up, so be it. Indeed, there are indications that such efforts are already under way. The Association of Schools and Colleges of Education in State Universities and Land Grant Colleges and Affiliated Private Universities has begun to look at ways to define teacher education at the better universities. In addition, the so-called "Holmes Group," a collection of about twenty deans of education from among the most prestigious institutions in the country, is meeting in an effort to set up optimal standards for teacher education, rather than resting content with minimal standards.

Any number of reformers have commented on the difficulty of attracting high-quality students into the teaching profession. On the whole, this is not something that colleges of education can address by themselves. The economic structure of the teaching profession and the low esteem in which teachers are held, along with the attractive opportunities outside of teaching, all work against high-quality students' entering the teaching profession. There simply can no longer be any question that over the years American education was built by shamelessly exploiting bright women. For many years during the growth of univeral public education, there were few professional opportunities for intelligent young women other than teaching and nursing. With the recent opening up of our social and economic system, these women now have many other opportunities and they are taking advantage of them.

At the same time, education has a very special advantage in attracting at least some students. While noting that many teachers expressed widespread disillusionment with much of teaching, survey after survey reveals a real commitment to teaching. Most teachers are in teaching because they have a calling—it certainly is not for the money. Simply put, they enjoy working with children and helping them to develop and learn. This strain of idealism can be utilized, along with at least some minimal financial reforms, to attract high-quality teachers.[14]

There are already a number of scholarship programs in place to attract teachers, and more are on the way. Where possible, local scholarships and incentives should be developed to supplement the state and federal initiatives, but these programs must emphasize quality rather than quantity. Unfortunately, marginal colleges of education have been even more aggressive than quality institutions in trying to attract students. There seems to be nothing so attractive to the president of a marginal institution than the belief that not only can anyone train teachers, but that it can be done inexpensively as well. If we are to improve the quality of teacher education, we must stop doing it in low-quality institutions, even if that means that many of them will go out of business.

CONTINUING PROFESSIONAL DEVELOPMENT

A final area in which the reform movement has implications for colleges of teacher education is that of continuing professional development for teachers.[15] Because of the centrality accorded to teachers and the teaching profession by much of the reform literature, the improvement of teaching occupies a central place as well. Although there are clear regional differences across the country in the relative emphasis to be placed on preservice teacher training versus in-service training, everyone seems to agree that continuing development of teachers is essential. It is essential both to update teaching areas, e.g., in computers and computer software, and to improve teaching skills, e.g., in bringing the results of research on effective instruction to the classroom. Continuing professional development will be particularly important in the Northeast and Midwest where student populations are declining and where current teachers will be on the job for ten to twenty more years.

Colleges of education have, of course, always been concerned with continued professional development for teachers. The standard modes for such involvement have been graduate courses at the colleges and workshops in the schools. Over the years, however, these methods of delivering continuing education have eroded considerably. Graduate courses will, of course, continue to have a place in the delivery system, but when most teachers in an area already have their master's degrees and are already at the top of the salary scale, the courses lose some of their attraction. In addition, such courses are often designed for the benefit of the college of education rather than for the practicing teacher. They may not be up to date with respect to the current research and, too often, the college professor talks down to the teacher.

Workshop sessions are often even worse. Typically, these are scheduled for a half day in the school and are put on by educational entrepreneurs who have developed an appealing style, but are often without much substance in what they present. Teachers are tired, they are often forced to attend the workshops by their administrators, and seldom is there the kind of follow-up that would be required for truly lasting change.

Both the traditional graduate course and the short workshop have come under increasing challenge by recent effective-schools research. We have learned that lasting change takes time to implement and must be accepted by those who must implement it. Change, especially educational change, cannot be implemented by fiat. Furthermore, the effective unit of change seems to be the individual school building, aided by a strong, educationally oriented principal. Teachers who gather willy-nilly in a college classroom seldom have the commonality of interests that results in effective change.

We have also learned that the culture of the school is very important to how teachers perform. Study after study has shown that the effects of the school climate on a teacher far outweigh the effects of either college classroom instruction or student-teaching experiences. The reality of the class-room and the mores of the school seem to swamp even the best teacher preparation programs. Theodore Sizer's *Horace's Compromise*[16] is particularly effective in detailing the effects of school climate.

What this indicates is that colleges of education must learn how to utilize one of the most important influences on teachers—the school climate in which the teachers work. Teacher preparation cannot stop at the edge of the campus when the prospective teacher receives a diploma. Rather, as many of the reports indicate, a variety of means must be found to continue teacher preparation into the field with internships, master teachers, and long-term commitments to working in the field. Without going quite so far as the headline-grabbing efforts of some colleges of education that are issuing one-year warranties to school districts that hire their graduates, the idea of closer school-college partnerships is the one that can and should be pursued.

Indeed, the reformist efforts to restructure the teaching profession to allow good teachers to stay in the classroom, instead of having to go into administration to get a pay raise, can be turned to the advantage of colleges of education. So-called "master teachers" in the schools can be identified, given special training responsibilities, and made adjunct faculty of colleges of education. There is no question that there is a growing body of knowledge about what makes a good teacher. Much of this knowledge is produced in graduate schools of education, and the other colleges of education should certainly be up to date on this research. At the same time, it is a long way between the research and its reasonable implementation in the classroom. Master teachers who also know the research and who are themselves knowledgeable about the constraints of the classroom can be invaluable additions to the teacher preparation process. They can give a touch of reality to college courses, and can continue the education of teachers via internships and intensive professional development activities when those teachers get into the classroom.

It should be noted that I am not here calling for a return to the old normal-school approach to training teachers. The fact that practicing teachers have an important role to play in teacher preparation should be no more surprising than that medical schools require extensive internships and practical training along with their university instruction. Similarly in teacher education, there is excellent reason why teachers must continue to be trained in colleges and universities. It is only there that teachers will have the time and opportunity to reflect critically upon their chosen profession and to acquire the skills to become lifelong learners in that profession. At the same time, however, it would be folly to continue to pretend that good teachers do not know a great deal about teaching and how to help other teachers become better.

All schools and colleges of education need to form long-lasting partnerships with schools nearby. Even the more prestigious graduate schools of education cannot remain above the fray. They can and should study education, but they must also remember that their scholarship must be thoroughly grounded in the real world of education. Scholarship in education is not simply "applied" psychology, or history, or philosophy, or administrative theory. The insights of those disciplines are of tremendous value for the study of education, but they are insights that must be grounded in a thorough appreciation of the practical affairs of education. If colleges of education take this seriously, new models of teacher education, both preservice and in-service, can be evolved in partnership with the schools and the liberal arts faculties at the institutions of higher education.

CONCLUSION

Teacher education per se has not been the center of attention in the recent national reports on education, but teachers and teacher quality have been. Thus, as the discussion has moved to the state and local level, policy discussions and initiatives have focused at least in part on issues of teacher preparation as one major way of affecting teacher quality. In this chapter I have attempted to highlight those issues that seem to have the most direct bearing on teacher education.

First, I noted that many seem to assume that learning how to teach is simply unnecessary. To the contrary, I have urged that the question is not *whether* one will learn how to teach, but rather *how* one will learn how to teach. Efforts must be undertaken to improve courses in pedagogy by utilizing connections with the liberal arts and recent educational research, or else colleges of education will find themselves increasingly under attack, and justifiably so.

Certification procedures must be improved and colleges of education must take the lead in insisting on higher standards. Research must be undertaken to demonstrate the efficacy of reflective pedagogical training as contrasted with certifying any liberal arts graduate who wants to teach. If we are convinced that we can teach teachers how to teach, let us prove it.

Tests, too, will have an important impact on teacher education. At the extreme, test scores of graduates of teacher preparation programs may be used to phase some of those programs out of existence. At a minimum, colleges of education must begin to overcome the widespread view that they are intellectually barren and attract only the weakest students. Some colleges of education are very good indeed, and they should say so. Others are fully deserving of the scorn heaped upon them, and they should be closed down. Teachers must have minimal competency, and complaints about the problems with tests do not, in the long run, do teachers or colleges of education any good. The limits of testing as a policy tool must be recognized, but where tests are appropriate, as in certifying minimal general knowledge, they must not be mindlessly resisted.

Any given institution can probably attract teacher education students of about the same quality as the institution as a whole. What this means is that the low, overall quality-indicators for teachers may be due to the fact that a disproportionate number of them are coming from third- and fourth-rate institutions. Higher-quality programs can no longer permit themselves to be lumped with lower-quality programs as if there were no differences between them worth noting. Indeed, in my view, perhaps a third to a half of current teacher preparation programs should be shut down. State education departments will be reluctant to take such steps, but the better colleges of education can apply pressure by insisting on rigorous standards and measurable results in their own programs.

Finally, the need for developing new models of continuing professional development for teachers has never been more apparent nor more amenable to action. Colleges of education should cooperate closely with their liberal arts colleagues and with schools in devising new programs that make use of the expertise to be found in all three areas. Master teachers associated with colleges and universities should be the rule, rather than the exception.

Colleges of education have a great deal at stake in the current wave of educational reform. If they take advantage of their opportunities, they can emerge stronger and more respected. If they fail, they may yet go out of business entirely. The critics are many and the friends are few. In order to take advantage of their opportunities, the colleges of education must basically do three things. First, they must cooperate as they have never done before, both with schools and with the liberal arts colleges on their campuses. Second, they must go to work on their curriculum, improving it where possible, jettisoning it where necessary. There is no reason that education courses should not be viewed as among the most intellectually stimulating and demanding in the university. And last but not least, colleges of education must somehow clean up their own act. There are too many of them of marginal and below-marginal quality. If they do not begin to impose higher standards on themselves, such standards will be imposed upon them by people who do not understand the difference between a good college of education and a poor one. Thus, the most important lesson of the educational reform movement for colleges of education may be that they need to reform themselves. Let us hope that they have the will to succeed.

NOTES

I am indebted to Paul Farber and to my wife, Dr. Carol A. Hodges, for the numerous helpful suggestions they made on this essay.
    1. Lawrence C. Stedman and Marshall S. Smith, "Recent Reform Proposals for American Education," *Contemporary Education Review* 2 (1983).

2. Ernest L. Boyer, *High School: A Report on Secondary Education in America* (New York: Harper & Row, 1983).

3. Task Force on Education for Economic Growth, *Action for Excellence: A Comprehensive Plan to Improve Our Nation's Schools* (Denver, Colo.: Education Commission of the States, 1983).

4. John I. Goodlad, *A Place Called School: Prospects for the Future* (New York: McGraw-Hill, 1983).

5. Jonathon Alter, John McCormick, and Nadine Joseph, "Why Teachers Fail," *Newsweek* 104 (24 September 1984): 64–70.

6. N. L. Gage, "What Do We Know About Teaching Effectiveness?" *Phi Delta Kappan* 66 (October 1984): 87–93, and David C. Berliner, "Making the Right Changes in Preservice Teacher Education," *Phi Delta Kappan* 66 (October 1984): 94–97.

7. Richard E. Ishler, "Requirements for Admission to and Graduation from Teacher Education," *Phi Delta Kappan* 66 (October 1984): 121–22.

8. Task Force on the Role of the Liberal Arts in Teacher Education, Draft Report (Association of Schools and Colleges of Education in State Universities and Land Grant Colleges and Affiliated Private Universities, 1984).

9. Ernest L. Boyer, *High School.*

10. C. Emily Feistritzer, *The Making of a Teacher: A Report on Teacher Education and Certification* (Washington, D.C.: National Center for Educational Information, 1984).

11. New York State Education Department, Certification Information (Fall 1983).

12. Linda Darling-Hammond, "Taking the Measure of Excellence: The Case Against Basing Teacher Evaluation on Student Test Scores," *American Educator* 8 (Fall 1984): 26–29.

13. C. Emily Feistritzer, *Making of a Teacher.*

14. See, for example, John I. Goodlad, *A Place Called School,* 171–73.

15. Madlyn Levine Hanes and Michael D. Rowls, "Teacher Recertification: A Survey of the States," *Phi Delta Kappan* 66 (October 1984): 123–26.

16. Theodore R. Sizer, *Horace's Compromise: The Dilemma of the American High School* (Boston: Houghton Mifflin, 1984).

Part 5

Historical Perspective

Considerations
Historical Perspectives on Reform in New York State

Gail P. Kelly and Maxine S. Seller

In the past two years a multitude of commissions on the nation's schools have issued reports calling for massive educational reform.[1] In 1983 and 1984, the New York State Regents held a series of meetings throughout the state and in August of 1984 issued an action plan that calls for changes in curriculum, high school graduation requirements, and educational standards.[2] These reforms are intended to herald an era of excellence and strengthen schooling's contribution to the state's economy. Other states have taken steps to upgrade their schools. Some have changed graduation requirements; others have moved toward changing course offerings, initiating more rigorous testing programs, and changing teacher recruitment and certification requirements.[3]

While there have been reforms mandated, it is by no means clear that the changes the states are initiating will be translated into practice or, if put into practice, that they will have their intended effect. Histories of school reform indicate that it will take more to change educational practice than enacting legislation that calls for curricular revision, higher standards, and "excellence." Reforms of the past have often been nothing but a series of paper recommendations that were revived, or forgotten, ten years hence.

This chapter is a case study of the history of school reform efforts in New York State in the twentieth century. Through a survey of the many commissions that sought to improve the state's schools, this chapter asks what lessons can be learned from past reform efforts that might inform today's policy makers. Are there characteristics that distinguish "successful" from "unsuccessful" attempts to change American schools? While our focus is on New York State, we believe that what can be said about the many well-intentioned efforts to change the state's school system and its educational outcomes has relevance to other states now trying to bring excellence to the schools in a time of scarce resources and erosion of public confidence in the public schools. What we can learn from the history of reform in this state can help guide policy makers elsewhere as they formulate reform programs and attempt to translate them into practice.

In this chapter we do not purport to study every reform ever attempted in New York State. Rather, we have selected those reforms that represent serious and wide-ranging attempts to change the quality and outcomes of primary and secondary education, as do the national reports on excellence of the 1980s. We therefore selected three of the major reforms that attempted to change schools in New York State before World War II: namely, the Hanus Report of 1911–1913, the Rural School Survey of 1922, and the Regents Inquiry of 1937. In the postwar era, we looked at statewide reforms instigated by the federal government—the National Defense Education Act of 1957 and Title I of the Elementary and Secondary Education Act—as well as state-initiated attempts to change the quality and distribution of education, namely, the Fleischmann Commission and its successors, and the Regents' Competency Testing Program. Unlike pre–World War II reforms, the reforms of the last two decades, like current reform efforts, were instigated largely by the federal government.

We have not organized this chapter chronologically; rather, we have opted to present our data topically, structured around what we have identified as the implications of New York State's history of school reform for current efforts. In the pages that follow we ask how reforms of the past have been affected by the specificity of their goals, their consistency, executive leadership exerted, resources, and provisions for accountability.

LOFTY, VAGUE GOALS AND REFORM

The various national commissions on education in 1983 and 1984 have set "excellence" as a goal for education, which is expected to reinstate "America's competitive challenge." The schools, many of the reports maintain, should prepare for the technological society of the future. No one contests such admirable goals for the schools; the question, however, is whether such goals can indeed be achieved as the states enact reform.

The history of reform movements in New York State suggests that attempts to reform schools have often been ineffective when their goals and recommendations were general, rather than specific, and when they called for knowledge no one possessed. The fates of the Hanus Report of 1911, the Rural School Survey of 1922, and the Regents' Inquiry of 1937, and of the attempts to equalize education in the 1960s and 1970s illustrate the impossibility of achieving commendable, but vaguely defined educational and social goals.

The first important twentieth-century reform commission was the Hanus Report that, while dealing with the schools in New York City, affected over half the public school children in the state. A detailed survey by experts from university education departments and municipal research bureaus, it set a precedent for other city surveys, for the multivolume Rural School Survey of 1922 and Regents' Inquiry of 1937, and for other more specialized commissions on school reform in the state. Unfortunately, the Hanus Report set a precedent for vagueness as well. It instructed schools to inculcate "those things which, if known, would insure intelligent cooperation and competition among men," but neglected to specify what those "things" were. It instructed schools to train "efficient citizens" who would "appreciate the common interests of our democratic society," but did not specify what made a citizen "efficient" or what those "common interests" were.[4] Similarly vague goals appeared in the Rural School Survey, which directed schools to give children "such training as will make them acceptable members of society," and in the 1937 Regents' Inquiry, which urged that children be taught "those qualities, attitudes and abilities that are essential for efficient living in an evolving industrial democratic society."[5] Local school officials may well have been perplexed as to what measures to enact to reach these worthy but imprecise goals.

Curriculum reforms that were specific rather than general, on the other hand, were more likely to be implemented. The Hanus Report's recommendation that social studies and vocational subjects be expanded was gradually carried out in the New York City schools. On the other hand, when the Rural School Survey made the general recommendation that the many subjects taught in rural elementary schools should be consolidated, the schools continued to teach the same subjects anyhow. A decade later, however, when the state education department issued two syllabi showing specifically how to consolidate school subjects, curriculum reform took place.

While the reports of the 1980s ask that the schools prepare students for new technologies, does anyone know what those technologies are, or how anyone might be prepared for them? In the past, commissions that have called for reforms based on knowledge no one possessed have seen their proposals shelved. For example, the Rural School Survey suggested replacing the locally elected "amateur" district trustees with state-appointed, professionally trained supervisors on the grounds that the latter would bring the benefits of "the science of education" to local school management. The author of the recommendation admitted, however, that "We cannot point to any organized body of printed material and say 'That is our body of education science.' It is yet largely in that empirical stage when it is mainly held in the minds of the professional workers, largely as the results of their professional experiences . . . ." Rural voters rejected the proposed change of administrative personnel; they were not convinced that the admittedly primitive "scientific" knowledge of the new professionals was better than the common sense of the old trustees, who at least could be controlled by their local constituencies.[6]

A second illustration of the importance of an adequate knowledge-base is the 1937 Regents' Inquiry's recommendation that all teachers systematically teach good character, using methods of "proven worth." Unable to recommend such methods from their own experience or from educational literature, the inquiry asked representative principals how they taught character in their schools. The resulting unannotated list of suggestions was then incorporated into the report for the benefit of other principals. The suggestions (none of "proven worth") ranged from "sports" and "encouragement of recreational and free reading" to "pictures on display," "arbor day programs," and "teaching of etiquette in lunchroom periods." It is doubtful whether the report's recommendations on systematic character education were implemented then or, given current knowledge, whether they could be today.[7]

The message from the past is clear: before American schools can prepare students for future technologies or teach excellence, greater specification of how they might be taught in school needs to occur. Of the current reports, only one suggested that care be taken to develop a knowledge base for implementing new curricula on science and technology. Most urge that such courses be taught forthwith.

INCONSISTENCY: THE BANE OF REFORM

The various reports urging reform in the nation's schools in the 1980s call for a myriad of changes. The history of school reform in New York State suggests that the extent to which the reforms posited are consistent strongly affects whether any reforms are implemented at all. Diverse initiatives and sources of reform at any given period in the past have produced commission reports with recommendations so diverse and conflicting that effective implementation was difficult, if not impossible. The recommendations of the Hanus Report, for example, reflected the varied and often conflicting interests of the city board of estimate and appropriations that initiated it, the educators who wrote it, and the businessmen and civic and women's organizations who served as unofficial consultants. The board of appropriations called for school budgets based on "facts . . . not educational opinion," for better accounting, and for elimination of waste and "frills." Educators wanted the schools divorced from city politics and called for "progressive" pedagogy. Business interests were reflected in the report's request that schools "act as a transmitter between human supply and industrial demand," and civic organizations hoped to make the schools social-service agencies to uplift, Americanize, and control the immigrant slum populations.[8]

Rather than choose among these viewpoints, the Hanus Report included something of each, with little regard for consistency.[9] Thus while recommending an enriched and differentiated curriculum to please progressive pedagogues, it also called for the elimination of specialty teachers who might teach such a curriculum in the elementary schools in the interests of economy. While expressing concern for the language problems of immigrant children, the report suggested that instruction in English grammar be struck from the elementary curriculum; progressive educators thought grammar too "abstract." The report recommended more vocational training *in* the schools; at the same time it urged investigation, in the interests of economy, of on-the-job training *outside* the schools. It advised corporal punishment, isolation, and early entry into the workforce for the recalcitrant student to prevent waste of classroom time, while advocating social and medical correction of student defects and a curriculum so "vital" (the Progressive Era equivalent of "relevant") that there would be no failures. Recommendations for expensive social services and vocational training could scarcely be reconciled with simultaneous demands for economy and efficiency. Not surprisingly, much of the Hanus Report was quietly shelved.

Reform efforts sometimes failed or became sidetracked not because of contradictory aims of reform, but because contradictory definitions of a seemingly agreed-upon goal were adopted, as were conflicting strategies to achieve these goals. This was exemplified in the more-often-than-not court-mandated attempts to provide educational quality in New York State since 1965.

While committed to "equality" on paper since the 1960s, New York State, like the rest of the nation, has been hard pressed to define what providing equality in education meant in actual practice. The Federal Elementary and Secondary Education Act (ESEA) of 1965, which brought appreciable funds to the state from the federal government, defined equality in terms of providing the conditions for children from "deprived" backgrounds, presumed to be at high risk for failure, to succeed in school.[10] ESEA defined equality in terms of programs made available to targeted populations, not in terms of whether equality of educational expenditure or outcome was assured. While ESEA, which was administered by New York State for the federal government, defined equality in terms of programs for targeted populations, subsequent state and federal legislation provided, at times, less than consistent definitions. The Bilingual Education Act, for example, defined equality as providing mother-tongue education to students whose first language was not English. This federal legislation argued that children needed to have equal access to knowledge, not necessarily equal educational processes in a common language. The notion of cultural deficit, central to ESEA, was implicitly rejected by New York State's own bilingual education legislation, which insisted that minority cultures were by no means an impediment to school success.[11] Not only did federally induced and state-promoted programs provide differing and conflicting definitions of equality, but additional state and federal legislation relating to handicapped children argued that equality meant that all learners ought to be entitled to participate in the same educational processes, regardless of their handicap.[12] Special schools for mentally and physically handicapped children, which the state had sponsored for decades, were perceived as counter to the very concept of equality.

While varying state and federally mandated programs carried their own, often less than consistent, versions of what constituted equality, New York

State initiated a series of commissions that sparked yet another debate about what equality entailed. In 1969 Nelson Rockefeller, then governor, appointed the now almost forgotten Fleischmann Commission.[13] Its 1973 three-volume report represented the first full survey of the state's schools since the 1940s. In it the commission called on the state to provide educational equality and defined it differently from the ESEA, the Bilingual Education Act, or the legislation that mainstreamed handicapped children into the public schools. The Fleischmann Commission defined equality in terms of educational expenditure, need, and tax burden. The commission argued that education in New York was unequal because districts with high property values were spending much more on education than districts with lower property values. Poor districts taxed themselves more heavily in proportion to their property values than rich districts and still had less to spend per student for schooling. In addition to the tax rate being higher in poor areas, the Fleischmann Commission found per capita cost of education in poor districts much higher than in wealthier districts because of the concentrations of bilingual, handicapped, and disadvantaged students, whose educational costs were over twice that of children from affluent English-speaking homes. Defining equality as the provision of educational monies according to a child's needs rather than a district's wealth or the size of the tax burden it could bear, the commission recommended that local property tax should not be the basis for determining how much was spent on schooling.

Through the 1970s New York State grappled with the issues raised by the Fleischmann Commission, while several cities litigated against the old state formulas for providing aid to local school districts.[14] In 1980 and again in 1982 the state issued reports on how equality in education might be provided. Meanwhile, differences in expenditures per student continued to widen between school districts. In 1974–5 per pupil expenditures varied from $1820 to $978.[15] By 1981–2, two commissions later, it ranged from $3560 to $1763. Equality, while state policy, remained elusive.

THE ROLE OF STRONG EXECUTIVE LEADERSHIP

The National Commissions on Excellence, like so many of the reports on the schools issued in 1983 and 1984, challenged parents, teachers, the community, and business to reform the schools. The question must be asked, however, to what extent do the reports acknowledge the role of committed, persistent executive leadership in bringing about successful reform? The history of educational change in New York State demonstrates that unless such leadership is exerted, schools are likely to resist change. The role of Governor Alfred E. Smith in rescuing the schools from the fiscal crisis of the early 1920s illustrates how important the executive office is in bringing about effective change. During the opening decades of the century and especially after World War I, the costs of local government had risen much faster than income. Local taxes, primarily property taxes, had soared, producing an outcry for tax relief throughout the state. Cities, whose property tax rates were limited by state law, were facing bankruptcy and the poorer rural counties had reached the limit of their resources.

While all areas of local government had become more expensive, education costs had risen most and were therefore most subject to criticism. In 1919, a legislative joint committee on taxation and retrenchment (better known as the Davenport Commission) noted "the extravagance of educational expenditures" and suggested the need for further investigation.[16] Rather than making political capital out of the drive for economy, the new governor asked the legislature for and received in 1919 and 1920 twenty-two million dollars to increase teachers' salaries.[17] This was not an isolated triumph but the first of a series of persistent efforts to solve the financial crisis of the schools. In the decades before Smith took office, the proportion of school expenses born by the state, as opposed to the local governments, had steadily declined until it reached a new low of 8 percent in 1919. Legislation passed under Smith's leadership reversed this trend, raising the state's contribution by 1930 to 38.6 percent. During this same period state aid to school districts increased from $7,474,440 to $102,000,000, permitting continuing expansion of education, especially at the secondary level.[18]

A precursor of the New Deal, Smith believed that the state should take an active role in meeting people's needs. He believed educational problems could not be solved without money and that this obligation could not be postponed because "time lost cannot be regained by the children who are injured by the states's failure to make adequate provision for their education."[19] Smith acted on the premise that voters would support additional spending if they understood its importance and were assured of value for their money; his administration sponsored a series of commissions on education, the most important of which were the Davenport and Friedsam Commissions, and lobbied successfully to implement their recommendations.

Reversing its earlier suggestion about educational extravagance, in its 1924 report the Davenport Commisison assured the public that the schools were not wasteful. Its recommendations became the Cole Law of 1925. Although it did not abolish the old "quota" system, whereby the state gave disticts financial "quotas" for more than a dozen different purposes, the Cole Law added a large state grant for each "teacher unit," greatly increasing state aid. In addition, the law gave each district enough money (above what the district raised by a mandated "equalized" tax rate) to provide a minimal per student education fund. With the Cole Law, the state for the first time assumed financial responsibility for a minimum educational fund for every child, no matter how poor the child's district, and provided for statewide "equalization" of the tax burden for the support of that fund.

When an economy-minded legislature refused his request to finance another commission on education, Governor Smith assembled an informal conference of educators and economists, including Michael Friedsam, president of B. Altman and Company. The conference became the Friedsam Commission, chaired and financed by Friedsam; and its recommendations, sponsored by the governor, became the Friedsam Law of 1928. The Friedsam Law raised the minimal state-supported educational fund, increased the state's contribution, and lowered the contribution required by the districts. In 1930 when the law took full effect, the old "quota" system—in which the state gave the districts many small grants for specific purposes, often unrelated to need—was submerged in the new "equalized" aid structure. Following the recommendations of the Friedsam Commission, Governor Smith lowered the state property tax, developed new sources of state revenue, and shared this revenue with local governments in unprecedented amounts. Thus Smith did more than advocate and lobby for increased state spending on education; he initiated fiscal policies that made local and state increases feasible.

The importance of strong executive leadership is underscored in more recent years in the failure of the state to implement the Fleischmann Commission recommendations. State government was ambivalent about what it would mean to move toward equalizing educational expenditure between school districts, with equality defined, as in the Fleischmann Report, as providing greater amounts of money to bilingual, poor, and handicapped students. The Fleischmann Commission had recommended that the state either take over all educational finance through the institution of a statewide property tax, or that the state begin immediately to equalize expenditures per pupil among and within districts by removing state aid from wealthy districts and leveling up poor districts. This would have meant that 40 percent of the districts in the state would probably lose substantial amounts of money, while 60 percent would either remain at current funding levels or gain state aid.[20]

The financial recommendations were politically explosive. Rather than take immediate action Governor Rockefeller, and after him Governor Carey, appointed various commissions to study the proposals.[21] They focused exclusively on the property tax and state-funding formulas, not because of strong leadership from the governor's office or the state legislature, but rather because of litigation that eventually led to the *Levittown* case of 1978. No agencies followed up on implementing the other recommendations the commission made proposing changes in curriculum and standards, which are echoed in the 1984 regents' plans for improving the state's primary and secondary schools.

In part there was little action on the curricular recommendations of the Fleischmann Commission because the commission did not propose that new monies be brought to the schools; rather, the commission implied that its recommendations could be enacted by increasing the "productivity" of the system through efficiency measures. The commission asked for massive change without increasing monies available to education. At the same time it urged that monies be redistributed among districts, significantly reducing state aid to many districts. It is little wonder that the executive leadership was tentative. Given the poor state of New York's economy and the declining federal aid to education, the state focused solely on the formula for aid to local districts and, though pressed by impending legal action, it moved very slowly indeed. Ten years after the Fleischmann Commission issued its report, its proposals on educational finance were only partly implemented; those regarding curriculum and standards were being proposed once again, although in changed form.

REFORMS AND RESOURCES

The extent to which resources for reform are specified for the schools affects quite strongly whether local districts change their practices. Even when the government has strongly and consistently urged specific reforms, local school districts have failed to implement them fully, not because they opposed the reforms, but because the changes they were asked to make entailed large and continuing new expenditures. New York State often requested the changes but failed to provide adequate and specifically earmarked funding for their execution. Examples of reforms frustrated by insufficient funding include plans for the introduction of a "practical" curriculum in the rural high school during the second and third decade of the century, and the implementation of the National Defense Education Act in the late fifties and early sixties, and, as discussed earlier, the Fleischmann Commission recommendations.

Participating in a nationwide trend toward more "practical" high school curriculum, the Rural School Survey of 1922 recommended that rural high schools change their traditional college preparatory curriculum to meet the needs of increasing numbers of students who would not go to college or even finish high school. Specifically, the survey recommended that agricultural and industrial arts courses be available for all boys, and that home economics be not only available but also required for all girls. The survey also recommended that the current concentration on Latin and mathematics be replaced, especially for the noncollege bound, with social studies, general science, and other useful subjects. Commissioner Groves wanted rural students to have all the opportunities available to their city counterparts. This would have meant the inclusion of more modern languages and laboratory sciences as well. The new curriculum did not materialize, however, largely because the states did not provide the necessary funding.[22]

The state began its effort to change the rural high school curriculum in 1910 with a law offering to pay two-thirds of the cost of the first teacher and half of the cost of the second teacher for agriculture programs. In 1917 the federal Smith Hughes Act provided additional subsidies for teachers of vocational subjects, including agriculture, industrial arts, and home economics.

Because of these special appropriations, by 1921 agriculture was taught in seventy-two rural high schools and in six separate state agricultural high schools.[23]

While advocates of the new "practical" education were pleased with this initial success, it is significant that in no part of the state did the percentage of rural high schools teaching agriculture exceed 14.5 percent in 1921. In most areas it was substantially less. That the Rural School Survey in 1922 recommended that agriculture should be available to all high school boys who wanted it made little difference; further growth in the 1920s was slight. Although state and federal subsidies made it possible to hire a well-trained, male high-school–level teacher of agriculture for half the cost of the usual female rural elementary school teacher, neither the state nor the federal government subsidized the considerable additional expense of equipment or operating costs. By 1922 the scattering of communities motivated enough to pay these additional costs already had programs. Most rural high schools were in villages, which saw no reason to spend their own money on programs of benefit mainly to nonresident, "open country" students. Hard pressed to pay for existing programs, they had other priorities.[24]

Closely tied to agricultural education, home economics programs also illustrate the important role of adequate outside funding in creating change at the district level. Although home economics was probably a more popular "practical" curricular reform than agriculture and its potential clientele was larger, the original state aid legislation of 1910 did not subsidize it independently. Early state-aided home economics programs had to be housed in agriculture departments, their teachers usually hired as the "second," and less heavily subsidized teacher. (Agriculture, however, could be taught and subsidized with or without home economics.) Because of the state subsidy law, almost all early high school home economics programs were in rural areas; after the state law changed in 1919 to finance home economics independently of agriculture the number of home economics programs increased both in rural and urban high schools. Still, as late as 1921, there were only seventy-four state-aided departments, forty-five of which were still subordinated to agriculture programs. Although home economics programs grew more rapidly than agriculture during the 1920s, the Rural School Survey's recommendation that the subject become mandatory for all girls in rural high schools was not carried out; perhaps 10 percent of all girls had access to the program. One reason for the slow growth was the fact that local communities could get subsidies under the Smith Hughes Act only if they offered a "vocational" program, one that took up almost half of a student's academic time. Few girls were interested in an extensive (and unremunerative) "vocational" home economics program, and even though subsidies were available for teachers' salaries, few communities were willing to commit themselves to the high equipment and operating costs of such a program.

Home economics and agriculture entered the curriculum of at least some rural high schools because they were partially subsidized by the state and federal governments. Reforms lacking subsidies were implemented even less fully, if at all. Studies of high school curriculum in 1927 showed that although courses taken in social studies had increased, Latin and mathematics were still prominent in student programs. Science, modern languages, and vocational subjects that were expanding in urban high schools were growing slowly, if at all, in their village counterparts. Despite increased state aid in the 1920s, many rural districts were poor. It was cheaper to teach Latin and algebra than to hire specially trained modern-language teachers or pay for the laboratories, special equipment, and high operating costs of the recommended "modern," or "practical," subjects. No new money was appropriated in the 1920s to finance the desired curricular reform, so little reform took place.[25]

Forty years later another effort to change curriculum, this time initiated by the federal government, was also less than successful because of inadequate funding. Congress passed the National Defense Education Act (NDEA) in 1957, following the Soviet Union's launching of Sputnik. The legislation proposed to upgrade the teaching of science, mathematics, and foreign languages in the schools and recommended a variety of means to do so, from more laboratory facilities in the schools to more advanced-placement classes in targeted subjects, especially science and mathematics. Under the terms of NDEA the federal government provided funds for local districts to purchase equipment for science, mathematics, and language laboratories. The state was to administer the funds, under broad federal guidelines, and to decide on the validity of local requests. The NDEA also provided matching funds for the states to improve supervisory and related services to the schools.

The New York State Education Department (SED) greeted NDEA with enthusiasm. The state established an ad hoc advisory council in science and technology in 1957 to study math and science programs. Between 1958 and 1963 the state revised curricula in the targeted subjects and developed instructional materials for the new curricula. In addition SED ran summer institutes to train teachers to use the new materials and established science and math demonstration centers.[26]

How much effect these efforts had in the state's classrooms is unclear, however. After much prodding of the districts, by 1964 the state education department had received and filled requests for 3494 pieces of science equipment, 2241 of math equipment, and 2409 of foreign-language equipment. Despite the SED effort, however, close to 25 percent of the districts refused to apply for equipment, stating lack of teachers qualified to use it as the reason.[27]

While NDEA did place government-financed equipment in many classrooms, science, mathematics, and foreign-language instruction in those classrooms was not necessarily strengthened. In part this was because the NDEA and the state did not provide districts with funds to hire additional math, science, or foreign-language teachers who could provide the upper-level instruction the reform hoped for, or use the advanced equipment the NDEA had paid for. Close to a third of all the state's science and math teachers remained individuals certified in subjects like physical education, English, and social studies. State-sponsored workshops and demonstrations reached only a fraction of these teachers; federal and state funds were too limited.

A 1965 evaluation carried out by SED concluded that while more students were enrolled in science courses (largely because the state had changed requirements for high school graduation), there was little evidence that instruction in mathematics, science, or foreign languages had improved.[28] The infusion of new equipment and materials did not stimulate enough additional expenditures at the local level to carry the proposed reforms to successful completion. Local districts felt that they could not afford to divert monies from basic school subjects to upgrade mathematics, science, or foreign-language instruction. In fact, the SED report complained that districts that did reallocate funds to science and mathematics caused "harm" to instruction in the language arts, civics, and health education. After 1965 the state sought to change NDEA to extend the program to all subjects (except art and music) at the elementary and secondary levels. In short, the state recommended unspecified grants to school districts for general "improvement of instruction."[29]

While the lack of total funding was responsible for the failure of NDEA to significantly improve high school science and mathematics instruction, education has been improved by state-mandated programs that districts could implement without additional taxing of local resources. This was the case in the regents-mandated Basic Competency Testing Program, which was put into effect in 1979. The program specified that a local district could not award high school diplomas unless students passed state-administered tests in mathematics, reading, and writing. (Tests in health and civics were optional.) The local districts were not required to do anything except withhold degrees from substandard students; the tests were graded as well as administered by the state.[30]

As the 1983 report of the Carnegie Foundation for the Advancement of Teaching indicated, the New York State competency testing program did insure that basic skills were taught.[31] The competency testing program, still in effect in 1984, demonstrates that if the state pays for a program, especially one limited to testing, it can change minimal standards on degrees it controls. Emphasis on minimal competency does not assure "excellence"; ironically, it may actually lower educational standards while improving only students' test-taking skills.

REFORM AND ACCOUNTABILITY

While the national commissions on education of the 1980s call for many reforms, the history of New York State suggests that the extent to which accountability or evaluation are part of reform may well affect the ways in which reforms are enacted. In New York State neither accountability nor evaluation at the local district level has been a distinguishing feature of past reform. Until the Elementary and Secondary Education Act of 1965, school districts have rarely been asked to account for programs they have put into effect, their educational standards, or how they allocated monies given them by the localities, the state, or the federal government; nor have districts been required to conduct studies to see if the programs they offer have achieved their intended objectives. Reform often has been limited to what districts say they will do to change practices or what the state or federal government hopes they will do. This has been the case whether or not the districts were given funds to bring about change. Schools rarely have reformed practice without strong, consistent impetus to do so from either state or national governments. Often districts have used state or federal money to pay for services they would normally have provided through locally raised funds. The end result has been not the improvement of educational services intended by the state or federal reformers, but rather local property tax relief and a lessening contribution of localities to the education of their children. Even when money has been spent as the state or federal government intended, absence of evaluation at the local level has made it difficult for either the planners or the executors of the reform to know whether the effort was worthwhile. Decisions to continue or to eliminate the reform, then, are based exclusively on political or budgetary rather than educational factors.

Although education has been considered a state function since 1795, throughout most of New York's history the state has chosen to delegate its responsibility in this area to the local districts. Originally, this choice was a necessity; the state had no machinery to make and enforce educational decisions at the local level in the large and primarily rural area under its jurisdiction. Later, necessity came to be viewed as a virtue and the decision-making autonomy of the local district was enshrined as American democracy in action. Early reformers shared this attitude. According to the Rural School Survey of 1922, "that which a citizen learns through operation of his own action becomes firmly established, while that which is forced upon him against his will he opposes more firmly. It is therefore fundamental in state aid that we leave final decision to the local community and leave them to choose what is best."[32]

Ironically, as state aid to education increased during the 1920s, state control over how the money would be spent decreased. In the opening decades of the century state aid came to the districts through a system of individual "quotas," most of which were for a specific purpose, such as hiring physical education teachers or purchasing library books, and districts were expected to spend the money for the designated purpose. Each district reported, for example, on its use of the library quota. Since there were only two supervisors to inspect elementary-and secondary-school libraries all over the state, however, reporting was essentially on the honor system.[33] During the 1930s nonspecific state aid granted to districts solely on the basis of the number of students in attendance became more important than the old "quota" grants, many of which were discontinued altogether in 1930. While the new system was intended to enable the districts to provide better educational programs without raising local property taxes, or even to allow hard-pressed districts to maintain educational services while reducing property taxes, it was not intended to defray local expenses for programs unrelated to education. The existence of this misuse of state aid to education is reflected in the Friedsam Law of 1928, which specifically prohibited "the application of state education funds in any city to the credit of the General Fund for the Reduction of Taxation, notwithstanding any provisions to the contrary contained in the charter of such city."[34]

The states' power to hold local districts accountable was rarely used, even after the abolition of the quota system. State-appointed district superintendents in rural areas had the authority to condemn substandard school buildings but, fearing the displeasure of local taxpayers, used their authority sparingly. The Regents' Inquiry of 1937 noted that "literally hundreds" of unsanitary, unsafe, substandard rural schools were still in use.[35] The same report noted that "there is no integrated systematic program for studying and appraising the work of the school."[36] Standardized tests were marked locally and were such unreliable guides to the quality of instruction that both the Rural School Survey and the Regents' Inquiry recommended their use be restricted or eliminated, and supervision of teachers by local or state authorities was sporadic and haphazard.[37] Accountability was further hindered by poor accounting systems at the local level. The Rural School Survey found that half the rural districts did not have budgets, and that the reports district supervisors sent to the state were based on "abstracts" sent to them by local officials, rather than receipts and other substantial data.[38] Cities had their own supervisory systems, and the district supervisors who represented the state in rural areas were careful not to antagonize local officials and taxpayers, believing that to exert state power over the local districts would be undemocratic, futile, and counterproductive. In such an atmosphere, it was difficult to tell whether normal operating directives from the state, much less special requests for reform, were being implemented.

An increased demand for accountability and evaluation came with increased federal spending for educational reform in the 1960s, specifically with the Elementary and Secondary Education Act (ESEA) of 1965. The implementation of Title I of this program through SED illustrates the fact that without accountability, even when monies are earmarked for specific purposes, intended reforms are not necessarily made in the local schools. The ESEA asked local districts (perhaps for the first time) not only how they proposed to spend funds granted through the state, but also how instructional practices and student outcomes changed as a result of the funded programs.[39]

Title I of ESEA provided monies for compensatory education, which would be allocated by state governments for programs to aid children who were from low-income homes or at least one year behind grade level in reading, writing, and mathematics. Considerable sums were involved. In 1972 ESEA paid the salaries of 45,426 teachers, aides, and supervisors throughout the state. In 1974-5 New York's share of ESEA funds amounted to $214,372,281, of which over $190,000,000 went directly to local school districts.[40]

Although responsible for administering and monitoring ESEA projects, the state education department seemed reluctant to do more than provide money for any proposals made by the districts. The state defined 99 percent of all districts eligible for ESEA monies and before 1972 conducted no routine site visitations, nor did the state require local districts to evaluate the impact of the new funds on the targeted populations. The only monitoring was by a mail questionnaire. Only when the federal government required an investigation because of charges of misallocation of funds did the state intervene.

In 1972 a state report stated bluntly that while ESEA funds reached 99 percent of the districts in the state, two-thirds of the targeted population remained outside of the funded programs. The reasons given were "political pressure" and "parental objection."[41] Because no accountability had been built into the program, the district used the funds to hire additional staff to bolster their entire programs, rather than to provide services directly to the children statewide who were identified as in greatest need of services and for whom ESEA monies were intended. The problem lay in the fact that monies were not given to individual schools or individual children within schools, but to the district as a whole. The federal government began to insist on clear-cut accounting. Specifically, it wanted to know how ESEA would serve children, not school districts, and whether the programs had any effect on targeted populations. By 1974-5, with ESEA funds at stake, stricter accountability became part of state practice. Annual reports began to delineate how funded programs were different from programs "not previously occuring in regular classroom activities funded by local and state levy monies."[43] Reports thereafter spoke of students served, rather than of the school districts that received monies.

Evaluation as well as accountability became a stronger part of the ESEA program. Under federal pressure, in 1972 and again in 1975 the state sought to find out whether the programs funded were effective. Such data were difficult to generate. Districts did not necessarily turn over test scores to the state and although there seemed to be improvement in the number of students reading at grade level, there was no way to tell, given the nature of district reportage, if this resulted from ESEA-funded intervention.[43]

Attempts to build accountability and evaluation into reform in the case of ESEA did help get programs to targeted populations, but not without creating a great deal of enmity on the part of the state and local districts toward the federal government in general and ESEA in particular. In its annual recommendations to Washington, *Federal Legislation and Education in New York,* the state education department asserted that the federal government should not set educational priorities. "Elementary and secondary education is the responsibility of the state," SED asserted, and the federal government "should not seek to direct the expenditure of state and local resources."[44] The state insisted that "requirements on state and local agencies have become excessive as related to the proportion of federal assistance available." In 1977 New York State began to ask for block grants from the federal government allocated on a per capita basis (as the local districts had been receiving from the state since 1930), to which the Reagan administration from 1980 was inclined to accede.

LESSONS FROM THE PAST

Our historical survey of reform in New York State has suggested that there are lessons for today's reformers from past efforts in the state that had at best mixed results and, more often, little to do with changes in school practices. Past reforms calling for "excellence," or some other well-intentioned but vaguely stated goal, have rarely succeeded; no one has ever quite been sure how to measure "excellence." More often than not, broad-ranging, vaguely articulated aims, however admirable, ended up promoting contradictory practices that not only undermined intended goals, but also often subverted preexisting programs of proven worth.

The reports of 1983 and 1984 call for greater rigor and more academic and scientific-technological training. It may be that the reforms of today will, like the NDEA of the 1950s, make students take more courses; but will such reforms insure that students learn more? Testing programs being urged today, like the Regents' Basic Competency Testing Program in New York State of the 1970s, may insure that more students fail to receive their diplomas, but will they guarantee excellence in education? Such programs in the past, as in the case of the regents' competency testing program, undermined academic standards and promoted solely test-taking skills.

New York State's history of educational reform also suggests that it is easier to call upon the schools to teach the skills of tomorrow than to have the schools actually teach those skills. The Rural School Survey of 1922, which called for "applying the benefits of the science of education" to school management, or the 1937 Regents' Inquiry, which asked teachers to instruct their students in "good character," both came to naught. A similar fate may await contemporary calls for teaching for the world of tomorrow, and for similar reasons. Everyone agrees it would be a good idea for schools to engage in such activities, but it will not be possible for the schools to do so without careful attention to curricular development.

The extent to which current reform efforts acknowledge the role of committed executive leadership will strongly affect the outcome of the excellence reports. In the past, calls for change that were not accompanied by strong leadership have not affected practice. Without strong leadership and financial resources earmarked for specific purposes, local districts have resisted, ignored, and/or subverted the numerous commissions that have laid the onus for reform on their shoulders. In the past, as we have shown, many calls have emanated from the federal government, the state, and the courts for New York State to equalize educational expenditure; countless committees continue to be appointed to study the issue, but no one has taken responsibility for reform. Until someone exercises strong executive leadership, inequality will continue to be studied but not redressed. American schools will be as uneven in quality ten years hence as they are today if all the responsibility for reform is placed upon local constituencies. As the NDEA-attempted reforms of the 1950s showed, some localities may prefer to ignore current appeals to change their schools, regardless of national and state charges that those schools are at best mediocre and put the nation at risk.

Most of the national reports of the 1980s express a faith that changes in school practice can be made without changes in the amount of money spent on education simply by asking districts or teachers to do more with the same funds, or even with less funding. If it was sometimes possible to do this with a limited reform in the past—the basic skills competency testing program in New York State, for example—it is scarcely possible to do so with the extensive changes suggested today. Although costs have risen so rapidly that taxpayers feel overburdened or the state, in a recession, perceives itself unable to afford its schools, the demands made upon the schools have increased more than the costs. Schools are asked to provide bilingual education, mainstream the handicapped, and offer remedial services to underachievers and enrichment programs to the gifted, while at the same time providing "excellence" in the form of more courses in science, mathematics, and technology and more advanced-placement courses. Our survey of the history of reform in New York State suggests that schools may be unable to meet new demands without substantial increments of additional monies. Otherwise, like the NDEA of the 1950s, programs that have proven benefit run the risk of being undermined so that new untested ones can be funded.

In reviewing the many reforms attempted in education in New York State in the twentieth century, we are struck with the fact that one reform follows so closely upon the other that the schools seem to be in a perpetual process of being reformed. Yet while many have been willing to "reform" the schools, few have taken the time or the trouble to evaluate past reforms, or even to see if they have actually been implemented. It is ironic that the memory of educators and politicians is so short. We find reformers in 1984 charging the schools with failure, when they may well have succeeded in large part in reaching some of the goals established within the last two decades. Just ten years ago in New York State the Fleischmann Report maintained that the state's system of education was "excellent," one of the finest in the world; that its standards were the highest; and that its only major blemish was the glaring inequalities in student outcomes. Today the reform efforts of ten years ago as exemplified by the Fleischmann Commission have been buried as new criteria are being used to determine whether past practices were adequate. New practices are being put into place without thorough knowledge of what "worked" in the past or of what goals from the past are worthy of continued pursuit.

Finally, the history of school reform in New York State indicates that reform movements, like those of today, are fraught with contradictions, not because politicians and pedagogues are blind to their inconsistencies, but because major reform efforts have diverse and contradictory sources. Discontent with the schools today, as in the past, is often in reality discontent about something else: crime, the state of the economy, racial unrest, poverty, an unfavorable balance of trade, or the country's position in the Cold War— complex issues on which the schools have little influence, but on which the national commissions on excellence nonetheless expect the schools to have a direct and salutary effect. In the past school reform has been noticeably unsuccessful when it has focused on social, political, and economic issues the schools could not and may never have been able to resolve. On the other hand, when reform has focused on exposing students to specific curricula or requiring minimal academic standards, it has been able to effect change. The reforms of the 1980s may not be able to make the United States technologically superior to Japan, but they may improve upon what schools try to teach students.

NOTES

This paper was prepared with funding from the Rockefeller Institute for Public Policy in Albany, New York. The authors wish to thank the Institute for its support; the views expressed here are the authors' alone. The authors wish to thank Nana Henne, Wasana Kangvalert, Jennifer Kelly, and Stuart Seller for their assistance in preparing this paper, and Lois Weis, Phil Altbach, and Hugh Petrie for their comments on an earlier draft.

1. See National Commission on Excellence in Education, *A Nation at Risk* (Washington: U.S. Government Printing Office, 1983); Mortimer J. Adler, *The Paideia Proposal: An Educational Manifesto* (New York: Macmillan, 1982); Educational Commission of the States, *Action for Excellence: Task Force on Education for Economic Growth* (June 1983); *Making the Grade, Report of the Twentieth Century Fund Task Force on Federal Elementary and Secondary Educaton Policy* (New York: Twentieth Century Fund, 1983); John A. Goodlad, *A Place Called School: Prospects for the Future* (New York: McGraw-Hill, 1984); National Science Board, Commission

on Precollege Education in Mathematics, Science and Technology, *Educating Americans for the 21st Century: A Plan of Action for Improving Mathematics, Science and Technology Education for All American Elementary and Secondary Students so that Their Achievement Is the Best in the World by 1995* (Washington: National Science Foundation, 1983); Theodore Sizer, *Horace's Compromise: The Dilemma of the American High School* (Boston: Houghton-Mifflin, 1984); National Academy of Sciences, National Academy of Engineering, Institute of Medicine, Committee on Science, Engineering and Public Policy, *High Schools and the Changing Workplace: The Employers' View* (Washington: National Academy Press, 1984); The College Board, *Academic Preparation for College: What Students Need to Know and Be Able to Do* (New York: The College Board, 1983); Ernest Boyer, *High School: A Report on Secondary Education in America: The Carnegie Foundation for the Advancement of Teaching* (New York: Harper and Row, 1983); Business-Higher Education Forum, *America's Competitive Challenge; The Need for a National Response: A Report to the President of the United States from the Business-Higher Education Forum* (Washington, D.C.: Business-Higher Education Forum, 1983).

2. New York State Board of Regents, *Proposed Action Plan to Improve Elementary and Secondary Education Results in New York* (Albany: State Education Department, 1983); New York State Board of Regents, *New Part 100 of the Commissioners' Regulations Re: Regents Action Plan* (Albany: State Education Department, 1984).

3. See U.S. Department of Education, *The Nation Responds: Recent Efforts to Improve Education* (Washington: U.S. Department of Education, 1984); "The States Consider Incentives for Teachers," *Politics of Education Bulletin 2* (Spring 1984): 9, 11.

4. See Paul Hanus, "The Report as a Whole," in New York City Board of Estimate and Apportionment, *Report of the Committee on School Inquiry,* 2 vols. (New York City: 1911-1913), vol. 1, pp. 57, 134.

5. The Joint Committee on Rural Schools, George A. Works, chairman, *Rural School Survey of New York State: A Report to the Rural School Patrons* (Ithaca, N.Y.: 1922): 74-75; Leo J. Brueckner, *The Changing Elementary School, The Regents' Inquiry* (New York: Inor Publishing Company, 1939): 64.

6. Charles H. Judd and others, *Administration and Supervision, Rural School Survey of New York State, Joint Committee on Rural Schools,* (Ithaca, N.Y.: 1923), Part IV, "Principles of Organization and Administration," by Franklin Bobbitt, pp. 327-28. For a general discussion of the survey's views on administration and its conflicts with local opinion, see pp. 263-412; see also George A. Works, *Rural School Survey of New York State: A Report to the Patrons,* 257-58.

7. Brueckner, *The Changing Elementary School,* 149-51.

8. Board of Estimate and Apportionment, *Report of the Committee on School Inquiry,* 14, 57, 17-18.

9. Board of Estimate and Apportionment, *Report of the Committee on School Inquiry,* especially pp. 17-21, 57-60, 64-65, 126-28, 137-42, 156-57. Valuable background on the conflicting views embodied in the Hanus Report can be found in Sol Cohen, *Progressives and Urban School Reform,* and Diane Ravitch, *The Great School Wars: New York City 1805-1973* (New York: Basic Books, 1974).

10. This discussion is based on the yearly reports on ESEA prepared by the State Education Department, Bureau of Urban and Community Programs Evaluation, which appeared from 1970 on. See, for example, the University of the State of New York, The State Education Department, Bureau of Urban and Community Programs Evaluation, *New York State, 1974-5, ESEA, Title I* (Albany: Author, 1975). For local studies, see The University of the State of New York, State Education Department, Office of Programs Analysis and Evaluation, *A Study of ESEA Title I in Selected*

School Districts (Albany, 1977).

11. The 1974 Supreme Court Decision, *Lau* vs. *Nichols* ruled that school districts are compelled under Title VI of the 1964 Civil Rights Act to provide meaningful education to children whose native tongue was not English. In May 1975, the state education department reprinted a federal publication written by the United States Commission on Civil Rights entitled *A Better Chance to Learn: Bilingual Bicultural Education* (Clearinghouse Publication No. 51). See also New York State Assembly, *Bilingual Bicultural Education, Preliminary Report of the Sub-committee* (Albany: October 1978). The issue of bilingual education had been raised earlier by the Fleischmann Commission. See *The Fleischmann Report on the Quality, Cost and Financing of Elementary and Secondary Education in New York State* (New York: Viking Press, 1973), vol. 1, pp. 3–52.

12. The many pieces of legislation affecting the mainstreaming of handicapped children, as well as federal and state legislation on bilingual education, are summarized yearly and published by the state. See the yearly *Summary of New York Legislation Affecting Education*, compiled by the Office of Counsel from 1975 (Albany: State Education Department). For federal legislation and New York State's reactions, see The University of the State of New York, The State Education Department, *Federal Legislation and Education in New York State* (Albany: Author, annual), especially from 1973 on.

13. *The Fleischmann Report*.

14. See New York Court of Appeals, Board of Education Levittown Free School District vs. Ewald Nyquist. 57 NY 2d 27, June 23, 1982.

15. See New York State Task Force on Equity and Excellence in Education, *The Search for Equity: Interim Report of the New York State Special Task Force on Equity and Excellence in Education*, 3 vols. (Albany, February 1982).

16. This following discussion of the fiscal crisis and school aid reforms of the 1920s is based on the following accounts: Harlan Updegraff, The Rural School Survey of New York State, *Financial Support* (Ithaca, New York, 1922); George D. Strayer and Robert Murray Haig, *The Financing of Education in the State of New York*, Education Finance Inquiry, Vol. I, under the auspices of the American Council on Education, Washington, D.C., (New York, Macmillan, 1923); Paul R. Mort, *State Support for Public School* (New York: Teachers College Press, Teachers College, Columbia, 1926); Alonzo G. Grace and G. A. Moe, *State Aid and School Costs* (New York: McGraw-Hill, 1938) (which contains a summary of all the state reports relating to school finance from 1920 to 1935); Paul E. Malone, *The Fiscal Aspects of State and Local Relationships in New York*, Special Report of the New York State Tax Commission, no. 13, (Albany, 1937); and Rose Naomi Cohen, *The Financial Control of Education in the Consolidated City of New York*, Teachers College, Columbia University, Special Contributions to Education #943 (New York: Teachers College Press, 1948).

17. Grace and Moe, *State Aid and School Costs*, 45–46.

18. For amounts of aid, see Rose Naomi Cohen, *The Financial Control of Education*, 162, 173; for percentages, see Paul E. Malone, *The Fiscal Aspects of State and Local Relationships in New York*, 204, 234.

19. Alfred E. Smith, *Up to Now: An Autobiography* (New York: The Viking Press, 1929): 276. On Smith's attitudes and public actions relating to education, see pp. 202–205, 276–79; on his financial policies, see pp. 334–53. See also David M. Ellis, James A. Frost, Harold C. Syrett, and Harry J. Carman, *A History of New York State* (Ithaca, N.Y.: New York State Historical Association and Cornell University Press, 1967): 393–406.

20. *The Fleischmann Report*, vol. 1, pp. 53–208; for recommendations on the curriculum, see vol 2, pp. 3–58; 59–101.

21. See, for example, Richard N. Bosivert, "The Impact of School Financing Reform on New York State Taxpayers" (Albany: 1973); New York State, Special Task Force on Equity and Excellence in Education, *An Interim Report,* September 1980; New York State Task Force on Aid to Education, *Report to Governor Hugh Carey* (Albany, January 1981); Charles W. deSeve, *Who Bears the Cost of New York's Schools? Measuring the Tax Burden: Report Prepared for the New York State Task Force on Equity and Excellence in Education* (Albany, 1980); *The Report and Recommendations of the New York State Special Task Force on Equity and Excellence in Education,* February 1982, 3 vols.

22. Emery Ferris, *The Rural High School,* Rural School Survey of New York State (Ithaca, N.Y., 1922): especially 47–51, 178–83; Theodore H. Eaton, *Vocational Education,* The Rural School Survey of New York State (Ithaca, 1922): 266–71.

25. Eaton, *Vocational Education,* 64. For the history of state and federal aid to agricultural and home economics programs, see pp. 13–25. See also University of the State of New York, *New York State Education Department 1900–1965* (Albany: State Education Department, 1967); 22–24

24. University of New York, *New York State Education Department,* 64–70.

25. Wayne W. Soper and Warren W. Coxe, *Trends in Secondary Education* (University of the State of New York Bulletin #961, December 1, 1930): 44–46; Thomas C. Norton, *Education for Work,* The Regents Inquiry (New York: McGraw-Hill, 1938): 51–52.

26. This discussion of the NDEA is based in part on the following sources: The University of the State of New York, State Education Department, *Regents' Program for Meeting Needs in Science, Technology and Education of the Talented* (Albany: Author, 1958); The State University of New York, the State Education Department, Bureau of Department Programs Evaluation, *National Defense Education Act, Title III: An Evaluation of the Program in New York State* (Albany: Author, 1965); New York State, Education Department, *Annual Narrative Report on Programs for Strengthening Instruction in the Critical Subjects—Science, Mathematics, History, Civics, Geography, Modern Foreign Languages, English and Reading for Fiscal Year 1965* (Albany: Author, 1966).

27. *NDEA, Title III Evaluation* (1965), 22.

28. *NDEA, Title III Evaluation* (1965). See also *Annual Narrative Report on Programs for Strengthening Instruction in Critical Subjects,* vol. 2, pp. 2, 10; vol. 3, p. 4.

29. *Annual Narrative Report.*

30. The discussion of the Basic Competency Testing Program (renamed the Regents' Competency Testing Program) is based in part on University of the State of New York, Office of the President of the University and Commissioner of Education, The Regents' Competency Testing Program. *Setting Standards in the Basic Skills as a Requirement for High School Graduation.* Information Brochure (Albany: Author, September 1978, mimeo); The University of the State of New York, the State Education Department, *The Regents' Competency Testing Program: Competency Testing, Remedial Instruction and High School Credentials—Regulations and Procedures* (Albany: Author, March 1979).

31. See Boyer, *High School,* chapter 1.

32. George A. Works, *Rural School Survey: A Report to the School Patrons,* 239–240. An excellent summary of the legislative and judicial basis for the state's primary responsibility for education is found in Rose Naomi Cohen, *The Financial Control of Education,* chapter 5, pp. 142–60.

33. Judd, *Administration and Supervision,* 205; Brueckner, *The Changing Elementary School,* 188.

34. Cohen, *The Financial Control of Education,* 174. For a summary of the quota system from 1920 to 1930, see Grace and Moe, *State Aid and School Costs,* 36–39.

35. Brueckner, *The Changing Elementary School*, 181. See also Julian E. Butterworth, *School Buildings and Grounds*, Rural School Survey of New York State (Ithaca, 1922): 124; and Judd, *Administration and Supervision*, 175.

36. Brueckner, *The Changing Elementary School*, 217.

37. On supervision, see Brueckner, *The Changing Elementary School*, 259; Judd, *Administration and Supervision*, 191–204; Grace and Moe, *State Aid and School Costs*, 91. On examinations, see Paul J. Kruse, "The State System of Examinations," in Judd, *Administration and Supervision*, 414–542.

38. Works, *Rural School Survey of New York: A Report to the Patrons*, 219–20; Judd, *Administration and Supervision*, 184. In both these volumes the tension between the attempt of the state to enforce minimal standards and the strong tradition of local autonomy is a recurring theme. State curriculum requirements for elementary schools are summarized in Brueckner, *The Changing Elementary School*, 100–101.

39. This discussion of Title I of the ESEA is based on the yearly reports prepared by the State Education Department, Bureau of Urban and Community Programs Evaluation, *New York State, ESEA, Title I* issued between 1970 and 1978.

40. The University of the State of New York, The State Education Department, Bureau of Urban and Community Programs, *Evaluation, 1971–1972 Achievement, ESEA, Title I* (Albany, 1972): 49; The University of the State of New York, The State Education Department, Bureau of Urban and Community Programs Evaluation, New York State, *1974–5, ESEA Title I. Annual Report, Section One: Program Descriptors* (Albany: Author, 1975): 2.

41. *Evaluation, 1971–2, Achievement, ESEA, Title I*, xiii.

42. *1974–5, ESEA, Title I*, 2.

43. See especially The University of the State of New York, State Education Department, *Evaluation, Elementary and Secondary Education. A Report to the Governor and Members of the Legislature Prepared Pursuant to Section 3602 of the Education Law* (Albany: Author, March 1974), especially p. 5, 8. See also the University of the State of New York, State Education Department, Office of Programs Analysis and Evaluation, *A Study of ESEA Title I in Selected School Districts* (Albany: Author, 1977).

44. University of the State of New York, State Education Department, *Federal Legislation and Education in New York State* (Albany: Author, 1977): 2.

The Excellence Debates
A Select Bibliography

Kowsar P. Chowdhury and Philip G. Altbach

The debates on excellence in education have generated not only many volumes of reports but also considerable commentary from educators, researchers, politicians, and even the president of the United States. So far, the literature seems to be limited to commentary and there is very little research evident. It is hoped that researchers will begin to seriously analyze the impact of the excellence debates on educational policy and practice as the reports begin to have effects on the educational system at all levels. If nothing else, this bibliography indicates that the excellence reports have produced a lively debate within the education community. The comments cover a variety of perspectives and reflect the diversity of opinion.

This bibliography is intended to provide a selected listing of the books and articles related to the excellence debates. We have included relevant books and articles that will be generally available. We have excluded most unpublished reports and documents. We have also excluded very short commentaries and articles from newspapers and general interest magazines.

The bibliography is organized in three parts. The first section includes as many of the reports that have been published in the past several years as we could locate. The second part consists of commentary and analysis of the reports in particular and the "excellence debates" generally. The third part is a listing of the interesting documents that were prepared by the National Commission on Excellence in Education and that are available from the ERIC System. As the literature is rapidly expanding, this bibliography is necessarily incomplete and provides a relatively early "snapshot" of a developing literature.

THE REPORTS

Adler, Mortimer J. *The Paideia Proposal.* New York: Macmillan, 1982.

Association of American Medical Colleges. *Physicians for the 21st Century.* Washington, D.C.: Association of American Medical Colleges, 1984.

Boyer, Ernest L. *High School: A Report on Secondary Education in America.* New York: Harper and Row, 1983.

Business–Higher Education Forum. *America's Competitive Challenge: The Need for a National Response.* Washington, D.C.: Business–Higher Education Forum, 1983.

College Board Educational Equality Project. *Academic Preparation for College: What Students Need to Know and Be Able to Do.* New York: The College Board, 1983.

Commission on International Education. *What We Don't Know Can Hurt Us: The Shortfall in International Competence.* Washington, D.C.: American Council on Education, 1983.

Education Commission of the States Task Force on Education for Growth. *Action for Excellence.* Denver, Colo.: Education Commission of the States, 1983.

Feistritzer, E. Emily. *The Making of a Teacher: A Report on Teacher Education and Certification.* Washington, D.C.: National Center for Educational Information, 1984.

Goodlad, John I. *A Place Called School: Prospects for the Future.* New York: McGraw-Hill Book Company, 1983.

National Commission on Excellence in Education. *A Nation at Risk: The Imperative for Educational Reform.* Washington, D.C.: U.S. Government Printing Office, 1983.

National Science Foundation. *Educating Americans for the 21st Century: A Plan of Action for Improving Mathematics, Science and Technology Education for All American Elementary and Secondary Students So That Their Achievement Is the Best in the World by 1995. A Report to the American People and the National Science Board.* Washington, D.C.: National Science Foundation, 1983.

New York State Education Department. *Proposed Action Plan to Improve Elementary and Secondary Education Results in New York.* Albany, N.Y.: New York State Education Department, 1983.

Sizer, Theodore R. *Horace's Compromise: The Dilemma of the American High School.* Boston: Houghton Mifflin, 1984.

"Text of New Report on Excellence in Undergraduate Education." *Chronicle of Higher Education* (October 1984): 35–49.

Twentieth Century Fund. *Making the Grade: Report of the Twentieth Century Fund Task Force on Federal Elementary and Secondary Education Policy.* New York: Twentieth Century Fund, 1983.

United States Department of Education. *Meeting the Challenge: Recent Efforts to Improve Education across the Nation. A Report to the Secretary of Education.* Washington, D.C.: United States Department of Education, 1983.

———. *The Nation Responds: Recent Efforts to Improve Education.* Washington, D.C.: United States Department of Education, 1984.

BOOKS

Adelman, Clifford. *College Curriculum: Shape, Influence, and Assessment. Staff Analysis of a Panel Discussion Conducted by the National Commission on Excellence in Education.* Washington: D.C.: National Commission on Excellence in Education, 1982.

Adler, Mortimer J. *Paideia Problems and Possibilities: A Consideration of Questions Raised by the Paideia Proposal.* New York: Macmillan, 1983.

————. *The Paideia Program: An Educational Syllabus.* New York: Macmillan, 1984.

American Association of School Administrators. *The Excellence Report: Using It to Improve Your Schools.* Arlington, Va.: American Association of School Administrators, 1983.

Etzioni, Amitai. *An Immodest Agenda: Rebuilding America Before the 21st Century.* New York: New Press/McGraw-Hill, 1983.

Finn, Chester E., Jr., Diane Ravitch, and Robert T. Fancher, eds. *Against Mediocrity: The Humanities in America's High Schools.* New York: Holmes and Meier, 1984.

Griesemer, J. Lynn, and C. Butler. *Education Under Study: An Analysis of Recent Major Reports on Education.* Chelmsford, Mass.: Northeast Regional Exchange, Inc., 1983.

Kelly, Gail P., ed. *Excellence, Reform and Equity in Education: An International Perspective.* Buffalo, N.Y.: Comparative Education Center, State University of New York at Buffalo, 1984.

Lake, Sara. *The Educator's Digest of Reform: A Comparison of 16 Recent Proposals for Improving America's Schools.* Redwood City, Calif.: San Mateo County Office of Education, 1984.

Levin, Henry M. *A Challenge for Action: National Leadership and Involvement in Education.* Stanford, Calif.: Stanford University California Institute for Research on Educational Finance and Governance, 1983.

Lightfoot, Sara Lawrence. *The Good High School: Portraits of Character and Culture.* New York: Basic Books, 1983.

National Commission on Excellence in Education. *Panel on Performance Expectations in American Education. Summary Report, Philadelphia, Pennsylvania, April 30, 1982.* Washington, D.C.: National Commission on Excellence in Education, 1982.

Nathan, Joe. *Free to Teach: Achieving Equity and Excellence in Schools.* New York: Pilgrim Press, 1984.

National Science Foundation. *Educating Americans for the 21st Century: A Plan of Action for Improving Mathematics, Science and Technology Education for All American Elementary and Secondary Students So That Their Achievement Is the Best in the World by 1995. Source Materials.* Washington, D.C.: National Science

Foundation, 1983.

Passow, A. Harry. *Reforming Schools in the 1980s: A Critical Review of the National Reports.* New York: ERIC Clearinghouse on Urban Education, 1984.

Ravitch, Diane. *The Troubled Crusade: American Education 1945-1980.* New York: Basic Books, 1983.

West, Edwin G. *Are American Schools Working? Distributing Cost and Quality Trends.* Washington, D.C.: Cato Institute, 1983.

ARTICLES

Albrect, James E., and Terry Duea. "What Price Excellence? The Iowa Experience." *Phi Delta Kappan* 65 (November 1983): 211-13.

Aldridge, Bill G., and Karen L. Johnston. "A Response to the National Reports." *NASSP Bulletin* 68 (March 1984): 20-24.

Ambach, Gordon M. "State and Local Action for Education in New York." *Phi Delta Kappan* 66 (November 1984): 202-4.

Bailey, Adrienne Y. "The Educational Equality Project: Focus on Results." *Phi Delta Kappan* 65 (September 1983): 22-25.

———. "Agenda for Action." *Educational Leadership* 41 (March 1984): 64-68.

Bell, Terrel H. "The Federal Role in Education." *Harvard Education Review* 52 (November 1982): 375-80.

———. "Leadership for Reform and Renewal of American Education." *American Education* 20 (March 1984): 5-94.

———. "American Education at a Crossroads." *Phi Delta Kappan* 65 (April 1984): 531-34.

Best, John Hardin. "Reforming America's Schools: The High Risks of Failure." *Teachers College Record* 86 (Winter 1984): 265-74.

Boiarsky, C., and C. Johnson. "The Excellence in Education Report: Connecting Reading, Writing and Thinking." *Curriculum Review* 22 (December 1983): 37-40.

Boyer, Ernest L. "Reflections on the Great Debate of '83." *Phi Delta Kappan* 65 (April 1984): 525-30.

Brandt, R. "On Excellence and Mediocrity: A Conversation with Milton Goldberg." *Educational Leadership* 41 (March 1984): 17-19.

Chandler, Harry N. "Just Among Us Teachers." *Phi Delta Kappan* 65 (November 1983) 181-82.

Clark, David L., Terry A. Astuto, and Paula M. Rooney. "The Changing Structure of Federal Education Policy in the 1980s." *Phi Delta Kappan* 65 (November 1983): 188-93.

Clinchy, Evans. "Yes, But What About Irving Engleman?" *Phi Delta Kappan* 65 (April 1984): 542-45.

Cohen, David K. "Policy and Organization: The Impact of State and Federal Educational Policy on School Governance." *Harvard Education Review* 52 (November 1982): 474-99.

Cross, K. Patricia. "The Rising Tide of School Reform Reports." *Phi Delta Kappan* 66 (November 1984): 167-72.

Dodd, Anne Wescott. "A New Design For Public Education." *Phi Delta Kappan* 65 (June 1984): 685-87.

Doyle, Dennis P. "Deregulation, the New Federalism, and Scarcity: The End of Additive Reform." *Phi Delta Kappan* 64 (September 1982): 54-58.

Ebel, Robert L. "Three Radical Proposals for Strengthening Education." *Phi Delta Kappan* 6 (February 1982): 375-78.

"Education in the Eighties: Political Trends—A Symposium." *Teachers College Record* 84 (Spring 1983): 669-752.

Eicholtz, Robert L. "School Climate: Key to Excellence." *American Education* 20 (January-February 1984): 22-26.

Elshtain, J. B. "Time to Reform the Schools." *American Education* 19 (June 1983): 38-41+.

Ericson, David P. "Of Minima and Maxima: The Social Significance of Minimal Competency Testing and the Search for Educational Excellence." *American Journal of Education* 92 (May 1984): 245-61.

Evans, H. Dean. "We Must Begin Education Reform Every Place at Once." *Phi Delta Kappan* 65 (November 1983): 173-77.

"Excellence in Education (Symposium)." *Instructional Innovator* 28 (September 1983): 14-36.

Farrar, Eleanor, J. E. Desanctis, and D. K. Cohen. "Views from Below: Implementation Research in Education." *Teachers College Record* 82 (Fall 1980): 77-100.

Finn, Chester E., Jr. "A Call for Quality Education." *American Education* 18 (January-February 1982): 31-36.

———. "The Drive for Educational Excellence: Moving Toward a Public Consensus." *Change* 15 (April 1983): 14-22.

———. "Teacher Unions and School Quality: Potential Allies or Inevitable Foes? *Phi Delta Kappan* 66 (January 1985): 331-38.

Finn, Chester E., Jr., and others. "The New Basics for Everyone?" *Educational Leadership* 41 (Ocotober 1983): 28-33.

Florio, David H. "Curing America's Quick-Fix Mentality: A Role for Federally Supported Educational Research." *Phi Delta Kappan* 64 (February 1983): 411-15.

Fowler, C. W. "Only Masochists Could Accept the Findings of the Excellence Commission." *American School Board Journal* 170 (September 1983): 43+.

Gardner, David Pierpont. "A Time for Re-examination and Renewal Commitments." *American Education* 18 (August–September 1982): 31–34.

Gardner, William E. "A Nation at Risk: Some Critical Comments." *Journal of Teacher Education* 35 (January–February 1984): 13–15.

Gates, James D. "A Response to the National Reports." *NASSP Bulletin* 68 (March 1984): 13–15.

Giroux, Henry A. "Public Philosophy and the Crisis in Education." *Harvard Educational Review* 54 (May 1984): 186–94.

Glazer, Nathan. "The Problem With Competence." *American Journal of Education* 92 (May 1984): 306–13.

Goldberg, Milton. "The Essential Points of a Nation at Risk." *Educational Leadership* 41 (March 1984): 15–16+.

Goldberg, Milton, and James Harvey. "A Nation at Risk: The Report of the National Commission on Excellence in Education." *Phi Delta Kappan* 65 (September 1983): 14–18.

Goodlad, John I. "A Study of Schooling: Some Implications for School Improvement." *Phi Delta Kappan* 64 (April 1983): 552–58.

———. "Access to Knowledge." *Teachers College Record* 84 (Summer 1983): 787–800.

———. "Improving Schooling in the 1980's: Toward the Non Replication of Non Events." *Educational Leadership* 40 (1983): 4–7.

Gordon, Shirley B. "A Nation at Risk: Community Colleges to the Rescue." *Community and Junior College Journal* 54 (September 1983): 14–15.

Graham, Patricia Aljberg. "The Twentieth Century Fund Task Force Report on Federal Elementary and Secondary Education Policy." *Phi Delta Kappan* 65 (September 1983): 19–21.

Gray, Dennis. "Whatever Became of Paideia? (And How Do You Pronounce It?)." *Educational Leadership* 41 (March 1984): 56–57.

Greene, Maxine. "'Excellence,' Meanings and Multiplicity." *Teachers College Record* 86 (Winter 1984): 283–98.

Hall, Peter M. "A Social Construction of Reality." *Elementary School Journal* 84 (November 1983): 142–48.

Hayden, Rose Lee. "A Response to the National Reports." *NASSP Bulletin* 68 (March 1984): 17–19.

Hedin, Diane. "A Nation at Risk: Is It Good for Students." *Journal of Experimental Education* 7 (Spring 1984): 22–27.

Heyns, Barbara L. "Policy Implications and the Public and Private School Debates."

Harvard Education Review 51 (November 1981): 519–25+.

"Higher Standard (Symposium)." *Education Leadership* 41 (October 1983): 3–12+.

Hipple, Theodore W., and others. "To Help a Nation at Risk, Try Boyer and Goodlad." *English Journal* 73 (April 1984): 22–25.

Howe, Harold II. "Education Moves to Center Stage: An Overview of Recent Studies." *Phi Delta Kappan* 65 (November 1983): 167–72.

Hunt, James B., Jr. "Action for Excellence—[Excerpt from Report by Task Force on Education for Economic Growth]." *Educational Leadership* 41 (September 1983): 14–18.

―――. "Education for Economic Growth: A Critical Investment." *Phi Delta Kappan* 65 (April 1984): 538–41.

Husen, Torsten. "Are Standards in U.S. Schools Really Lagging Behind Those in Other Countries?" *Phi Delta Kappan* 64 (March 1983): 455–61.

Hymovitz, L. "Schools for Survival in the Twenty-First Century (Implications of Report entitled 'Global 2000 Report to the President: Entering the Twenty-First Century')." *The Clearing House* 55 (September 1981): 32–34.

Justiz, M. J. "It's Time to Make Every Minute Count." *Phi Delta Kappan* 65 (March 1984): 483–85.

Kaplan, George R. "Some Cranky Fulminations on Reagan and Education." *Phi Delta Kappan* 9 (May 1982): 592–95.

―――. "Hail to a Chief or Two: The Indifferent Presidential Record in Education." *Phi Delta Kappan* 66 (September 1984): 7–12.

Kerr, Donna H. "Teaching Competence and Teacher Education in the United States." *Teachers College Record* 84 (Spring 1983): 525–52+.

Kraft, Richard J. "A Summary of the Major Reports." *Journal of Experimental Education* 7 (Spring 1984): 9–15.

Labaree. David F. "Setting the Standard: Alternative Policies for Student Promotion." *Harvard Education Review* 54 (February 1984): 67–87.

Lachance, Roger. "'A Nation at Risk'—A Principal's Viewpoint." *NASSP Bulletin* 68 (March 1984): 45–48.

Langberg, Arnold. "A High School Principal Looks at the National Reports." *Journal of Experimental Education* 7 (Spring 1984): 32–35.

Leonard, G. E. "The Great School Reform Hoax." *Esquire* 101 (April 1984): 47–52+.

Levin, Henry M. "Federal Grants and Educational Equity." *Harvard Education Review* 52 (November 1982): 444–59.

Lieberman, Myron. "Here's Why the Key Recommendations of the Excellence Commission Never Will Become Reality in Most Local School Systems." *American School Board Journal* 171 (February 1984): 32–33.

Loucks. Susan F. "At Last: Some Good News From a Study of School Improvement." *Educational Leadership* 41 (November 1983): 4–5.

Maker, C. J., and S. W. Schiever. "Excellence for the Future." *Gifted Child Quarterly* 28 (Winter 1984): 6–8.

Merseth, Katherine K. "From the Rhetoric of Reports to the Clarity of Classrooms." *Educational Leadership* 4 (December 1983–January 1984): 38–42.

Metzger, Christa. "Gummibears Instead of Sour Grapes: A Positive Response to the National Reports on School Reform." *Phi Delta Kappan* 66 (November 1984): 177–82.

Minter, Thomas K. "The Importance of the Federal Role in Improving Educational Practice: Lessons from a Big-City School System." *Harvard Education Review* 52 (November 1982): 500–13.

Mondale, Walter F. "The Mondale Strategy for Excellence in Education." *Phi Delta Kappan* 66 (June 1984): 16–19.

Nash, Robert J., and Edward K. Ducharme. "'Where There is No Vision, the People Perish': A Nation at Risk." *Journal of Teacher Education* 34 (July–August 1983): 38–46.

"A Nation at Risk: The Imperative for Educational Reform." *American Education* 19 (June 1983): 2–3, 5–17.

"A Nation at Risk (Symposium)." *Independent School* 43 (October 1983): 13–17+.

"A Nation at Risk: The Imperative for Educational Reform." *Elementary School Journal* 84 (November 1983): 112–30; discussion, 131–48.

"A Nation at Risk: Implications for Educational Measurement." *Educational Measurement: Issues and Practice* 2 (Winter 1983).

"A Nation at Risk (Symposium)." *NASSP Bulletin* 68 (March 1984): 1–59.

"National Reports on Education: A Round Table Discussion." *American Education* 20 (March 1984): 38–45.

Neill, G. "Quality of Math, Science Teaching—Federal Commission Studied Problem." *NASSP Bulletin* 66 (October 1982): 41–48.

"A New Basics for Everyone? A Symposium on Curriculum Recommendations of the Commission on Excellence." *Educational Leadership* 41 (October 1983): 28–33.

Odden, Allan. "Financing Educational Excellence." *Phi Delta Kappan* 65 (January 1984): 311–18.

Ohanian, Susan. "Huffing and Puffing and Blowing Schools Excellent." *Phi Delta Kappan* 66 (January 1985): 316–20.

Page, Homer. "Two Perspectives on the Crisis in Education." *Journal of Experimental Education* 7 (Spring 1984): 36–39.

"The Paideia Proposal: A Symposium." *Harvard Education Review* 53 (November

1983): 377–411.

Passow, A. Harry. "Tackling the Reform Reports of the 1980s." *Phi Delta Kappan* 65 (June 1984): 674–83.

Pellicano, Roy R. "Literacy for Modern Times." *Educational Leadership* 41 (December 1983–January 1984): 67–69.

Peterson, Paul E. "Did the Education Commissions Say Anything?" *Brookings Review* 2 (1983): 3–11.

Ravitch, Diane. "The Continuing Crisis: Fashions in Education." *American Scholar* 53 (Spring 1984): 183–93.

Reagan, Ronald. "Excellence and Opportunity: A Program of Support for American Education." *Phi Delta Kappan* 66 (September 1984): 13–15.

"Recent Reports on Education: A Digest." *Change* 15 (November–December 1983): 38–43.

"Reflections on the Future of American Education (Symposium)." *Peabody Journal of Education* 59 (January 1982): 69–92.

Reisler, R. F. "Education Agenda for the Eighties [Report of the President's Commission for a National Agenda for the Eighties]." *Phi Delta Kappan* 62 (February 1981): 413–14+.

"Reply to 'A Nation at Risk' [Report of the CEC Ad Hoc Committee to Study and Respond to the 1983 Report of the National Commission on Excellence in Education]." *Exceptional Children* 50 (April 1984): 484–94.

Rethinking the Federal Role in Education: A Special Issue of *Harvard Education Review* 52 (November 1982): 371+.

Resnick, Daniel P., and Lauren B. Resnick. "Improving Educational Standards in American Schools." *Phi Delta Kappan* 65 (November 1983): 178–80.

Rosenholtz, Susan J. "Political Myths About Education Reform: Lessons from Research on Teaching" *Phi Delta Kappan* 66 (January 1985): 349–55.

Schuster, Jack H. "Out of the Frying Pan: The Politics of Education in a New Era." *Phi Delta Kappan* 63 (May 1982): 583–91.

Schlechty, Phillip C., and Victor S. Vance. "Institutional Responses to the Quality/Quantity Issue in Teacher Training." *Phi Delta Kappan* 65 (October 1983): 94–101.

Scribner, J. D. "Defining A Nation at Risk: Excellence Costs." *Education Digest* 49 (December 1983): 10–12.

Seaborg, G. T. "A Call for Educational Reform." *Science* 221 (July 1983): 219+.

Seeley, David S. "Educational Partnership and the Dilemmas of School Reform." *Phi Delta Kappan* 65 (February 1984): 383–88.

Shanker, Albert. "Taking the Measure of American Education Reform: An Assessment of the Education Reports." *American Journal of Education* 92 (May 1984):

314–24.

Shreeve, William, and others. "Citizens and Educators Should Assess Local Strengths in View of National Report." *NASSP Bulletin* 68 (March 1984): 30–36.

Slavin, Robert E. "Realities and Remedies." *Elementary School Journal* 84 (November 1983): 131–38.

Smith, G. Pritchy. "The Critical Issue of Excellence and Equity in Competence Testing." *Journal of Teacher Education* 35 (March–April 1984): 6–9.

Spock, B. "Coercion in the Classroom Won't Work [Critique of Report]." *Atlantic* 253 (April 1984): 28–30+.

Stedman, Lawrence C., and Marshall S. Smith. "Recent Reform Proposals for American Education." *Contemporary Education Review* 2 (Fall 1983): 85–104.

"Symposium on the Year of the Reports: Responses from the Educational Community." *Harvard Education Review* 54 (February 1984): 1–31.

Taber, Gary Davisson. "The Affective Domain and 'A Nation at Risk'." *NASSP Bulletin* 68 (March 1984): 49–52.

Tanner, Daniel. "The American High School at the Crossroads." *Educational Leadership* (March 1984): 4–13.

"Teacher Responds to Commission Reports (Symposium)." *English Journal* 73 (March 1984): 22–25.

Tesconi, Charles A., Jr. "Additive Reform and the Retreat from Purpose." *Educational Studies* 15 (Spring 1984): 1–10.

Thomas, H. "Essay Before a Course: Against the Commission's Report." *Lutheran Education* 119 (January–February 1984): 154–59.

Toch, Thomas, "The Dark Side of the Excellence Movement." *Phi Delta Kappan* 66 (November 1984): 173–76.

Tollett, Kenneth S. "The Property of the Federal Role in Expanding Equal Educational Opportunity." *Harvard Education Review* 52 (November 1982): 431–43.

Turnbull, Brenda J. "The Federal Role in Educational Improvement." *Harvard Education Review* 52 (November 1982): 514–28.

Tye, Kenneth A., and Barbara Benham Tye. "Teacher Isolation and School Reform." *Phi Delta Kappan* 65 (January 1984): 319–22.

Vik, Phil. "A Response to 'A Nation at Risk': More Looking and Less Leaping." *NASSP Bulletin* 68 (March 1984): 53–59.

Walker, B. F. "A Nation at Risk! Again?" *Contemporary Education* 55 (Winter 1984): 119–20.

Watt, D. G. "Some Thoughts on Educational Reform and Renewal." *American Education* 19 (July 1983): 26–30.

Weckstein, Paul. "Democratic Economic Development Is the Key to Future Quality Education." *Phi Delta Kappan* 64 (February 1983): 420–23.

White, Daphne Siev, and Jay Sommer. "The Agenda for Excellence." *American Educator* 7 (Fall 1983): 32–35, 42.

Williams, Dennis A., and others. "Can The Schools Be Saved?" *Newsweek* 9 (May 1983): 50–58.

Wood, Fred H., Gil Johnson, and Tom Paden. "Will This New Round of Recommendations for High Schools Make a Difference?" *Educational Leadership* 41 (March 1984): 69–72.

Yutvin, J. "Two Muddled Recommendations from A Nation at Risk." *Principal* 63 (March 1984): 41–43.

DOCUMENTS COMMISSIONED BY THE NATIONAL COMMISSION ON EXCELLENCE IN EDUCATION

(These materials are available through the ERIC System. ERIC document numbers are included.)

Adelman, Clifford. "Diffusion and the College Connection: A Study of High School Transcripts, 1964–1981." 81pp. ED 228-244.

Adelson, Joseph. "Twenty-Five Years of American Education: An Interpretation." 41 pp. ED 227-108.

Ailes, Catherine P. "A Summary Report on the Educational Systems of the United States and the Soviet Union: Comparative Analysis." 40 pp. ED 227-106.

Astin, Alexander W. "The American Freshmen, 1966–1981: Some Implications for Educational Policy and Practice." 59 pp. ED 227-070.

———. "Excellence and Equity in American Education." 30 pp. ED 227-098.

Blake, Herman. "Demographic Change and Curriculum: New Students in Higher Education." 42 pp. ED 225-994.

Brod, Richard I., N. Farnham, W. Mayer, and R. McCaughey. "University Entrance Examinations and Performance Expectations: A Comparison of the United States, Great Britain, France and West Germany." ED 227-102.

Cusick, Philip. "Secondary Public Schools in America." 34 pp. ED 227-105.

Doyle, Walter. "Academic Work." 87 pp. ED 227-097.

Duckworth, Kenneth. "Intelligence, Motivation, and Academic Work: An Operations Perspective." ED 227-109.

———. "Some Ideas About Student Cognition, Motivation and Work" [A Critique of the Symposium on *The Student's Role in Learning*]. 20 pp. ED 228-240.

Eckstein, Max A., and S. Shafer. "A Comparative Review of Curriculum: Mathematics and International Studies in the Secondary Schools of Five Countries." 115 pp. ED 227-068.

Farrar, Eleanor, B. Neufeld, and Matthew B. Miles. "A Review of Effective Schools Research: The Message for Secondary Schools." 44 pp. ED 228-241.

Gamson, Zelda. "A Little Light on the Subject: Keeping General and Liberal Education Alive." 74 pp. ED 225-993.

Gardner, William E., and John R. Palmer. "Certification and Accreditation: Background, Issues Analysis, and Recommendations." 52 pp. ED 226-003.

Holsinger, Donald B. "Time, Content and Expectations as Predictors of School Achievement in the U.S.A. and Other Developed Countries: A Review of IEA Evidence." 58 pp. ED 227-077.

Good, Thomas L. "What Is Learned in Schools: Responding to School Demands, Grades K-6." 88 pp. ED 227-100.

Good, Thomas L., and G. M. Hinkel. "Schooling in America: Some Descriptive and Explanatory Statements." ED 228-246.

Howey, Kenneth R. "Charting Directions for Preservice Teacher Education." 51 pp. ED 226-004.

Hurd, Paul DeHart. "An Overview of Science Education in the United States and Selected Foreign Countries." 128 pp. ED 227-076.

Hurn, Christopher J., and B. B. Burn. "An Analytic Comparison of Educational Systems: Overview of Purposes, Policies, Structures and Outcomes." 82 pp. ED 225-991.

Husen, Torsten. "A Cross-National Perspective on Assessing the Quality of Learning." 56 pp. ED 225-992.

Karweit, Nancy. "Time on Task: A Research Review." 88 pp. ED 228-236.

London, Howard. "Academic Standards in the American Community College: Trends and Controversies." 47 pp. ED 227-071.

Maehr, Martin L. "Motivational Factors in School Achievement." 79 pp. ED 227-095.

Miles, Matthew B., and others. "The Extent of Adoption of Effective Schools Programs." Vol. II. Review of Effective Schools Programs. 58 pp. ED 228-242.

Neumann, William. "College Press and Student Fit." 30 pp. ED 227-112.

Pace, C. Robert. "Achievement and Quality of Student Effort." 40 pp. ED 227-101.

Prokop, Harvey L. "Intelligence, Motivation and the Quality and Quantity of Academic Work and Their Impacts on the Learning of Students: A Practitioner's Reaction." [A Critique of the Symposium on *The Student's Role in Learning.*] ED 227-103.

"Public Hearing—Language and Literacy: Skills for Academic Learning." Houston,

Texas, April 16, 1982. 330 pp. ED 225-996.

Public Hearing on Science, Mathematics and Technology Education. (Stanford, California). 1982. 299 pp. ED 227-096.

Resnick, Daniel P., and Frederick Rudolph. "Educational Excellence—The Secondary School–College Connection and Other Matters: An Historical Assessment." 30 pp. ED 225-995.

Resnick, Lauren B. "Standards, Curriculum, and Performance: A Historical and Comparative Perspective." 53 pp. ED 227-104.

Rudolph, Frederick. "Educational Excellence: The Secondary School–College Connection and Other Matters: An Historical Assessment." ED 225-995.

Sjogren, Clifford. "College Admissions and the Transition to Post-secondary Education: Standards and Practice." 32 pp. ED 227-094.

Snow, Richard E. "Intellegence, Motivation and Academic Work." [A Critique of the Symposium on *The Student's Role in Learning.*] 15 pp. ED 227-107.

Sternberg, Robert J., and R. K. Wagner. "Understanding Intelligence: What's in It for Education?" ED 227-110.

Stipek, Deborah. "Motivating Students to Learn: A Lifelong Perspective." 56 pp. ED 227-111.

Torney-Purta, Judith, and John Schwille. "The Values Learned in School: Policy and Practice in Industrialized Countries." 83 pp. ED 227-072.

———. "The Years Between Elementary School and High School: What Schooling Experiences Do Students Have?" 51 pp. ED 228-239.

Warren, Jonathan. "The Faculty Role in Educational Excellence." 55 pp. ED 227-069.

Whitla, Dean K. "Value Added and Other Related Matters." 34 pp. ED 228-245.

Yanger, Sam J. "Inservice Education." 63 pp. ED 227-075.

Zimiles, H. "The Changing American Child: The Perspective of Educators." 54 pp. ED 227-099.

Contributors

PHILIP G. ALTBACH is professor in the Faculty of Educational Studies and Director of Comparative Education Center, State University of New York at Buffalo.

MICHAEL W. APPLE is professor of curriculum and instruction, University of Wisconsin, Madison.

ERNEST L. BOYER is president of the Carnegie Foundation for the Advancement of Teaching and former United States Commissioner of Education.

DENNIS L. CARLSON is assistant professor of education, Rutgers University, Newark, New Jersey.

KOWSAR P. CHOWDHURY is a doctoral student in the Comparative Education Center, State University of New York at Buffalo.

CARL A. GRANT is professor of curriculum and instruction, University of Wisconsin, Madison.

RICHARD C. HUNTER is Superintendent of the Dayton Public Schools, Dayton, Ohio. He was formerly Superintendent of Schools in Richmond, Virginia.

GAIL P. KELLY is professor in the Department of Educational Organization, Administration and Policy, State University of New York at Buffalo.

LINDA M. MC NEIL is assistant professor of education at Rice University, Houston, Texas.

PAUL E. PETERSON is the director of the governmental studies program at the Brookings Institution, Washington, D.C.

HUGH G. PETRIE is Dean of the Faculty of Educational Studies, State University of New York at Buffalo.

ROSEMARIE V. ROSEN has served as Deputy Superintendent for Finance and Administration for the Boston Public Schools. She is currently Director of Human Resources, Department of Mental Retardation, State of New York.

MAXINE S. SELLER is professor in the Department of Educational Organization, Administration and Policy, State University of New York at Buffalo.

ALBERT SHANKER is President of the American Federation of Teachers, AFL-CIO.

SHEILA A. SLAUGHTER is associate professor in the Department of Educational Organization, Administration and Policy, State University of New York at Buffalo.

CHRISTINE E. SLEETER is assistant professor in the Department of Education, Ripon College, Ripon, Wisconsin.

JOEL SPRING is professor in the College of Education, University of Cincinnati, Cincinnati, Ohio.

LOIS WEIS is associate professor in the Department of Educational Organization, Administration and Policy, State University of New York at Buffalo.